The Dance of the Comedians

The Dance of the Comedians

The People, the President, and the
Performance of Political Standup
Comedy in America

PETER M. ROBINSON

University of Massachusetts Press

AMHERST AND BOSTON

Copyright © 2010 by University of Massachusetts Press
ALL RIGHTS RESERVED
Printed in the United States of America
First printed in paperback 2011

LC 2009048474
ISBN 978-1-55849-733-7 (cloth); ISBN 978-1-55849-785-6 (paper)

Designed by Steve Dyer
Set in Electra by House of Equations, Inc.
Printed and bound by Thomson-Shore, Inc.

Library of Congress Cataloging-in-Publication Data

Robinson, Peter M., 1958–
The dance of the comedians : the people, the president, and the performance
of political standup comedy in America / Peter M. Robinson.
p. cm.
Includes bibliographical references and index.
ISBN 978-1-55849-733-7 (cloth : alk. paper)
1. Presidents—United States—Humor—History. 2. Political satire, American—
History. 3. Stand-up comedy—United States—History. 4. American wit
and humor—History. 5. Presidents—United States—Public opinion—
History. 6. Public opinion—United States—History. I. Title.
E176.1.R644 2010
973.09'9—dc22
2009048474

British Library Cataloguing in Publication data are available.

To Beth, Ryan, and Sarah,
for their love of a comedian.

CONTENTS

ILLUSTRATIONS

ACKNOWLEDGMENTS

I am grateful to the many people whose expertise, patience, and good humor helped to make this book possible. First, the guidance and encouragement extended by the History Department at Miami University in Oxford, Ohio, were extraordinary. I am particularly grateful to Andrew Cayton, William Doan, Sheldon Anderson, and Peggy Shaffer, who improved this project through its many early stages with critical eyes and supportive words. All are extraordinary scholars whom I am thankful to count among my colleagues and friends. I also owe thanks to LeRoy Ashby at Washington State University, Stephen Kercher at the University of Wisconsin at Oshkosh, and Edward Stern, producing artistic director at the Cincinnati Playhouse in the Park, who commented on earlier versions of the manuscript with constructive support and whose expertise in American popular culture, postwar liberal satire, and performance studies offered invaluable perspective.

The superb staffs at the American Antiquarian Society in Worcester, Massachusetts; the John F. Kennedy Presidential Library in Boston; the Franklin D. Roosevelt Library in Hyde Park, New York; the Film and Television Archive at the University of California, Los Angeles; and the Billy Rose Theatre Collection of the New York Public Library provided vital assistance. I am especially grateful to William Schurk and Susannah Cleveland at the Music Library and Sound Recording Archives at Bowling Green State University in Bowling Green, Ohio, and to William McNitt at the Gerald R. Ford Library in Ann Arbor, Michigan, for their quick and resourceful attention to my many requests.

I have great appreciation for the entire staff at the Will Rogers Memorial Museum in Claremore, Oklahoma, for their help and generosity. Michelle Lefebvre-Carter, former executive director of the Museum, and Joseph Carter rendered one kindness after another during my stay to conduct research. I am enormously indebted to Steven Gragert, the Museum's archivist, historian, and current executive director, whose knowledge saved me time, whose expertise served to bring Will Rogers into clearer focus, and whose hospitality turned hard work into an absolute pleasure. Steve and the

Museum also provided generous funding that allowed me to present some of my findings at the Southwest/Texas Popular Culture Association meeting in early 2008.

I owe others special thanks. This project could not have been completed without the support of the College of Mount St. Joseph in Cincinnati. Travel funds from the Mount allowed me to share my work and collaborate with scholars around the country, and a reduced teaching load during one busy semester gave me valuable time to research and write. Most of all I am thankful to Tim Lynch at the Mount, whose passion for the craft of history is contagious and who read each chapter with care and inexhaustible good cheer. Other colleagues — Sister Margaret McPeak, Elizabeth Barkley, and Fran Harmon — were particularly helpful in accommodating my need for writing time with understanding and words of encouragement. Drew Shannon, Father John Amankwah, Robert Bodle, Jennifer Morris, Michael Klabunde, and other friends on the Mount faculty kept my spirits high and my research current by passing along the latest joke from the Internet. Several students in my course on the history of American humor also provided helpful feedback, and I am grateful to Charles Patrick Coggins for his editorial assistance.

Bruce Wilcox, Carol Betsch, and the expert staff at the University of Massachusetts Press have been a joy to work with throughout. Amanda Heller brought her meticulous skills to the copyediting process. I am particularly thankful to my editor, Clark Dougan, for his superb guidance and no small measure of patience.

I am happy to thank the many wits who have informed my comicview over the years with their punch lines and performances. They include my sister Ellen Noyes, my brothers Dave Robinson and Jim Robinson, and a cast of others who inspired this book in various ways. Tony Freeman, Phillip Waller, Peter Meekins, Paul Kassel, Layne Beamer, Shelley Russell, Georgia Herrmann, Eric Lowry, Kate Mullins, R. Scott Shriver, Pat and Sarah Mahoney, Mark Gyorgy, and Jed Grisez have done more for me than they know.

Finally, two people were absolutely indispensable to this project and remain so as I continue in my academic career. Words fail to express my gratitude to Allan Winkler, who has been the ideal teacher, mentor, guide, and friend. His knowledge, experience, and meticulous approach to history are surpassed only by his astounding generosity of spirit. Last but foremost, my wife, Beth, has humored me throughout this endeavor. I thank her for her love, for the expressions of encouragement that are far too numerous to count, and for the joy that has brought me strength and plenty of laughs along the way.

The Dance of the Comedians

PROLOGUE

"I'm not kidding"

WITHOUT WARNING to her audience, and with even her husband uncertain of exactly what was coming, first lady Laura Bush took the stage and stole the show at the annual White House Correspondents' Association dinner on April 30, 2005. In a performance widely applauded by supporters and critics on both sides of the culture wars, Mrs. Bush made open fun of the policies, the foibles, and, indirectly, even the sexual performance of the president of the United States. Just as George W. Bush was approaching the podium as entertainer in chief, a role increasingly prescribed for the president by the developments of the previous century, Mrs. Bush reversed expected performance roles—and challenged lingering gender expectations where first ladies are concerned—when she pushed him aside and addressed the crowd:

> Ladies and gentlemen, I've been attending these dinners for years, and just quietly sitting there. Well, I've got a few things I want to say for a change. . . . George always says he's delighted to come to these press dinners. Baloney! He's usually in bed by now. I'm not kidding. I said to him the other day: "George, if you really want to end tyranny in the world, you're going to have to stay up later."[1]

As the ten-minute routine proceeded, Mrs. Bush bemoaned her evenings spent married to "Mr. Excitement" by identifying with one of the year's most popular television shows and by sharing her solution for invigorating White House domestic life, touching on the president's more private shortcomings in the process:

> Ladies and gentlemen, I *am* a desperate housewife. I mean, if those women on that show think they're desperate, they ought to be with George. One night, after George went to bed, Lynne Cheney, Condi

Rice, Karen Hughes, and I went to Chippendale's. I wouldn't even mention it, except Ruth Ginsburg and Sandra Day O'Connor saw us there. I won't tell you what happened, but Lynne's Secret Service codename is now "Dollar Bill."

The laughter swelled and it quickly became clear that Laura Bush was a hit. Occasionally she cast glances left or right toward President Bush, Lynne Cheney, or some other target, perhaps with a wink of reassurance that all was in jest, but she never did so apologetically. She was clearly enjoying her moment in the spotlight, the studied graciousness of her smile failing to mask completely a sense of impish glee she telegraphed with each joke and every roar of approval from the crowd of journalists. At the climax of her act, with her confidence high and her comic role by now firmly established, she ventured into more volatile political territory with her description of Bush on their ranch in Crawford, Texas:

> We like it down there. George didn't know much about ranches when we bought the place. Andover and Yale don't have a real strong ranching program. But I'm proud of George. He has learned a lot about ranching since that first year when he tried to milk the horse. What's worse it was a male horse. Now, of course, he spends his days clearing brush, cutting trails, taking down trees, or as the girls [Bush daughters Jenna and Barbara] call it: "The Texas Chainsaw Massacre." George's answer to any problem at the ranch is to cut it down with a chainsaw, which I think is why he and Cheney and Rumsfeld get along so well.[2]

Although Laura Bush's material was crafted by White House speechwriter Landon Parvin and well rehearsed in advance, she displayed the comic chops of a pro. Her lack of formal experience notwithstanding, her delivery was focused and smooth. She showed a polished sense of timing as she allowed the laughter and applause from one joke to crest and proceed just past its peak before she continued, never allowing silence to kill the comic rhythm. Cedric the Entertainer, one of the nation's most popular comedians and purportedly the evening's headliner, could only sit and try to enjoy being upstaged by a comic novice who had her act down cold.

Laura Bush's performance as a seasoned standup comic was due not only to her rehearsals in the days leading up to the dinner but also to her awareness—like that of her husband and his administration—of the potency of the live comedic event as political theater in the early twenty-first century. By standing in front of an audience that received and responded to her jokes about the president, and simultaneously in front of the president himself—the object of the humor—the first lady turned comic became an agent for mediating the dynamic relationship between the American presidency and the American people, represented at the dinner by members of the White House press corps. In this comedic ménage à trois, Laura Bush the comedian stood in command at center stage.

This mediation through standup comedy had been incubating since before the founding of the republic, but it resonated most potently during the middle years of the twentieth century. As prominent participants in American politics, the Bushes had long been schooled in and victimized by such humor, but they learned about the multifaceted political force of one-liners alongside their fellow citizens during a period when such ridicule of the presidency became prominent, even ubiquitous, on the American cultural landscape. Today most Americans at least acknowledge as common cultural currency the skewerings of the presidency on *The Daily Show with Jon Stewart*, *The Colbert Report*, or *Saturday Night Live*, the ridicule that is the staple ingredient of monologues on *The Tonight Show* or the *Late Show with David Letterman*, and the parody scattered across the World Wide Web on blogs and other sites that seem to proliferate daily. Fewer Americans, however, recall the humor of Mort Sahl and Dick Gregory, whose standup routines, along with the impersonations of Vaughn Meader, prompted millions of Americans in the 1950s and 1960s to redefine their attitudes toward the chief executive. And fewer still remember the Compass Players and others whose mischievous experiments with improvisation and performance in the 1950s paved the way for the widespread success of presidential satire on stage and television. There are other comic icons as well, notably Will Rogers, who played a watershed role not only in bringing presidential humor into the mainstream but also through his masterly exploitation of every performance medium at his disposal, thereby initiating a popular new dynamic that brought the American public and the president into a closer and more equitable proximity, if not necessarily a more amiable one. Rogers encouraged his fellow citizens to understand the performance and reception of humor as a site of cultural exploration, creativity, and even political resistance, however tame by modern standards. Presidents and their supporters, along with their critics and even their wives, have responded by getting in on the act, perceiving the power of such humor to define, reinforce, and otherwise affect popular opinion.

The merry, mocking, and often contested anarchies of standup political comedy precipitated by Rogers and his beneficiaries have locked humorists, presidents, and their fellow Americans in an improvisational and often ambiguous three-way dance that has been formative to modern political and popular culture in the United States. Laura Bush's routine at the Washington

Hilton simply was emblematic of this interaction. This book explores this tripartite bond of reciprocal and dynamic performance, its origins, its leading players, and its rise to cultural prominence.

The Dance of the Comedians examines standup comedy—particularly its ramifications for the presidency and Americans' perceptions of that institution—as a uniquely compelling form of cultural performance. While the term "performance" has taken on overlapping pleats of meaning in the arts, humanities, and social sciences in recent years, here it refers primarily to an encounter in which participants congregate in community with one another to display and respond to patterned behaviors and roles. Part ceremonial ritual, part playful improvisation, the performance of comedy empowers its participants to reexamine, renegotiate, and often redefine the roles of all concerned. At the White House correspondents' dinner, Laura Bush presented herself before an audience in the surprising role of comedian for the purpose of "simple" entertainment. In the process, however, she commanded a complex and multilayered cultural transaction. She deployed comedy to tweak her audience's perception of President Bush, but just as significantly—with Bush also present and on display as the object of the laughter—the president was humbled by being called on to participate, however briefly, in a less imperious and more vulnerable relationship between himself, those in the media, and the American people at large. The institutional formality of the presidency—and the attendant deference accorded it—was upstaged by images of the comical humanity of the president himself. With the masturbatory reference to Bush naïvely milking a male horse, his wife even challenged his carefully crafted persona of the experienced rancher, the self-made master of his own Texas domain. While this particular moment may not have permanently affected the presidency or people's perceptions of it, the cumulative impact of earlier performances by other comedians, other presidents, and other Americans *has* affected American popular and political culture in profound ways. In May 2005 Laura Bush, her husband, and her audience simply danced the steps first choreographed by the comic pioneers who appear in this book.

In examining the act of performance—the "dance" itself—and not just the performers or their material, the chapters that follow recognize what comedians, politicians, demagogues, actors, the clergy, musicians, and other producers of public theater—but few historians—have long understood, namely, that there is enormous power and dynamism to be found in performance. Far more than a site of benign leisure and simple amusement, the threshold space between performer and audience fairly crackles with energy and unpredictability. In this crucible of margins where a performer's creativity fires the imagination of an audience, whose response in turn reflects energy back to the performer through laughter, applause, or other reaction, new cultural possibilities are given license and may be freely shaped, embraced, accepted, or dismissed before the audience reemerges onto the thoroughfare of everyday life. Performance can be likened, as anthropologist Victor Turner has pointed out, to a loop in a culture's linear progression "when the social flow bends back on itself, in a way does violence to its own development, meanders, inverts, perhaps lies to itself." Effectively delivered, performance becomes an arena of cultural struggle, or what I prefer to describe as a vibrant and fleeting dance between a performer's creative acts and an audience's spontaneous and equally creative response. Standup comedy cavorts along this dynamic threshold in particularly audacious ways that have shaped political discourse, most significantly where it concerns the changing American presidency.[3]

Certainly not every performance—comedic or otherwise—disturbs the established order of things in any radical way. As the complexities of the twentieth century combined with the proliferation of electronic mass media and Americans' burgeoning access to them, however, public sites of performance became more numerous and volatile. This often led Americans not to cultural affirmation but rather to new interrogations and, increasingly, to new conclusions about themselves and their relationship to virtually every facet of their culture, including their most prominent political leaders. Standup comedy emerged from the 1910s to the 1980s as both an increasingly prominent means of cultural performance and a more influential site for Americans to make such political interrogations.

In exploring the growing acceptance then embrace of humor directed at the presidency, I also trace the evolving intersection of two types of performative processes: "ritual" and "play," terms frequently considered to be antithetical to each other in the Western tradition, yet which are intricately intertwined and whose interplay is key to examining the effectiveness of standup comedy. Ritual, the performance of a widely practiced, often sacred ceremonial process, typically marks a time-honored rite of passage from one social or spiritual status to another. Ritual is rigidly structured and conservative by definition; it uses the power of performance to *preserve* a culture's most cherished values, and its very survival depends on the engaged participation of the community. Ritual is hard work.[4]

Play, by contrast, is inherently anti-structural, the very antithesis of work or rigidity. Its hallmarks are spontaneity, freedom, fantasy, experimentation, disorder, and even subversion of conventional assumptions. Play may serve as catharsis, the "letting off of steam" in response to too much order, thereby maintaining or even buttressing those assumptions, but it may also pursue more dangerous ends, encouraging significant cultural upheaval. Play, as it turns out, is much more than mere fun and games.[5]

The historical boundaries between play and ritual have become progressively porous, especially during the past 150 years, and despite the desperate attempts of industrial societies to codify and segregate the two. Traditionally the ritual of work has been exalted in this country by both Protestant orthodoxy and industrialized capitalism by sacred virtue of its regimentation and resulting productivity, while play—as "non-work"—is commonly denigrated as idle, profitless, and profane. Nevertheless, while the structure of ritual and the anti-structure of play can and do exist separately in industrialized societies, they are always close to each other and in fact reside in symbiotic alignment. Industrialized society and its attendant forces of capitalism and nationalism segment people into various workaday functions, classes, and affiliations. Workers go about their business and are expected to perform their prescribed ritualized roles. Play, with its particularly free-wheeling—even rebellious—potential, complements ritualized behaviors by offering necessary liberation from these roles and, according to theorist Brian Sutton-Smith, serves to make the ritualized status quo tolerable while keeping people flexible and open to the possibility of cultural change. While it may commonly be seen as wholly distinct from the ritual of work and may be associated with inconsequentiality or "mere fun," in fact play infiltrates ritual and critiques it for the necessary and subversive joy of it, frequently inverting long-accepted societal hierarchies in the process. Play cloaks itself in workaday ritual, often to comical extremes, as in the ornate trappings of professional football's Super Bowl—a game, after all, but one that trumpets the gladiatorial labors of the athlete even as it reinforces and venerates American leisure culture. At their most effective, theater, concerts, and comedy routines all flirt with the predictabilities of public ritual, but their true power resides in the playful and unpredictable dance on the narrow, exciting threshold of possibility between performer and audience.[6]

Standup comedy hovers at these intersections of ritual and play in particularly stealthy and effective ways. Its audiences tend to gather for the most ordinary of reasons—to fulfill ritualized norms of behavior, not to engage in hit-and-run guerrilla raids on political culture or the presidency. Going to a comedy show is something that is fun to do—or, as with banquets or roasts, it can often be a ritualized obligation. Ostensibly the White House correspondents and their guests congregated in formal attire at the Washington Hilton in April 2005 to fulfill another work-related role, to put in an appearance at yet another professional function, albeit a prestigious one. They left, however, with a good laugh and good copy about a first lady transformed into a first-rate cutup. They also became co-conspirators in a playful act of cultural havoc, however small. For a few fleeting hours the predictabilities of work cavorted with the improvisational characteristics of play as laughter and applause reverberated from Laura Bush's punch lines and gave all those involved a glimpse of alternative perspectives on the presidency. Play reverted to work once again as the journalists reported on the evening's events, offered glowing critiques of the first lady's surprise performance, and mined the evening for every nugget of consumer appeal until after a few days the news cycle turned toward fresher material. The performance itself played on, however, proliferating through the Internet, which allowed a wider public to log on and laugh along.

Conversely, at first blush it can be said that Laura Bush was "simply kidding" or "playing around" in joking about the president, her objectives being pleasure and the desire to facilitate a cathartic if temporary truce in the rancorous battles fought daily within the Washington Beltway. Such assessments are legitimate, of course, as far as they go. They may even reflect her sincere intentions. Yet such trivialization is beguiling (often to the delight of those complicit in the humorous act, who hope that political humor, by its very definition, will fall below the radar and escape earnest scrutiny). As Joseph Boskin, Arthur Power Dudden, Stephen Kercher, and other scholars of American humor have argued, the comical is not to be confused with the trivial. The laughter and good cheer accompanying humor belie its political and cultural potency. In fact political comedy has often been where the serious work of democracy is done.[7]

Even though dismissive attitudes toward humor and its legitimate contributions to public discourse stubbornly persist, a sense of this potency has been increasingly accepted by interpreters of American culture in the early twenty-first century and by the American public at large. According to polls by the Pew Research Center for the People and the Press, the audiences of comedy programs such as *The Daily Show* and *The Colbert Report* are among the most knowledgeable about current affairs. These programs also have been cited by a growing number of young Americans as primary sources for political news and information. The number of people aged eighteen to twenty-nine who said that they learned about presidential campaigns from such shows doubled between 2000 and 2004, continuing the trend of young people accessing the presidency through political humor which began five decades earlier. Similarly, in the wake of Laura Bush's performance at the White House correspondents' dinner, many interpreted her comedy as a calculated hit-and-run raid in the culture wars. One blogger concluded that the first lady, whose approval ratings were considerably higher than her husband's, had been sent onstage by Bush strategist Karl Rove in a covert attempt to win back moderate Republicans and independent voters through her engaging use of humor, specifically with the racy references to *Desperate Housewives* and milking the male horse. *New York Times* columnist Frank Rich not only was not laughing at her jokes but also decried what he called "the press corps' eagerness to . . . serve as dress extras in what amounts to an administration promotional video." Standup comedy—even (or especially) that sweetened by an endearing first lady—reasserted itself as a weapon in the political and cultural battles of 2005, and it continues to play a starring role today.[8]

In fact the Bush performance and the subsequent debate about its motives and significance were merely derivative of earlier groundbreaking performances by past comedians on either side of the footlights, both in and out of the Oval Office. During the first third of the twentieth century, humorist Will Rogers—costumed in the homespun simplicity of a "ropin' fool" and disclaiming, "All I know is what I read in the papers"—was a master at exploiting the potential of stage and radio performance to insinuate himself between Americans and their elected leaders during a period of crisis and redefinition. In the process he permanently recast the roles of citizen and president alike and encouraged both to engage each other with a new sense of equality. Rogers's ubiquity in American mass culture during the early twentieth century initiated unprecedented discussion about the power and propriety of poking fun at the presidency. His jokes touched Americans in their workaday rituals through the pages of hundreds of daily newspapers. His humor also accompanied them in their newfound proclivity for play, whether from the vaudeville stage, where he starred for the first quarter of the century; on the screen, where he was the top box office attraction during much of the 1920s and 1930s; or over the radio airwaves, which he dominated for the first fifteen years of commercial radio's existence. Rogers rose to stardom at precisely the same moment that the mass distribution of "show business" began to blur the boundaries between work and play, and his dominance of the mass media married entertainment culture to political culture, especially where Americans' perceptions of the presidency were concerned.[9]

Following Rogers's lead, during the 1950s and early 1960s "new wave" political comedians such as Bob Newhart, Dick Gregory, and others, deceptively costumed in the ritualized suit and tie of the day (Mort Sahl, in his sweater and slacks, was the notable and prescient exception), once again cross-pollinated comedy and presidential politics, this time with the increasing acidity befitting a postwar America haunted by communists, consumerism, and the prospect of nuclear annihilation. Sahl's audacious routines at

Dwight Eisenhower's expense earned the comic a growing following among Americans who were often disquieted by the nation's leadership during the variable fortunes of the Korean War, the hysterics of Joseph McCarthy's witch-hunts, the early struggles of the modern civil rights movement, and mammoth changes in virtually all aspects of American life. In 1962 Vaughn Meader's hilarious impersonation of John F. Kennedy during the cathartic months following the Cuban missile crisis brought popular culture and the presidency into such close proximity that many Americans thought that the president and the comic were one and the same. More than anyone since Will Rogers, Sahl and Meader defined during the mid twentieth century how and why Americans laugh at their president in the early twenty-first.

Like Rogers, these later comedians exploited the new media at their disposal. These included television and film to some extent, although with the United States transformed into what historian Lizabeth Cohen has termed a "consumers' republic" by the 1950s and television firmly established as a vital means for promoting patriotism by purchase, political standup got scant play for fear it would alienate sponsors and their customers. Instead it was the appearance of the long-playing record in 1948 and its sensational popularity during the comedy album boom of the 1950s and 1960s that brought these comics before large numbers of people. Meader's album *The First Family* marked the popular zenith of the comedy record when it became the bestselling album in American history to that time. The LPs usually were recorded live, capturing not only the comic in performance but also the audience, whose presence completed the circuit. The live crowd's infectious laughter and applause energized listeners at home and encouraged them to spread the merry contagion by listening again and again, playing the records at parties, and repeating their favorite jokes to friends and co-workers. Consequently, although the comedians' live performances often were relegated to clubs such as San Francisco's claustrophobic hungry i—a broom closet compared to the palatial New Amsterdam Theater, where Rogers played—and to less dominant media than those at Rogers's command, jesters such as Sahl, Newhart, Meader, and Gregory nevertheless popularized a new and more acerbic brand of political humor that seemed well suited to uncertain times. Their increasingly mordant performances on records and in nightclubs reestablished the political comedian as a cultural hero wielding punch lines to empower Americans and to interrogate their relationship to the highest office in the land.[10]

As for Frank Rich's lament in 2005 over the Bush administration's manipulation of the media by punch line, the first lady's performance is reminiscent of Franklin D. Roosevelt's and John F. Kennedy's pioneering use of humor to mesmerize and neutralize a potentially hostile press and, by extension, to win over a nervous or dubious public. When it served their purposes to do so, both presidents could seize the performative moment for themselves and work a crowd as skillfully as a professional comedian works a room. In fact, while both men possessed deep wells of personal humor that they drew from instinctively, they were students of professional comedians as well—Roosevelt of Will Rogers and Kennedy of Mort Sahl—however unwittingly. Both presidents understood the ability of humor to divert or obfuscate for short-term political gain, yet they were also cultural arbiters who prompted a more permanent shift in Americans' attitudes toward the office and those who hold it. Their humor was sometimes in league with that of the professional comedians and often in opposition to it, but like Rogers, Sahl, and others, Roosevelt and Kennedy recognized and actively harnessed the potency of laughter. Their effective use of mass media toward this end and Americans' widespread acceptance of it meant that future presidents would also have to master such humor (as Ronald Reagan did) or be mastered by it (as Lyndon Johnson and Richard Nixon discovered). Far from dismissing humor as trivial or distracting, Roosevelt and Kennedy understood its value to the modern presidency and employed it more discerningly than any other president since Abraham Lincoln. If, by the time of his death in 1935, Will Rogers had proved social critic and former *Punch* editor Malcolm Muggeridge's observation that power is inherently laughable, then by the time Laura Bush took the stage in 2005, presidents and their handlers had learned well the complementary lesson that Roosevelt and Kennedy taught: that laughter is inherently powerful. These two chief executives showed that presidents too could lead the dance.[11]

In fact the Roosevelt and Kennedy administrations and the years that frame them are definitive cultural watersheds, periods when wellsprings of humor emanated from the presidents and the comics alike, with the American public increasingly complicit in the act of cultural performance. These years put the long-standing rituals of presidential deference most profoundly in play, as all three—the people, the presidents, and the comedy professionals—danced their way through the tensions between traditional reverence for the presidency and ridicule of it. Standup comedy could both alleviate these tensions and exacerbate them, often simultaneously. During these years, political standup played a central role in this destabilization. Everyone involved in the act of telling the joke was increasingly cognizant of its value and conspired in unleashing the latent force to be found in such seemingly insignificant humor. These were particularly fascinating moments, when Americans recognized that the performance of political comedy had tremendous worth—and potentially enormous costs—for those on all sides of the punch line.

• • •

The Dance of the Comedians is about the origins and development of this mutual recognition. During the first decades of the republic, when the burgeoning geographic frontier marked the threshold of an America literally performing itself into existence, newspaper editor Charles Farrar Browne cast himself as the "Old Showman" Artemus Ward. In his travels from Maine to Ohio to California, he pioneered the performative relationship between the emergent American humorist and the nascent American audience, even as his hilariously semiliterate observations helped to shape the definition of popular humor. During the 1860s his "lectures" on diverse subjects, including "pollertics" and its various "candydates," both entranced and transformed those who sold out lecture halls and theaters nationwide to watch him perform the pseudonymous identity that had made him famous initially in print. Abraham Lincoln, whose own use of humor was as much calculated for effect as it was legendary, was a devoted reader who found in Ward's playful jests the ideal palliative for the afflictions of the presidency. After briefly tracing the opportunities and impediments that informed a uniquely American political humor, this book begins with an analysis of Ward in performance, his effect on a nascent American public, and his imagined but significant association with the presidency. Ward's (and Lincoln's) audiences were paltry by modern standards. Nevertheless, the origins of the dance are found here.[12]

Its climax came with the commodification and institutionalization of political standup comedy during the mid-1970s. By this time, thanks to presidents, comics, and the public—performers all during the previous half-century—not only was presidential humor accepted currency in the American cultural marketplace but also it had a consumer value that was recognized and distributed by mass communication channels in ways that led directly to today's widespread embrace of presidential humor and ridicule. Lyndon Johnson's prosecution of the Vietnam War and the resulting credibility gap between citizens and the White House, Richard Nixon's Watergate, and Gerald Ford's pratfalls all became fodder not only for comedians, now adept at capitalizing on jokes at the expense of an institution perceived as more laughable than laudable, but also for audiences that were increasingly receptive to such jokes in the wake of assassination, scandal, and imperial behavior in the executive branch. The cultural legitimacy of presidential humor was still debatable to many, but its commercial value was no longer in question.

This commodification crystallized relatively quickly. In 1968 presidential candidate Richard Nixon, one of the most humorless men ever to seek the office, momentarily conceded the powerful influence of comedy on his political fortunes when he agreed to a one-line cameo appearance on *Rowan and Martin's Laugh-In*, the most popular show on television. His incredulous reading of the catchphrase of the year—"Sock it to *me?*"—earned him votes and further cemented the show's ratings supremacy. More significantly, it affirmed ridicule of the presidency both as a staple component of national campaign strategy and as a commodity to be bought and sold in volume on the mass consumer market. This process was intimated by Artemus Ward in the nineteenth century, initiated by Will Rogers during the 1910s, rediscovered and further refined by Mort Sahl during the 1950s, and finally brought to fruition by Vaughn Meader—and, unwittingly, Kennedy—only a few years before *Laugh-In* debuted. By 1969 the wealthiest and most powerful man in American popular culture was neither a musician nor an author nor a filmmaker but a standup comedian named Johnny Carson, who could claim at least as many viewers as the president of the United States could claim voters. In 1974 Carson delivered an ultimatum to NBC, demanding that it stop airing reruns of *Tonight Show* material on Saturday nights. Driven by economic necessity, the network gave license to Lorne Michaels, a former *Laugh-In* writer, to assemble the ingredients for *Saturday Night Live*, which permanently made presidential satire a centerpiece of American popular culture. It also made household names of Chevy Chase, Dan Aykroyd, and many more from the Second City comedy troupe, which had been inspired by the work of the Compass Players and others beginning in the mid-1950s. By 1976, with the show's dominance solidified—largely thanks to the program's ridicule of Ford and the first mock presidential debate between Chase (playing Ford) and Aykroyd (as challenger Jimmy Carter)—the "dance of the comedians" began the transition from its dramatic climax toward its denouement.

During the years that followed, presidential comedy became increasingly ubiquitous, mass distributed, and ready for prime time and late-night alike, as the huge popularity of programs such as *The Daily Show, Late Show with David Letterman, Real Time with Bill Maher,* and the cable network Comedy Central attests. Routines on the late-night comedy shows have become just that—routine—for those who would be president, as demonstrated by Bill Clinton's appearance on *The Arsenio Hall Show* in 1992 and John McCain's decision to announce his candidacy between punch lines on the *Late Show with David Letterman* in 2007. Once in office, presidents are obliged to cast themselves as comedians in chief, whether in their working interactions with the media or at functions such as the White House correspondents' dinner, as a strategy for courting public opinion, advancing policy, or stemming criticism. Franklin Roosevelt, John Kennedy, and Ronald Reagan assumed the role most naturally, but all have had to learn the part.[13]

The perception and reception of political standup changed dramatically during the middle decades of the twentieth century. Will Rogers's declaration "All I know is what I read in the papers" is a relic of the past. Today a growing percentage of postmodern audiences quickly and unashamedly concede that all they know about the news—and much of what they know about their president—comes not from conventional news sources but rather from the political comedy they consume on late-night network television or Comedy Central, whether as live broadcasts or "viral video" sources on YouTube and other Internet sites that circulate the humor among millions of viewers within hours. In 1962, although many Americans were outraged, millions were tickled by Vaughn Meader's uncanny impersonation of Jack Kennedy, their cultural sensitivities piqued by the prospect that the presidential identity could be co-opted so mischievously—if lovingly—for comedic gain. By comparison, by 1992, with comedian Dana Carvey's imitation of George H. W. Bush on *Saturday Night Live*, presidential impersonation and presidential identity had been conflated in Americans' minds, with many claiming that the comic played the president better than the president played himself. In 1952 Dwight Eisenhower publicly lambasted his opponent, Adlai Stevenson, for denigrating the dignity of the office by introducing humor into the presidential campaign, but by 2005 the White House itself was shrewdly casting the first lady as standup comedian for what it considered to be the vital purpose of infusing the presidency with humanity through self-ridicule. So much has changed, it is now often hard to tell the comedians apart, at least without a dance card.[14]

In this book I seek to explore the improvised choreography that precipitated this change. It has been a dance to be sure, often reminiscent of the playful scene from *The Bartered Bride* that inspired the title of this history. The opera by Czech composer Bedřich Smetana, which follows the time-honored formula of true love surviving the vicissitudes of rash conclusions and mistaken identities, is set amid the excitement of a festival day, when ritual is ostensibly celebrated and yet anything can (and therefore does) happen. *The Bartered Bride* is essentially a protracted marriage dance, with leaders, followers, and interlopers shifting roles dynamically, each vying for the others' attentions and trying to command the moment. "The Dance of the Comedians" is a pivotal scene in the opera in which a ringmaster introduces his troupe of energetic circus performers, who infuse further disorder into the story while paradoxically providing a key to its resolution. It is an exuberant, unsettling, and defining moment. Similarly during the twentieth century, the standup comedian served as both the minister of ritual and the ringmaster of play to join the people and the presidency in unprecedented—if contested—ways through live performance. The dance was at times a relatively harmonious waltz, at others a frenetic dervish in which the dancers could not avoid tripping over one another and themselves. The structure of my narrative highlights the comics and presidents who have shaped this cultural dance most profoundly. As for the audience, its role as comic interloper is visible throughout; here are the ticket buyers, theatergoers, record listeners, and television viewers who laughed, pointed fingers, mimicked the mimics, repeated the funniest material to co-workers, classmates, or neighbors, and in the process of helping to redefine the modern American presidency became comedians themselves, creating what social historian Joseph Boskin has termed "people's humor." Today these citizen-comedians have taken the stage in increasingly sophisticated ways, through amateur contests at comedy clubs as well as via e-mail, blogs, text messages, and homemade videos whose audience is but a mouse click away on YouTube.[15]

There are pitfalls to writing histories about comedy and its many variants, which may explain why a relatively small—although growing—number of scholars has stepped up to the task, even among those who otherwise champion the study of popular culture. Like Rodney Dangerfield, humor often "don't get no respect"; we still tend to eschew the study of humor as not "serious," and therefore not "important." The valuable (and serious and humorous) work of many across the fields of history, anthropology, and literary criticism offers welcome and overdue correctives. I hope this study will make a modest contribution as well.[16]

Perhaps the most daunting challenge, however, is that humor—especially political humor—tends to be tightly bound to time and place and is therefore highly perishable. Essayist E. B. White once compared examining humor to discover why it is funny with dissecting a frog in order to discover why it jumps: the endeavor can be valuable, but the subject tends to die on the examination table. The lifeless glob of component parts does not simply cease to jump; it bears little resemblance to the sprightly frog, and the process itself tends to dissipate interest in the subject. While it may be too much to hope that the jokes and satire discussed here will leap off the page with the same vitality they had as they jumped across the stage or airwaves, my hope is that the task at hand can still elicit an occasional laugh.[17]

1

An American Company of Comedians

NOT LONG after the election of 1860 Artemus Ward paid a visit to Abraham Lincoln at his home in Springfield, Illinois. The courtesy call by America's favorite humorist on the "President eleck of the United States" was bedlam from the outset, and the zany confusion for readers was hilariously compounded by the frayed homespun dialect that Ward used to retell it:

I found the old feller in his parler, surrounded by a perfeck swarm of orfice seekers. . . .

"Mr. Ward, [said Lincoln,] sit down. I am glad to see you, Sir."

"Repose in Abraham's Buzzum!" sed one of the orfice seekers, his idee bein to git orf a goak at my expense.

"Wall," sez I, "ef all you fellers repose in that there Buzzum thare'll be mity poor nussin for sum of you!" whereupon Old Abe buttoned his weskit clear up and blusht like a maidin of sweet 16. Jest at this point of the conversation another swarm of orfice-seekers arrove & cum pilin into the parler. . . . I thought Old Abe would go crazy. . . .

The house, door-yard, barn & woodshed was now all full, and when *another* crowd cum I told 'em not to go away for want of room as the hog-pen was still empty. . . .

"Good God!" cride Old Abe, "they cum upon me from the skize— down the chimneys, and from the bowels of the yearth!"

The showman Ward stepped boldly to Lincoln's aid:

"Can't you giv Abe a minit's peace? Don't you see he's worrid most to death! Go home, you miserable men, go home & till the sile! . . . Stand not upon the order of your goin,' but go to onct!" . . . You ought to hev seen them scamper. . . . In five minits the premises was clear.[1]

This "cordyul" meeting between the gaggle of office seekers, Lincoln ("he at the hellum [helm] of the ship of State"), and Ward ("at the hellum of the show bizniss") was fiction. For that matter, so was Artemus Ward. Both the man and the tale about a humorist coming to the rescue of a president besieged by those who elected him originated in the antic mind of Charles Farrar Browne, a soft-spoken newspaper man who became the country's first nationally known standup comedian. Yet the fabricated encounter lived plausibly and vividly in the imaginations of the tens of thousands who devoured the "Interview with President Lincoln" when it first appeared in the New York magazine *Vanity Fair* in late 1860 and when it was reprinted in the bestselling collection of Ward-isms, *Artemus Ward, His Book* in 1862. The vision of Ward—the semiliterate "Old Showman"—at the center of a farcical ballyhoo between the president and the electorate, as well as that of "Old Abe" blushing "like a maidin of sweet 16," were images that people could both accept and appreciate in the crucible of improvisation called the United States of America. Many could even recognize themselves in the melee, and Lincoln, whose own humor was already legendary, was among them. *Artemus Ward, His Book* was one of his prized possessions; he turned to it often as relief from the horrors of the Civil War, frequently beginning cabinet meetings by reading from it aloud. The president of the United States—engaged not only as the object of the joke but also as part of its audience and as a fellow humorist attuned to the symbiosis of politics and comedy—was an avid fan.[2]

By the time of his sudden death from tuberculosis in 1867 at age thirty-three, thousands more of Browne's fans had also seen Artemus Ward in performance (although Lincoln, whose penchant for the theater was as real as it was fatal, was never among them). Browne toured the nascent country tirelessly from coast to coast, playing with audiences and their fluid conceptions of themselves and "others," and with their competing ideas of amusement versus propriety. As he attracted sold-out crowds from Lewiston, Maine, to San Francisco, California, Browne pioneered a wholly new and uniquely American brand of humorous performance, shaping his audiences' conception of the presidency in the process.

Charles Browne and his alter ego stand at the nexus of politics and humor and at the genesis of political comedy performance in America. He was the personification of a new nation that found itself betwixt and between in virtually all things during the first half-century of its existence, and one that increasingly recognized humor and laughter as valuable tools for both expressing democratic liberty and easing the tensions inherent in the process of self-definition. He was born in 1834 on the northern frontier of Maine, a state still newly minted fourteen years after its admission to the Union as free territory in exchange for Missouri's entry as a slave state. Maine was well aware of its role in the tenuous compromises between North and South, between eastern moral reformers and western expansionists, and as a native son Browne was able to dance along such sectional and psychological divides with disarming good cheer. He was a man of the country but only felt the full rush of personal possibility in the new and growing cities, mimicking a nation that stood mesmerized on the borderlands between frontier and metropolis. Given a puritanical upbringing and imbued with a fierce work ethic, he was nevertheless entranced by the liberating siren song of the theater and by those who inhabited it, and he remained in lifelong tension between propriety and mischief, recklessness and respectability, work and play. In all these things he was the American spirit writ small.[3]

Most significantly, Browne invented Artemus Ward and introduced him into popular culture at the precise moment when Americans were most feverishly auditioning roles of their own, casting themselves both in the ensemble as part of an emerging general *public* and in the star turn as that new creation known as the individual *citizen*. With the spiritual zeal of the Second Great Awakening stressing personal faith and responsibility, the disappearance of widespread property restrictions on voting rights for men, and the audacious exuberance of Andrew Jackson's new Democratic Party all galvanizing the young nation and its people during the first decades of the nineteenth century, the American electorate ballooned, and voter participation in presidential elections surged threefold. Literacy gained importance as a deliberate expression of democracy and became more widespread in America than anywhere else in the world. Newspaper circulation and readership mushroomed in tandem, harnessing this newfound political consciousness to the new mass medium of popular print and its economic impetus, capitalism. Browne's beginnings as a typesetter, journalist, editor, and freelance writer on the make gave him front-row access to, and a small measure of control over, the development of what Benedict Anderson terms the "print capitalism" that brought news and ideas to the masses and profit to those who could produce and distribute them quickly. His travels took him into the streets, newspaper offices, and bars that became his second home, where the papers were dissected and debated, and where a wholly American public sphere was starting to crystallize.[4]

Browne and the bustling American public that became his audience seemed to understand naturally that the glue holding together both good copy and good conversation was humor. Quips, anecdotes, tall tales, and other stories—whether related in person or in print—provided more than ephemeral amusement or diversion; they were central to the formation of this individual and collective identity. As historian Daniel Wickberg has shown, the very notion of "humor" and an individual possessing a "sense of" it were just beginning to assume their modern meaning during the middle third of the nineteenth century. Humor began to be more than an objective characteristic, as it had been understood during the medieval and early modern periods; it took on increasing subjective value as a highly desirable trait, a distinguishing mark of individualism. Although Americans took much of their comic tradition from Great Britain, they attuned this evolving appreciation of humor to their peculiar social, economic, environmental, and political conditions, using it to inform a personal and national sense of themselves. The ability to spin a good yarn revealed a certain wisdom and a knack for creative enterprise. It exhibited the power to produce something increasingly valued as constructive—laughter—out of challenging, contradictory, even fearful situations that were common in the new and constantly changing America. Humor implied courage and freedom itself: the personal liberty to revel openly—even defiantly—in the oddities of life and to react freely with snickers or guffaws when others did the same. As a result, humor not only defined the individual but also tended to ingratiate him or her to those gathered round. Constituent members of the group in turn revealed their individual sense of humor (or lack of it) in how they responded, and the degree of similarity in these responses served further to conjoin these individuals into a unified whole. When Browne and others engaged in humorous exchange, then, they were in fact gauging one another individually while simultaneously inducting one another into fluid social and political networks. The ability to *make* a joke as well as to *take* one—the individual skill to laugh at some person or situation delicately balanced with the ability to join the communal act of laughing *with* others—was beginning to acquire significant value for the individual citizen and the general public alike.[5]

As Alexis de Tocqueville famously observed after visiting the new country in 1831, it also was a time when Americans—again both individually and collectively—were beginning to exert "political sovereignty," a more direct and autonomous control over political power. In addition to newspapers, civic ceremonies, taverns, and other forums of democratic debate, theaters and halls in large cities and small towns alike were especially potent as political spaces—and humor the political means—for rehearsing and crowning oneself a sovereign citizen. If learning to read and buying one of the more than a thousand newspapers that appeared between 1790 and 1835 gained one access to the collective local and national print discourse, then buying a ticket to a minstrel show, play, or other performance earned one admission to a shared spectacle that offered even more. Such shows invited men—and increasingly women—into immediate merry association with fellow Americans. They allowed them to put themselves at center stage, both in the guise of the comic performer and through the echo of their own laughter, and to hone their citizen's sense of humor and sense of community. Audiences soon understood that these performances contained significant power by virtue of a humorist's ability to hold court and get laughs. Starting with Thomas Dartmouth "T. D." Rice's sensational debut performance of "Jumping Jim Crow" in 1832, white working-class Americans developed an insatiable appetite for blackface minstrel shows. These were highly participatory programs—in which white men "blacked up" in burnt cork—that offered a distraction from the rituals of work by portraying absurdly broad stereotypes of African Americans' reputed simplicity and ignorance to mock the increasingly complex and dehumanizing effects of industrialization. Soon Jim Crow shared the stage with other stock blackface characters such as the comical Zip Coon, who symbolized the pretentious urban dandy, and Brudder Tambo and Brudder Bones, musician-jokers who poked fun at the hollow pretensions of elitism and power with puns and one-liners. A comic monologue known as "the stump speech" further spoofed these targets by mangling the oratorical style of speakers who pompously railed on about religion, politics, or moral reform. The audience got involved from the start, roaring its approval or displeasure from the house, demanding encores, throwing objects, even taking the stage to dance and sing along, determined, as "sovereigns," to "have the worth of our money when we go to the theater." From their rowdy participation in blackface minstrelsy to their antic and freewheeling reception of Falstaff and other fools in performances of Shakespeare's plays, which also were wildly popular at the time, Americans began to invent their own hurly-burly brand of popular show business and cast themselves as director, stage manager, and star.[6]

Charles Farrar Browne and his alter ego sprang from these innovations and traditions. Browne combined the country's burgeoning infatuation with humor and showmanship with its companion zeal for democracy to create Artemus Ward—a barely educated but entrepreneurial and wisecracking everyman—who became a one-man sensation during the 1860s. He allowed his audience to see themselves in sum as the public; and by appearing to be merely playing himself (most people did not differentiate between Charles Browne and Artemus Ward onstage), he allowed them to see themselves individually as the citizen. He modeled humor as a release mechanism and as an expression of personal liberty, hinting at its potential for cultural and political subversion. He playfully parodied national institutions—religion, politics and the presidency, even performance itself—and by reducing them to objects of laughter that his audience could share, he gave license for his fellow citizens to do the same. What is more, Browne poked fun at these institutions not just as they were still aborning but during the Civil War, when their very existence was in dire jeopardy. He thereby demonstrated to his countrymen and women that the mechanisms of democracy are necessarily forever undergoing revision, and that even in such moments of crisis (or especially during them), jokes, satire, and ridicule can render a restorative pruning effect that allows democracy to grow and adapt. Browne encouraged Americans to recognize humor as both a tonic to ease the immediate symptoms of the nation's pain and a prescription for its re-creation.

•   •   •

Charles Browne was the first solo performer to conjoin political humor with live performance for personal profit, but he certainly did not invent American political humor or laughter directed specifically at the presidency. Anglo-Americans' mockery of British oppression in general and the Crown in particular was a staple of the Revolutionary era and offered liberal precedent for Americans to align laughter forever after with political protest. Although most colonists remained loyal to George III and were loath to make fun of him directly in the years before war broke out, cheaply produced "jest-books," newspapers such as James Franklin's *New-England Courant*, and almanacs, including James's younger brother Benjamin's enormously popular *Poor Richard's Almanack*, introduced political one-liners to the reading public as early as the 1720s (an early zinger: "The greatest monarch on the proudest throne, is oblig'd to sit upon his own arse"). Of course, most gibes directed at British abuses were circulated in person—live between joker and audience—wherever two or more disgruntled colonists gathered together to denounce Parliament or the king directly once war broke out. These original spontaneous performances have been lost, of course, but their echoes can certainly be heard in the folk journalism of the day and the jest-books that continued to proliferate in the new nation toward the end of the eighteenth century. One of the more popular, *Feast of Merriment*, published in 1795, recounts the last illness of George II, who reportedly said to his physician, "You have, Sir, I suppose, helped many to another world." "Not so many as your Majesty," replied the doctor who evidently could not help but administer another parting dose of dry sarcasm, "nor with so much honor to myself." In his preface the editor of *Feast of Merriment* championed humor as essential to the new American spirit, insisting that "if [one] should chance to be a little squeamish at the stomach, it will prove an excellent remedy for the spleen, or the belly-ach [sic] of despair. In a word," he concluded with a nod to the empowering effects of a good laugh:

> [This book is] for the benefit of those who may be disposed to dance and sing; to add glee to the short pittance of life, to improve the social virtues; to heighten the charms of the big-bellied decanter, and to frighten

haggard care and her wry-faced train to a distance. Depend upon it, Reader, that with a few glasses of wine in your head, a pretty lass upon your knee and the *Feast of Merriment* in your hand, you will be a thousand times happier than any monarch in the universe.

At least according to this early American wag—no longer fettered to British tyranny but clearly still culturally influenced by it—kingly power could not hope to compete with the liberating power of a good joke.[7]

Simultaneously with their growing ridicule of the Crown, Americans began to create a heroic class from the Revolutionary ranks, and, with equal parts adulation and loving ridicule, they exalted their fellow countrymen's exploits even as they acknowledged their foibles, thus recognizing themselves and celebrating the common exceptionalism discernible in every American. Patriot-heroes of all ranks appeared in the jest-books and almanacs. Among them was Ethan Allen, the hero of Ticonderoga, whose ego was clipped in *Beers's Almanac* for 1793. One of seven brothers, Allen reportedly observed that never before had seven such been born of any woman, to which a Scottish officer replied, "You are mistaken. Mary Magdelen [sic] was delivered of seven exactly like you," a reference to Christ having cleansed Mary of seven demons. While cutting Allen's pride down to size through ridicule, the comment simultaneously championed the audacious swagger that Americans saw both in their heroes and in themselves.[8]

Wit was applauded in the new American hero. Early almanacs and jest-books not only recorded the exploits of warriors who did battle on the field but also touted those whose industriousness, practical education, and prowess with words equipped them to wage war on paper and win battles through laughter. No one was mentioned more frequently in this regard than Benjamin Franklin. Franklin's humor was the lodestar around which revolved all other competing and contradictory perceptions of this iconically paradoxical American. Franklin was many things: a printer, inventor, statesman, and scientist. He spent the first forty-two years of his life in private business and the last forty-two in public service. A man whose intellect was tempered by pragmatism, he wrote more than perhaps any other American of his day, yet he had largely taught himself to write. He exalted thrift when he famously spoke of pennies saved being pennies earned, yet he freely admitted that he could not practice thriftiness himself. He was both devoted to his wife and ever the flirt. Yet his humor and its many manifestations—wit, parody, satire, and puns at the expense of King George III, Parliament, and the foibles of humankind in general—did not excuse or reconcile these incongruities and contradictions in his character as much as celebrate them. In Franklin's hands, humor indicated heroic defiance, mastery over the follies and flaws of both others and oneself by virtue of being able to recognize them and replace the harm they might do with ridicule or resignation as the occasion demanded. As a young man Franklin tried to break this "habit I was getting into of prattling, punning, and joking," but to no avail. Whatever else he was or was not, Franklin epitomized the conviction that it was humor that made the man, and his fellow Americans strove to fashion themselves in his image.[9]

Early jest-books are replete with paeans to Franklin's tweaking of all manner of authority. His inventive efficiency was celebrated even at a young age and at the risk of offending his parents and the Almighty when, after enduring long prayers by his father before each meal, he reportedly said one year after all the winter's provisions had been stockpiled and salted: "I think, father, if you said grace over the whole [warehouse]—once and for all—it would be a vast saving of time." Another anecdote reveals Franklin serving as president of the Pennsylvania Constitutional Convention in 1776, when a law was proposed to forbid Episcopalians from praying for the king. Franklin, believing such a law might cause more of a disturbance among the public than it was worth,

> thought it quite unnecessary; for, added he, "those people have, to my certain knowledge, been praying constantly these twenty years past, that 'God would give to the King and his counsel wisdom,' and we all know that not the least notice has ever been taken of that prayer; so that it is plain they have no interest in the court of Heaven." The house smiled, and the motion was dropt.

In lionizing Franklin—the first celebrity comedian—alongside celebrity leaders Ethan Allen, Henry "Light-Horse Harry" Lee, Horatio Gates, and others, Americans enshrined humor in their pantheon of treasured national virtues. Indeed, Americans' adulation of Franklin and his mix of humor, politics, and performance prepared the way for Artemus Ward and the generations of political comics that followed.[10]

At first, sustained or large-scale efforts to redirect political humor from the British political elite to that of the new nation were halting and ambivalent, reflecting the conflict between the infant country's Old World pedigree and its adamant strivings for independence. Newfound freedoms still vied with time-honored deference to political and religious authority in the minds of many Americans, especially during the formative years of constitutional debate, popular rebellions, and foreign threats from England and France. As former subjects, Americans grappled with their simultaneous loathing for paying tribute and their long-standing fascination with empire, aristocracy, and titles. Franklin himself had hoped for reconciliation with England as late as 1775. Immediately after George Washington's inaugu-

ration in 1789, the Senate acknowledged this tension when it wrestled at
length over what to call the new president. A committee suggested "His
Highness the President of the United States of America and Protector of
the Rights of the Same." John Adams, who concurred with the committee
in believing that a reverence for titles ran deep in human nature, favored
the briefer but no less regal appellation "His Majesty the President." These
new Americans—those best positioned to define the institutions of political power in the United States and who were accustomed to either paying
deference or having others defer to them—remained captivated by nobility
and rank. For all their talk of equality, these were, after all, still the cultural descendants of those early Virginians who had convicted one Richard
Barnes of "base and detracting speeches concerning the governor" in 1625
and, prior to banishing him, had his arms broken and his tongue "bored
through with an awl." Patience for political criticism—even that ostensibly
couched in the pleasantries of good humor—was often scant. Many, including George Washington, whose deification as the gentleman commander
of the Revolution largely exempted him from even the soft ridicule of the
early jest-books and almanacs, had been weaned on "Rules of Civility" that
included the admonition, "Mock not, nor Jest at any thing of Importance[;]
break no Jest that are Sharp Biting, and, if you Deliver any thing witty and
Pleasant, abtain [sic] from Laughing thereat yourself." The Sedition Act of
1798, which a nervous Federalist Congress passed with President Adams's
approval to stifle opposition during the crisis of that year's war with France,
prohibited the "uttering or publishing [of] any false, scandalous, and mali-
cious writing or writings against the government of the United States, . . . or
the President," and presented a further chilling counterpoint to the Constitution's First Amendment right of free speech.[11]

Although such ambivalence toward authority and dissent continues to
some extent to the present day, the cut and thrust of a maturing political
discourse during the early nineteenth century nevertheless ensured that
eventually ridicule of the president would grow in direct proportion to the
stability and power of the republic and the presidency. By the time Charles
Browne took his first job as a printer's apprentice for the Skowhegan, Maine,
Clarion in the mid-1840s, presidential humor was firmly within the purview
of the fourth estate. Even Washington—no longer the leader of popular
revolution after his election but now the symbol of institutionalized federal
power—suffered the barbs of an increasingly partisan press. Editorial cartoonists began earning their long and well-documented reputation for presidential ridicule with an anonymous caricature in 1789 called "The Entry"
that showed a messianic Washington on a donkey being led into New York
by his aide David Humphreys, with an accompanying couplet that read,

"The glorious time has come to pass, / when David shall conduct an ass." Revolutionary War officer John Armstrong wrote to General Horatio Gates advising the ever decorous Washington to meet such attacks "with firmness and good nature," counsel that would be echoed by future presidential advisers and heeded in varying degrees by future presidents. The unavoidable political passions endemic to democracy made such humor part of the American landscape from the very beginning, cultural sensitivities and tradition notwithstanding.[12]

This paradoxical reverence for both radical egalitarianism and conventional aristocracy was at the heart of America's Revolution two and a half centuries ago and it remains foundational to political humor to the present day. As Tocqueville observed in 1835, Americans could see no "middle course between the sovereignty of all and the absolute power of one man," yet in their passion for collective equality they also naturally sought to be recognized individually as strong and respected. Such simultaneous striving for equality and distinction, Tocqueville continued, "tends to elevate the little man to the rank of the great [and] . . . leads the weak to want to drag the strong down to their level." These political maneuverings are visible in the heroic motif of the almanacs and jest-books; they also inspired a new generation of popular print humorists as the new nation began to coalesce during the early 1800s. The great American everyman—be he the shrewd, taciturn Yankee from Down East New England, the swaggering frontiersman of the Old Southwest (present-day Kentucky, Tennessee, and points south), or something in between—emerged in popular culture as a national emblem precisely because he was a *common* American, or at least had sprung from common stock. The legendary Davy Crockett parlayed his Tennessee roots, bravery, horse sense, and prodigious love of liquor and violence into three terms in the United States Congress and martyrdom at the Alamo. Washington Irving's Rip Van Winkle, a simple, good-natured idler with a shrewish wife, slept through the Revolutionary War in New York's Catskill Mountains and somehow wound up "reverenced as one of the patriarchs of the village." Exuding rustic earthiness through tall tales and pronouncements of cracker-barrel wisdom, the American everyman at the center of such humor danced merrily and confidently along the precarious middle course between the egalitarianism of popular sovereignty and the exceptionalism of individual supremacy. He triumphed as one who—in his sagacious simplicity—was the genius-fool, the simple man on the verge of greatness.[13]

This archetypical character took a decidedly political turn with the humor of Seba Smith. Born in Buckfield, Maine, in 1792, Smith was a journalist and publisher who founded the first daily newspaper printed north of Boston, the *Portland Daily Courier*, and with it gave himself a vehicle for

exposing the confused and regularly ridiculous doings of Maine politics—
and by extension national government as well. In 1830 Smith created Jack
Downing, a simple Yankee farm lad who stumbles into the political fray and
becomes nothing less than the confidant of presidents from Andrew Jackson
to Franklin Pierce. As Downing recalled later in his faux memoir, *My Thirty
Years Out of the Senate*, the odyssey began in 1829, when the impulsive and
adventurous young Jack "tackled up the old horse, . . . packed in a load of
ax-handles and a few notions [to sell] . . . and drove off for [Maine's largest
city,] Portland." He continues:

> I hadn't been in Portland long before I happened to blunder into the
> Legislater; and I believe that was the beginning of my good luck. I see
> such queer kinds of carrying on there that I couldn't help setting down
> and writing to cousin Ephraim to tell uncle Joshua about it. . . . So I
> went to the editor of the Portland Courier and asked him if he would
> send it . . . and fact, he went right to work and printed it in the Courier
> large as life. . . . Well, this kind of got me right into public life at once;
> and I've been in public life ever since, and have been writing letters and
> rising up along gradually, one step after another, till I've got up along
> side of the President, and am talked of now pretty strong for President
> myself, and have been nominated in a good many of the first papers of
> the country.[14]

This tale of Downing's introduction to political life is a quintessential one
in presidential humor. The image of a rustic coming to town looking to sell
ax handles, "mother's cheese, and cousin Nabby's bundle of footings [stock-
ings]," then strolling into the Maine legislature, being quickly recognized
as one of the keenest minds in the room, and soon being propelled into a
stellar political career, projects an incongruity that was at once ridiculous
and completely plausible in the burgeoning democracy of 1830s America.
With his ability to make the transition quickly and naturally from bump-
kin to presidential aide and then to presidential contender, he illustrated
for Americans not only the relatively short distance between these stations
but also indeed their comical equivalence. In one letter written during
President Andrew Jackson's sensationally popular tour of the Northeast in
1833, the loyal Downing reported that he even shook hands in place of the
president, who was exhausted by the press of thousands of admirers wanting
to see and touch "the man of the people." He stood behind Old Hickory
and extended his right arm under Jackson's, with the throngs of star-struck
well-wishers none the wiser. In his meteoric rise, coming "up along side of
the President" (effortlessly attaining the ranks of captain and major in the
process), Smith's everyman increasingly subsumed the presidency itself; the

common citizen rose to greatness even as the president's aching arm and general fatigue revealed the human limitations of executive power. Downing's close dances with the presidency—and their contradictory signals as to who was leading and who was following in the dance—anticipated the fictional association between Artemus Ward and Abraham Lincoln a generation later, but even more significantly, they set the stage for the work of future comics who would get their laughs and earn their livings exploiting a foundational joke of American political culture: the apparently ridiculous contradiction of granting someone unequaled power over a nation of equals. Jack Downing's exploits also presaged in print the later live performances of presidential impersonation and the mock presidential campaigns of comedians from Will Rogers in the 1920s, to Pat Paulsen and his hilariously deadpan crusades for the White House in 1968 and 1972, to Stephen Colbert's brief candidacy in 2007–8.[15]

• • •

One year after Jack Downing and Andrew Jackson's tour through the Northeast, less than twenty miles from Seba Smith's native Buckfield, and in the very shadow of Downing's imaginary hometown of Downingville, Charles Farrar Browne was born in Waterford, Maine. The proximity represented more than mere coincidence; the dynamic Maine frontier—emblematic of the fragile compromise between slavery and abolition since the state's admission to the Union in 1820, and still on the threshold between settlement and wilderness—seemed to beget humor as a means of affording its inhabitants a way to reconcile the region's cultural contradictions as well as rebel against them.

Similarities to Smith pervade much of Browne's career. He was apprenticed to a printer at the age of thirteen and was completely steeped in the newspaper business as a type compositor, reporter, and editor by the time he was twenty-three. Like Smith and many of his countrymen (and reminiscent of Jack Downing), he did not see his future in his rural origins and instead gravitated toward the expanding political and cultural spheres of urban life, traveling to Boston, where he wrote his first pieces for the humor weekly *The Carpet-Bag* and then—upon its demise—to Tiffin, Ohio, then Toledo, and eventually to Cleveland, where he became associate editor of the *Plain Dealer*. He reveled in the discourse and debate that seemed to explode out of newsrooms, bars, and courthouses, and he found great comedy in the melee. At the *Toledo Commercial* he began to write humorous bits regularly ridiculing the city's political confusions, opting—according to one nineteenth-century biographer—for good-natured sarcasm to make his arguments, in contrast to the rival *Toledo Blade*, which chose "violent vituperation." Browne's comical strategy earned the *Commercial* more readers and him the beginnings of a following. While at the *Plain Dealer* he again followed Seba Smith and other humorists of the day when he began to cloak his gibes at American politics and culture in the guise of a genial if semi-literate "Old Showman" named Artemus Ward, who hailed from the fictional but quintessentially American town of Baldinsville, Indiana. Browne's indebtedness to Smith and others is extensive, to be sure, but he would build on Smith's precedent to revolutionize the performance of humor and to introduce Americans to the political power of laughter.[16]

Artemus Ward gained national fame during Browne's three years at the *Plain Dealer* owing to the continued meteoric rise of newspaper distribution and voracious readership. By 1860 the paper's daily circulation was more than 65,000 copies in a city that numbered only 43,000 residents and in a wider region that also sustained four other dailies. Even more significantly, the humor of Artemus Ward spread across the country thanks to the most widespread national postal system in the world and congressional legislation that not only granted newspapers deeply discounted postage rates but also allowed for the free exchange of material in the interests of encouraging a national news network and a better-informed populace. Readers from California to Browne's home state of Maine began to follow the humorous musings of the Old Showman as he traveled from town to town with his eccentric menagerie of oddities, which included "three moral Bares, a Kangaroo, . . . wax figgers of G. Washington . . . [and] several miscellanyus moral wax statoots . . . ekalled by few & exceld by none," all the while waxing comical on the events of the day, political and otherwise. Artemus Ward was becoming a star, and though his comedic celebrity did not equal the mythic status bestowed on Benjamin Franklin a half-century before, it was more widespread as a result of the increasing ubiquity and sophistication of print capitalism. As the presidential election of 1860 approached, it is likely that at least as many Americans had heard of the entertainer Artemus Ward as knew of the politician Abraham Lincoln.[17]

Yet few knew Ward's creator, Charles Browne. The free newspaper exchange of the day precluded any hope for royalties, and as associate editor of the *Plain Dealer*, he earned a paltry fourteen dollars a week. He started to entertain the possibility of capitalizing on America's growing love affair with all manner of amusements by taking his Old Showman on the road for real, via live performance. After a final attempt to negotiate with *Plain Dealer* publisher J. W. Gray to keep Browne in Cleveland and Ward exclusively in print (Browne offered to sell the Artemus Ward brand to the paper for $1,200 a year; Gray refused), Browne left Ohio for New York City and what his alter ego called "the show bizniss." His homely looks and soft-spoken demeanor notwithstanding, he believed he could earn himself the celebrity that had always captivated him and a much better living, even attain real wealth. Humor now had proven commercial value in America, and so Browne did as thousands of others were doing in this impatient and opportunistic country on the make: he re-created himself in his own sovereign image.[18]

For all his apparent confidence, Browne's romance with performance was an uneasy one. He had been enthralled by the stage since his days in Boston. He knew every play that passed through and kept happy company with the actors and artists of the day, but doubts about joining their ranks plagued him. He was by nature painfully shy. In Ohio he had once been unexpectedly called upon to speak at a banquet and found he could only sit petrified in his chair, silently shaking his head. In the next day's paper—safely out of the limelight and back behind the pen—he managed a hilarious recovery when he wrote, according to one biographer: "'We scorn the imputation of vanity, but we say our speech was a dignified and striking effort. In answer to a "response" call, we spoke felicitously as follows,' and the 'as follows' was three column-inches of blank space with the words 'immense and prolonged applause' at the bottom." Determined to conquer his fears, Browne purchased a copy of *The Western Orator*, a bestselling release that cashed in on the new popularity of public speaking, and began to study the basics of oratory in anticipation of his new career in front of a live audience.[19]

Browne's other misgivings about performance reflected in microcosm one of the nation's most enduring dilemmas. Born into a staunchly puritanical family, he was deeply influenced, even chastened by this part of his heritage, yet it was predictably at odds with his fascination for the stage. Speaking as Artemus Ward, Browne later declared, "I believe we are descendid from the Puritins, who nobly fled from a land of despitism to a land of freedim, where they could not only enjoy their own religion, but prevent everybody else from enjoyin his." Such jabs aside, he considered his religious roots with a mixture of veneration and satire—a tension he was never able to reconcile fully. At the same time, this conservatism instilled in him a work ethic that drove his sense of perfectionism and a feverish performance schedule that no doubt led to his early death. He was enthralled by stage life but was never completely convinced that such performance was entirely respectable.[20]

Most of his native New England—and the nation—shared his reticence. Browne's Puritan ancestors did not ban frivolity outright, but theirs was a decidedly ascetic brand of fun and came with so many theological strings attached that leisure was often accompanied by equal measures of guilt and fear. Levity, for those first New Englanders, was intended for advancing and preserving morality. The only good mirth, in the paradoxical admonition of one minister, was "sober mirth." It was to be "free" but "pure," "cheerful" yet "grave." Just as humor was to glorify God, it must not mock any representative of ecclesiastical or civil authority. Succeeding generations, including Browne's, inherited the spirit if not the letter of these restrictions. Many Americans still considered the phrase "the legitimate theater" to be similarly oxymoronic. In 1778 the Second Continental Congress resolved that because "frequenting play houses and theatrical entertainments has a fatal tendency to divert the minds of the people from a due attention to . . . the preservation of their liberties," any government official found attending such shows "shall be deemed unworthy to hold . . . office, and shall be accordingly dismissed." After extended debate the resolution was narrowly defeated, but nearly a century later the popularity of attractions such as plays, minstrel shows, and P. T. Barnum's American Museum in Manhattan—whose waxworks, live animals, and other novelties were the inspiration for Artemus Ward's traveling menagerie—was still countered by long-standing prescriptions against such frivolity.[21]

This antipathy took on an increased spiritual urgency in the nineteenth century, especially among those of the burgeoning northern middle class who sought moral calm amid the tempestuous changes brought about by industry and capitalism. Famed minister and reformer Henry Ward Beecher condemned the theater—explicitly recognizing its cultural potency—when he described it as "the gate of debauchery . . . [and] the door to all the sinks of iniquity." After all, amusements and those who performed them challenged established orthodoxies where gender, authority, and propriety in general were concerned. Even though much of the country was beginning to reject the proscriptions of Beecher and others, many remained convinced that having fun was a dubious enterprise at best, or that it simply was not worth the pain.[22]

Browne believed that he had to address such lingering antagonism, especially if he wished to attract a middle-class audience. His solution revolutionized popular performance and inaugurated the standup comedic form in America. Whereas "theatricals" that entertained were suspect, "popular lectures" that edified and promoted virtue were enthusiastically received by the middle class. Beecher, reformist publisher Horace Greeley, and legions of other cultural and Christian soldiers—aghast at the host of social ills they saw besieging the nation and increasingly adamant over the abolition of slavery—took to the public lecture platform at lyceums and athenaeums and drew tremendous crowds of people increasingly willing to be improved for the price of a ticket. Indeed, much of Artemus Ward's humor in print sprang from the incongruous image of the Old Showman's rustic ignorance juxtaposed with the "grate Moral Entertainment" he offered through his traveling collection of exotic animals and wax figures (which included the twelve apostles and other biblical characters). When Browne took to the stage, he decided not to "act" the persona of Artemus Ward, the portly rustic with the receding hairline, the sideshow dress, and the delightfully twisted way with words. He put on no makeup, costume, or vocal affectation; he was not "performing" per se. Instead, although Ward got all the billing, Browne appeared as himself: quiet, gaunt, bookish, and dressed in the sober garb of the lecturer. He appeared intent on lecturing; indeed he did lecture, but the frolicsome nonsense that he dispensed—as he stood before the crowd addressing them directly—did not edify, at least not in predictable terms. Rather, as he tweaked both the form and content of public lectures as well as what he saw as the moral extremism of those who delivered them, it gradually became clear that his purpose was to delight and to merrily subvert the ritual of such performances. He often would take to the podium and stand staring at the audience for long moments of uncomfortable silence as if he had forgotten his lines. Soon the crowd would begin to murmur, squirm, or cough nervously, and then just as the din was rising toward a peak he would chide: "Ladies and gentlemen. When you have finished with this unseemly interruption, I shall be glad to continue." By all appearances Browne was a minister and protector of the ritualized conventions of the day with his apparent homage to the lecture form, but in fact he was choreographing a playful new brand of cultural criticism, and audiences eagerly joined in the dance.[23]

In parodying the lecture in a daring yet disarming and wholly unprecedented way, Browne prophesied the coming of a new type of performance and performer. Comic stage actors, though prevalent in the theater by the 1860s, were generally confined to a specific role that the audience accepted as artifice, and they were subservient to the larger production around them. Similarly, the joker of blackface minstrelsy—while his timing and material were foundational to the patter that would mark standup comedy—was cloaked in a stock character and moved within performance expectations that had become ritualized by the mid-1800s. His dependence on set routines and fellow performers who might alternate as the joker or straight man makes him the harbinger of the comedy teams of vaudeville and beyond. Browne popularized something different and unique. With his Artemus Ward came the solo standup comedian, whose topical treatments of culture and politics could both mitigate the troubles of daily life and critique the status quo using the guerrilla tactics of humor. Here was the unadorned American everyman, speaking his mind and getting public laughs from laborers and the middle class alike as the sovereign star of his own show.

Browne debuted in Connecticut and Massachusetts in late 1861, and the Boston press reported that audiences were "kept in a constant roar of laughter." His "lecture" title, "Babes in the Wood," was a comedic misdirection, for Browne never quite got around to discussing the classic folktale, although the name was appropriate given his mischievous manipulation of an infant American audience learning to laugh at its own quirks and inconsistencies in the midst of civil war; culturally, his listeners were still "babes in the wood." During the performance he righteously endorsed the concept of temperance hotels, for example, although he lamented that "they sell worse liquor than any other kind of hotels." Everyone—whether Yankee or Confederate, white or black, male or female—seemed to fall prey to his genial ridicule. Religious fervor also took it on the chin. The Quakers were targets; so were the Mormons, both in Browne's onstage references to polygamy and on the complimentary passes he issued for a later show, "Among the Mormons," which read, "Admit the Bearer and One Wife." Purveyed as it was with such disarming and self-effacing good cheer, Ward's foolishness was embraced with enthusiasm, even by the Mormons, who welcomed him hospitably to Salt Lake City during his western tour in early 1864 and sanctioned his use of the local hall for a performance that included Brigham Young beaming from the audience.[24]

More orthodox American boorishness also came under attack. Crowds heard the same sorts of gibes from the stage that they appreciated in the pages of Ward's letters and essays, which Browne—like many of his contemporary humorists—wrote in the eccentric vernacular of the everyman. One told the story of the oafish fellow in Utica, New York, who physically attacked the Old Showman's collection of wax figures depicting the Last Supper, pummeling the effigy of Judas Iscariot while demanding of Ward:

> "What did you bring this pussylanermus cuss here fur?"
>
> "You egrejus ass," shouted Ward, "that air's a wax figger—a representashun of the false 'Postle."
>
> "That's all very well for you to say, but I can tell you, old man, that Judas Iscarrot can't show hisself in Utiky with impunerty by a darn site!"[25]

This was one of Browne's most popular stories. Through such silliness, whether recounted in print or performance, Americans were learning to laugh at one another in public, and in recognizing their own contributions to the eclectic and often eccentric national personality, they were also beginning to laugh at themselves as the object of the joke.

● ● ●

Even the president was laughing. Abraham Lincoln never attended "Babes in the Wood" or any other of Browne's shows, but he was a devotee of Artemus

Ward in print. When *Artemus Ward, His Book*, a collection of the Old Showman's writings, appeared in May 1862, Lincoln acquired one of the forty
thousand copies published and consulted it often. He reportedly began the
cabinet meeting of September 22 of that year by buoyantly reading aloud the
tale about the "High-Handed Outrage at Utica" before turning to the main
business of the meeting: the Emancipation Proclamation.[26]

Lincoln's appreciation of Ward's joke is understandable, for he shared
much with Browne and many other of his fellow citizens. Born in humble
circumstances on the Kentucky frontier, he ascended to the presidency using
the strategies of self-invention that were so familiar to Benjamin Franklin,
Seba Smith, Charles Browne, and their contemporaries. Lincoln's experiences and instincts taught him the desirability—even the imperative—of
humor in determining his fortunes. He relied on getting laughs from his
earliest days to ingratiate him to residents of the Illinois community where
he practiced law, to compensate for what has been described as his almost
majestic physical ugliness, and—like Browne—to ward off the cold disad-
vantages of his meager rural upbringing. By all accounts his talents for storytelling and mimicry were prodigious, and his seemingly endless reservoir
of anecdotes and tall tales appealed to both northern working-class ideals
and the middle-class sensibilities to which Lincoln subscribed. He famously
used one-liners and extended narratives to disarm foes affably, but he also
could employ invective—less frequently but no less effectively—to mock
detractors. When an early campaign speech was repeatedly interrupted by a
critic in the audience, Lincoln retaliated:

> I don't object to being interrupted with sensible questions, but I must say
> that my boisterous friend does not always make inquiries which properly
> come under that head. He says he is afflicted with headaches, at which
> I don't wonder, as it is a well-known fact that nature abhors a vacuum,
> and takes her own way of demonstrating it.

The candidate from Illinois could squelch a heckler as well as any other
standup comedian.[27]

Lincoln, therefore, had a keen understanding of the essential threefold
perspective on political humor. First, as a reader and citizen, he knew
what his fellow citizens were discovering, namely, the therapeutic ability of
humor to anesthetize audiences—at least momentarily—against the dilemmas of the day and to salve the despair of a horrific war. Second, as president
of the Union and therefore both at the center of such dilemmas and the
object of criticism or ridicule concerning them, he felt the potency of such
ridicule and, far from dismissing it, was generally equipped to receive it with
empathetic joviality. (When told that Secretary of War Edwin M. Stanton

had called him a fool, Lincoln reportedly replied: "Well, I guess I had better go over and see Stanton about this. Stanton is usually right.") Finally, as a fellow humorist by both instinct and design, Lincoln was able to blunt barbs aimed at him because he was always able to give much better than he got, and he understood the use of humor to deflect criticism and accumulate political capital. His ability to joke, and to be joked at, subtly mitigated his administration's unprecedented wielding of executive power during the Civil War. His humor became a positive measure of Lincoln's humanity that countered for many (at least many in the North) the utter contempt in which he, as the face of the Union, was held by the South and softened some of the wartime measures thought draconian by many, such as his suspending the writ of habeas corpus in border states, declaring martial law in several instances, and emancipating the slaves. By necessity Lincoln redefined the presidency, and by instinct he included humor in the definition.[28]

Given all this and his particular admiration for Browne's craft, Lincoln saw the benefit of coupling an Artemus Ward tale with the serious business of state. He also no doubt reveled in occasionally being the butt of an Artemus Ward joke. The account of the outrage at Utica in *Artemus Ward, His Book* appeared only pages away from the fanciful "Interview with President Lincoln" which began this chapter. The meeting—with the helpless president practically violated by a whirlwind of office seekers crawling down his chimney and between his legs, and consequently having to be protected by the valiant showman—was pure farce, and Lincoln was at its center. The idea that the president of the United States was powerless but for the authority of a comedian, or that he could just as easily be on the receiving end of a joke as any anonymous fool in Utica, had been gaining traction since the days when Seba Smith's Jack Downing came to the aid of an exhausted Andrew Jackson, but Browne's work made a wider mass audience much more receptive to such notions.

And Browne went even further: he shared the stage with the president. Lincoln may also have read Browne's 1863 contribution to *Vanity Fair* titled "Artemus Ward in Washington," which included a visit to the White House:

I called on Abe. He received me kindly. I handed him my umbreller, and told him I'd have a check for it if he pleased. "That," sed [Lincoln], "puts me in mind of a little story. There was a man, out in our parts who was so mean that he took his wife's coffin out of the back winder for fear he would rub the paint off the doorway. Wall, about this time there was a man in a adjacent town who had a green cotton umbreller."

[Ward interrupts:] "Did it fit him well? Was it custom made? Was he measured for it?"

"Measured for what?" said Abe.

"The umbreller?"

"Wall, as I was sayin," continnered the President, treatin the inter-ruption with apparent contempt, "this man sed he'd known that there umbreller ever since it was a pyrasol. Ha, ha, ha!"

"Yes," sed I, larfin in a respectful manner, "but what has this man with the umbreller to do with the man who took his wife's coffin out of the back winder?"

"To be sure," said Abe—"what was it? I must have got two stories mixed together, which puts me in mind of another lit—"

"Never mind, Your Excellency. . . . " I took my departer.

"Good-bye, old sweetness!" sed Abe, shakin me cordgully by the hand.

"Adoo, my Prahayrie flower!" I replied, and made my exit.

This merry patter is proto-vaudevillian. Here were two comedians sharing the limelight and vying for laughs. In this small corner of Browne's world, the president played the comic and the comic willingly played the foil, at least until the limits of presidential talent killed the joke and thus *became* the joke. As they said their silly, fawning good-byes, bosom buddies after all, Americans laughed at both comedians, one—"His Excellency" the president—having been humbled to the rank of showman, the other ele-vated to the partner of presidents.[29]

Browne and Lincoln never met, and there is no evidence that Ward's treatment of the president ever went beyond the printed page into Browne's live performances. Still, through their merry fictional associations they shared the stage as equals in the American popular imagination, however briefly, each benefiting from the other's celebrity. The showman gained political legitimacy as the politician learned the benefits of showmanship. At the conclusion of the manic "Interview with President Lincoln" (fig. 1) the grateful president-elect asked Artemus Ward who should fill his cabinet: "Fill it up with Showmen, sir! Showmen, is devoid of politics. They hain't got any principles. They know how to cater for the public. They know what the public wants, North & South. Showmen, sir, is honest men." Show-men may have been in short supply in Lincoln's cabinet, but the exigencies of the twentieth century and the mass media channels of radio and televi-sion ensured that future presidents would heed Ward's advice and bring showmanship—and increasingly the skills of a comedian—to the presi-dency itself.[30]

Neither Charles Browne nor Artemus Ward is well remembered, but Browne's legacy is ubiquitous in American culture today. He refined what the almanac jesters had first discovered during the Revolutionary era and Seba Smith had mined in the 1830s: the power of humor not only to equate

FIGURE 1. *Artemus Ward's imagined "Interview with President Lincoln" illustrated for* The Complete Works of Artemus Ward. *The artist is unknown.*

the egalitarian and the authoritarian impulses within a democracy but also to satirize bare humanity while simultaneously celebrating it. Browne demonstrated this not only with his gentle mocking of the presidency but also with his ridicule of the Mormons and the zealot from Utica. His hilariously awkward presence onstage gibed at those who presumed the authority to elevate themselves onto the lecture platform. He exposed the common foibles of those who would claim in some way to have special access to or province over the ideals of freedom and justice. He articulated for a growing American public what literature scholar Louis Rubin Jr. later termed "the Great American Joke," that is, the inherently laughable incongruity between the *promise* of unalloyed independence and the base *realities* of human nature that impose all manner of limitations on it. Americans may have imbued their nation with the most perfect of ambitions, yet they have entrusted their attainment to imperfect creatures like themselves. Ward, and later his student Mark Twain, brought the Great American Joke before a public increasingly torn between denying this incongruity and bursting into laughter over it.[31]

What is more, Browne's was the first solo act to bring live comedy to the American marketplace in a concerted form, both confirming and commercializing French philosopher Henri Bergson's observation that laughter "appears to stand in need of an echo. . . . Our laughter is always the laughter of a group." As the conduits by which humor was transferred from the page to the stage, Charles Browne and Artemus Ward taught Americans to laugh in community and to "entertain" themselves, a verb that means, as anthropologist Victor Turner reminds us, "to hold [possibilities] between." In the echoes of Browne's words and their own laughter, his countrymen heard themselves and auditioned new cultural and political possibilities concerning their relationship with their highest elected leader. Browne's humorous lectures would later mix with immigrant styles and other influences to render a wholly American form: standup comedy. An American company of comedians—citizens and presidents, led by the new standup humorists—was performing itself into existence.[32]

2

$\mathcal{D}$ance $\mathcal{P}$artners

IF CHARLES BROWNE was the first meteor of standup comedy to appear over the American landscape, Samuel Clemens was the comet. While Browne's fame as Artemus Ward was as brilliant as it was short-lived, Clemens's as Mark Twain burned on into the twentieth century, and his humor came to be celebrated by the nation and much of the world as quint-essentially American. Author and critic William Dean Howells once described Charles Browne as "the humorist who first gave the world a taste of the humor that characterizes the whole American people," while for one of his biographers, Browne's comedy defined "the genus American." But while Browne offered a taste, Clemens served up a progressive feast, seasoning American humor with liberal measures of authenticity, exuberance, irony, and cynicism that reflected the bittersweet experiences of a nation staggered by its own success.[1]

Clemens—whose birth coincided with the appearance of Halley's Comet in 1835 and whose death came with its return in 1910—alternately celebrated, kidded, and openly mocked the wholesale upheavals in the ways Americans worked and played during this dynamic time. He also challenged how they governed themselves through the presidency, though not as directly or consistently as would later comedians. Still, inspired by Browne and others but confronted by wholly new contingencies, he refined the national humor to address what he observed as the abuses of unbridled industrialized capitalism at home and the exploitations abroad that accompanied the United States' war with Spain and its first imperial adventures in Cuba and the Philippines at the turn of the twentieth century. It was Twain the humorist who lent the period its name—"the Gilded Age"—after the title of the satirical novel he coauthored in 1873. The sobriquet seemed fitting to describe a society in which, by 1893, 9 percent of American families owned 71 percent of the wealth, and which had been blinded, in the opinion of many, to massive injustice by a paper-thin but highly burnished veneer of affluence. To much of his audience, as Twain himself admitted, his humor often vanished in the face of his black fury over the greed, racism, and political corruption he saw consuming the nation. Yet this bitterness—most virulent during the last two decades of his life—was offset in the minds of the wider public by the hallmark themes that had made Twain America's bestselling author, favorite humorist, and most quoted sage since Benjamin Franklin. The idyllic boyhood exploits of Tom Sawyer, the comical yarns about backwoods frontiersmen, and Twain's own raucous adventures as a miner and riverboat pilot—all captured in the natural speech of real Americans—forever aligned ambition and sturdy individualism with defiant humor in the national character, even more firmly than had the words of Franklin, Washington Irving, or Seba Smith. In short, as the gulf between the American ideal and the American reality yawned to an unprecedented width, Twain's work ultimately upheld even as it ridiculed that keystone of the Great American Joke: an archetypical faith in the nation's potential. For not simply preserving America's humor during this period but reimagining it and inspiring its people to do the same, Twain became, for Howells, "the Lincoln of our literature." Through his articles, letters, short stories, books, and performances, "the genus American" first articulated by Browne was evolving into a more complexly funny species.[2]

· · ·

By the turn of the century most agreed with Twain's own boast that he was "the most conspicuous person on the planet," and this was both because and in spite of a host of changes that began to define the modern American audience even as his influence helped define the modern standup comedian. The public sphere where Americans informed, confronted, and entertained one another was growing exponentially, evolving to meet the needs and desires of an expanding and increasingly heterogeneous society. In the process, humorists and presidents—and the notion of both as "showmen"—progressed well beyond the whimsy of Artemus Ward, and Mark Twain retained a starring role through it all.[3]

The world of print still dominated this public sphere. Although he delivered nearly a thousand lectures and speeches to live audiences, Twain, "the people's author," appeared primarily through the words Americans read by or about him. Literacy continued to expand, aided by industrialization, which created the need for a managerial class able to read and write instruction manuals, run the factories, and keep the books. This mass of new readers tended to flock not to the traditional classics but to more accessible literature, including novels and other popular books sold through subscription marketing, the method that accounted for much of Twain's readership. Popular magazines thrived as printing processes improved and costs came down. The combined per issue circulation of monthly periodicals alone soared from 18 million to 64 million in the years between 1890 and 1905. The number of daily newspapers ballooned from fewer than 600 in 1870 to 2,226 at the turn of the century in an effort to keep pace with Americans' appetite for print, and as this competition for readers grew, so did innovation. Publishers introduced new features, including separate pages for sports coverage and advice columns. In 1896 publishing magnate William Randolph Hearst introduced an eight-page multicolored comic supplement called "The American Humorist" to his Sunday *New York Journal* which became the progenitor for comic strip sections that would have Americans laughing at favorites from the "Katzenjammer Kids" to "Li'l Abner" to "Peanuts." Editorial cartoonists—most famously Thomas Nast in *Harper's Weekly* and Joseph Keppler in the new humor magazine *Puck*—made political ridicule and satire widely accessible with their cutting drawings exposing social ills and corrupt politics, those of presidents included. Columnists likewise gained large followings with the rise of circulation and nationwide syndication. Among them was Finley Peter Dunne, who, in the guise and brogue of fictional Martin Dooley, a sagacious Irish barkeep on Chicago's industrial South Side, used comedic satire and mimicry to link working-class immigrant Americans to their leaders, be they the local alderman or the president of the United States.[4]

In addition to print, all manner of entertainments were born out of cultural necessity and economic opportunity to accommodate the demands and the pocketbooks of a massive and diverse working class, many of whom could not read English. The infant "show bizniss" of Artemus Ward's day began to gain large-scale economic traction, and there quickly arose an intricate and popular—if not completely legitimate—entertainment industry that offered escape even as it mirrored the broader economic and social trends toward centralized mass production. In their playful attendance at circuses, amusement parks, organized baseball and football games, Wild West shows, and other big-time attractions—all of which emerged in the four decades after the Civil War—Americans found themselves liberated from ritualized work schedules, prescribed boundaries of behavior, and the stares of the bosses and other "superiors" who lorded over these and seemingly all other aspects of their lives. During the early 1870s, as a severe depression closed many dramatic theaters, entrepreneurial producers began to package variety programs mixing specialty acts, dance numbers, comedy, and songs. They called the result vaudeville, hoping the refined reference to the France's Valley of Vire—or vau-de-Vire, where such songs were first popularized—would attract all segments of the mass audience, women and the middle class as well as workingmen. It did. Vaudeville houses, then networks of affiliated theaters called circuits, multiplied to meet demand. A decade later two New Englanders—Benjamin Franklin (B. F.) Keith and Edward Franklin Albee—began to monopolize vaudeville with a circuit of theaters in the East that eventually controlled the acts booked into hundreds of venues. Similarly the Orpheum Circuit, begun by California impresarios Gustav Walter and Morris Meyerfeld Jr., came to dominate the West and Midwest.[5]

Vaudeville stole the show for the next fifty years, and—along with the proliferation of print and other cheap amusements—began to cultivate a sophisticated mass audience. Diversity—of both the public itself and the entertainments available to it—muted the sense of group identification within audiences that had been so prevalent before the Civil War in favor of a more private, individualized experience. The commercial imperative to earn good press coverage and protect profits by attracting high-quality paying audiences prompted vaudeville producers to attempt to manage audience behavior by imposing house rules and presenting fare that was noncontroversial and decidedly apolitical (Keith-Albee theaters were nicknamed—not always flatteringly—"the Sunday School Circuit" for their family-friendly fare). As sociologist Richard Butsch has argued, these developments tended to subordinate the earlier sense of political sovereignty and solidarity within audiences in favor of a new culture of consumption, which became even more pronounced in the twentieth century. Yet if such trends made audiences comparatively more fragmented, passive, and less political than they had been a half-century earlier, their broader and more frequent attendance at shows made them—and the performers who played to them—more discriminating and sophisticated, particularly in their sense of humor. As selective consumers, audience members were no longer mere receivers or appreciators of humor in a broad sense; they were becoming critical interpreters of it. Both the production and reception of laughter grew more calculated and multilayered. Those who laughed and those who were laughed at learned to distinguish the chuckles of joyful release and the howls of approval from the jeers of mocking derision. If laughter was temporarily diminished as an expression of political sovereignty, it became a more potent declaration of economic independence, and performers had to play to these realizations or else, in the parlance of vaudeville, they "got the hook." As for political humor, it resided for the time being in the world of print, where, thanks to the efforts of cartoonists and columnists and the incendiary wit of Mark

Twain, Americans were gradually becoming as discriminating as readers as they were as members of an audience.[6]

All kinds of political performers, and eventually presidents, got in on the act. Political theater was on the rise as a result of the same seismic changes that were affecting all other aspects of American life. Union victory in the Civil War made dashing heroes of the military and political leaders who won it and stock villains of those in the defeated Confederacy. Congress, eager to reassert its power over the presidency, jousted with Abraham Lincoln's successor, Andrew Johnson, over Reconstruction and the limits of executive power, producing a knock-down, drag-out public drama that climaxed with Johnson's impeachment and near conviction. After barely clinging to the presidency with the election of Rutherford B. Hayes (described by one heckling critic as "a third-rate nonentity whose only recommendation is that he is obnoxious to no one"), Lincoln's Republican Party abandoned Reconstruction and public reform to promote private interest and industrial, continental, and then international expansion. As a result, depending on one's loyalties, Republicans were cast as either the champions of prosperity or the conservative stooges of robber barons such as John D. Rockefeller, Andrew Carnegie, and J. P. Morgan, who propagated monopolistic trusts in oil, steel, and finance. For their part, Democrats applied industrial mechanization to civic government by consolidating their support among immigrants and the urban working class into political "machines" that dominated many regional and city governments, spawning corruption and making famous (or infamous) the bosses who controlled them. The most notorious of these was Tammany Hall, the machine that controlled New York City politics throughout the nineteenth and early twentieth centuries. Thomas Nast's brilliant caricatures of its most infamous ringleader, William M. "Boss" Tweed, kept the cartoonist's national audience transfixed as the cartoons put a ridiculous human face on political fraud. Owing largely to Nast's humor, Tweed was ultimately arrested, convicted, and laughed out of office.[7]

The continuing explosive rise in print media highlighted not only the monopolistic, conservative, or corrupt actions associated with the Gilded Age but also the reformist reactions to them. Farmers and other rural Americans saw their way of life—traditionally the foundation of American identity—upstaged by government support for industrialization. In 1892 they formed the People's or Populist Party to rescue their agrarian interpretation of democracy and curb what they saw as rampant political corruption that favored huge corporations. Although the Populists failed to score significant wins nationally, several of their reforms were ultimately adopted, including the direct election of U.S. senators, and they produced a bona fide political icon in William Jennings Bryan, the "Great Commoner," whose oratory and crusades against the gold standard and imperialism kept him a prominent figure in American life for three decades and made him a nominee for president three times. The Progressive movement, which lasted until World War I, enlisted middle-class reformers at all levels of political rank to tackle societal ills such as urban pollution and overcrowding, child labor, graft, and the dehumanizing exploitation of immigrants. Progressive leaders such as Wisconsin's governor Robert M. La Follette, New Jersey's Woodrow Wilson, and settlement house pioneer Jane Addams earned prominence in the movement. In the South, former slave Booker T. Washington gained fame advocating moderate measures to counter the racism of Jim Crow from his Tuskegee Institute in Alabama, and journalist Ida B. Wells launched her fearless anti-lynching campaign. Women continued to advocate for equality. In 1872—a half-century before women were granted the right to vote—the Equal Rights Party nominated Victoria Woodhull as the first woman to run for president, with former slave and civil rights champion Frederick Douglass as her running mate. Of course most considered the very notion of a woman or an African American running the country to be a joke.

In the limelight of the expanding print media and in the gaze of a new mass audience, the performance of politics now included an eclectic cast of characters, but the president was not prominent among them in the early years of the Gilded Age. With the reallocation of official power to Congress, big business, city bosses, and state leaders, the chief executive was largely removed from the life of the people; Americans had nearly as hard a time distinguishing between James Garfield, Chester Arthur, and Benjamin Harrison in their own day as we do in ours. Circumstances brought a change. With the country becoming a titanic force in both the global economy and the race for empire, political power began to gravitate toward the executive branch, and the nation's attention started to orbit more closely around it. William McKinley's administration, and especially Theodore Roosevelt's, interacted deliberately with the print media and with the public directly and more frequently, out of reluctant necessity in McKinley's case, but more out of personal effusiveness as well as deliberate calculation in Teddy Roosevelt's.

Two humorists were particularly well equipped and well positioned to comment on this shift. Through his syndicated newspaper columns, Finley Peter Dunne and his loquacious saloonkeeper Mr. Dooley brought working-class immigrants into contact with presidential policies with such jovial authenticity that they could practically hear the bartender's voice. As for Twain, his theatrics—the drawling delivery, the everyman persona that identified him as neither an easterner nor entirely western, and, in later years, his signature white suits—complemented the literary celebrity that

made him the most famous humorist in American history. Once his fame
as a writer was firmly established in the early 1870s, he largely spurned live
performance and returned to it only out of economic imperative or to promote a new book. Still, if Twain's stage appearances became rarer, his stage
presence remained a fixture of American culture. He was in reality always
performing, projecting a force of personality that eclipsed not only Samuel
Clemens but everyone else as well. Twain firmly established the comedian
as a formidable cultural force in American society. His dominating influence and his proximity to presidents, captains of industry, and the literati
of the day lent unprecedented legitimacy to humor as social criticism. Not
only did this immortalize Twain, but also it afforded political comedians
who came after him the chance to earn wide authority within mass culture.
This included most notably Will Rogers, the cowboy comedian who dominated popular and political culture in the early twentieth century.

•   •   •

As a performer, Mark Twain was as much the professional progeny of
Artemus Ward as he was the progenitor of a new form of live humorous
performance. Twain was not just Ward's immediate heir; he was his student.
Samuel Clemens and Charles Browne became fast friends in late 1863,
when Browne paused for several days in Virginia City, Nevada, on a triumphant western tour at the height of his popularity. Clemens was working as
a reporter for the *Territorial Enterprise*, Nevada's first and most successful
newspaper, and had just recently begun to sign his more humorous articles
"Mark Twain." As a veteran printer and journalist, Browne made it his custom always to visit the local print shop and newsroom upon his arrival in
town in order to get the lay of the land and drum up free publicity, although
by this time in his career his national celebrity had certainly preceded him.
Assigned to write the advance notice of Ward's performance, Twain became
the humorist's unofficial guide to the region for the next fortnight. On the
evening of the first lecture (popular demand dictated that a second show
be added), Twain took a seat in the "printer's pew," a row near the front of
house reserved for the press, and, according to a colleague, watched the
performance in front of him with his mouth agape, so entranced by Artemus
Ward's technique that he would bellow with laughter only as the rest of the
audience was already quieting down. Afterward he wrote that "the man who
is capable of listening to [Ward's show] 'Babes in the Wood' from beginning to end without laughing either inwardly or outwardly must have done
murder, or at least meditated it at some time during his life." Fifteen years
later, when asked to assess Ward's onstage humor in comparison to his own,
Twain maintained that "Babes in the Wood" was the funniest thing he had

ever seen. By the time Browne left Virginia City several days later, the comedian's visit had persuaded the young writer to do two things. The first was to send his stories east, where Browne predicted they would be embraced. The following spring Twain sent him a tale titled "Jim Smiley and His Jumping Frog," which Browne helped to get published the next year as "The Celebrated Jumping Frog of Calaveras County," launching Twain's reputation as a national talent. Second, after observing Browne in performance, Twain became more determined to take to the platform himself. Artemus Ward's lecture demonstrated how a master performer could completely capture an audience by the clever manipulation of technique and timing. Twain, seeing that both fame and money could be earned by dispensing humor from the stage, resolved to follow Browne's lead.[8]

His first opportunity came less than a month later, at the end of January 1864, when he addressed the Nevada Territorial Legislature in a ceremony that required him to dance among the roles of reporter, comedian, and president of a sort: as a reporter charged with covering Nevada's Constitutional Convention, he had become so popular with the legislators that they elected him "President of the Third House" as the formal business of the convention drew to a close. The office was purely honorary; nevertheless, a speech was expected. Twain delivered it, and while no reliable record of his comments survives, his and others' later references to the speech indicate that he leveled some good-natured ridicule at territorial governor James Nye (who was not present) and that his comments were taken kindly. In the wake of the sold-out performance, which was billed as a benefit for the local Presbyterian church, the writer-president-comic had raised two hundred dollars for the cause, had drawn a bigger crowd to the same hall that Artemus Ward had played a few weeks before, and had shown that not only was he capable of delivering jokes at the expense of the local political elite but also an enthusiastic audience was prepared to pay to hear them.[9]

Twain's eagerness to establish himself as a writer, however, monopolized his time. His more purposeful debut on the lecture circuit came two years later, following his return from a plum assignment in the Sandwich (to be known thirty years later as the Hawaiian) Islands, where he had been sent by the *Sacramento Union* to write about the exotic qualities of the United States' new protectorate. In October 1866 he relented to his friends' insistence that he give a public talk about his experiences, which had already captivated readers in print. With a promise to mix "amusement with instruction," and a self-penned advertisement that advised, "The doors open at 7 o'clock. The Trouble to begin at 8 o'clock," Twain delighted a capacity San Francisco crowd for just over an hour with descriptions of Hawaiian natives, zealous Christian missionaries, and the volcano of Kilauea. The response was sensational. Fellow writer Bret Harte celebrated Twain's triumphant arrival as a lecturer: "His humor . . . is . . . of the western character of ludicrous exaggeration and audacious statement, which perhaps is more thoroughly national and American than even the Yankee delineations of [James Russell] Lowell." Twain found the money good (he netted four hundred dollars from the evening's performance) and discovered that the laughter infused him with a sense of power and—unlike his writing—placed him in live community with people whose responses he could immediately see and hear. He found that he enjoyed his time onstage and followed the San Francisco appearance with a brief, frenetic tour of California and Nevada. When his mounting fame persuaded him—as it had Charles Browne—to move to New York City shortly thereafter, he likewise appeared throughout the East, including at Cooper Union Institute in 1868, where Abraham Lincoln's national reputation had been established eight years before. The next year Clemens signed on with James Redpath, founder and co-owner of the Boston Lyceum Bureau, the most prominent booking agency for lecture tours, and he kept a busy schedule of appearances until 1874. His popularity even prompted Thomas Nast to suggest an innovative scheme whereby the cartoonist and the humorist would appear together onstage, with Nast drawing illustrations in response to Twain's comments, all in full view of the audience. Twain declined the offer.[10]

Despite his success, Twain quickly came to detest the lecture circuit. More specifically, he hated the strain and family separations that came with it and the distraction it caused from what he termed his primary "'call' to literature." In 1870, with the lucrative reception of his first book, *The Innocents Abroad*, he told Redpath, "I am not going to lecture any more forever." While he did return to the stage and the after-dinner dais frequently, it was usually because he needed the money.[11]

Mark Twain's stage career is most significant for its further popularizing and legitimizing of what Charles Browne's "Old Showman" Artemus Ward had initiated during the mid-1860s. Browne had exploited the media, the entertainment business, and the issues of his day to their accepted limits so as to introduce a new national audience to the concept that a lone performer could use humor legitimately and popularly to critique cultural assumptions, and he did so before audiences of many hundreds at a time. Only a few years later, Twain and his promoters were able to capitalize further on these comparatively humble beginnings thanks to Twain's enormous presence and to the rapid advances in the print, transportation, and entertainment industries that accompanied the expansion of the nation. Whereas *Artemus Ward, His Book* was considered a bestseller when it sold 40,000 copies in 1862, the publisher of Twain's *Innocents Abroad* sold more than 82,000 copies in its first eighteen months on the market. Cooper Union Institute, the site of his first major eastern lecture, had a seating capacity of 1,500; by the next year he was routinely appearing in theaters as large as Boston's Music Hall, which seated 2,500. By the 1870s a larger and more discriminating mass public than that which applauded Artemus Ward was becoming increasingly comfortable with the notion of the standup humorist as a fixture of popular culture and with the stage as the forum for commenting on the funny incongruities of the human race in general and the American genus in particular. Twain's star power lent lasting legitimacy to the addition of the humorist-comedian to the burgeoning variety of American entertainments. This was true even if only a small fraction of Americans ever had the opportunity to see him on-stage and if fewer still could afford the one- to two-dollar ticket price. It was also true even though, by the last years of his life, much of Twain's humor had been consumed by rage.[12]

In *The Mysterious Stranger*, published posthumously in 1916, Mark Twain eloquently articulated both the power of humor and humankind's inability or unwillingness to use it:

> You [humans] have a mongrel perception of humor, nothing more.
> . . . [Y]our race, in its poverty, has unquestionably one really effective
> weapon—laughter. Power, money, persuasion, supplication, persecution
> —these can lift at a colossal humbug . . . but only laughter can blow it
> to rags and atoms at a blast. Against the assault of laughter nothing can
> stand. . . . Do you ever use [it]? No; you leave it lying and rusting. As a
> race, do you ever use it at all? No; you lack sense and the courage.

By 1900, embittered by personal travails including the sudden death of his daughter and infuriated by his country's emergent craving for empire, Twain appeared to have lost not the sense or the courage to use humor but the patience to play with it. He railed—without attempting to craft any palliative humor into his attacks—against the injustice and moral cowardice he saw being embraced by the nation. He worked on a lengthy essay to be called "The United States of Lyncherdom" assaulting racial violence in the coun-try and the herd mentality that licensed it (it was not published in its entirety until 2000). Although he was initially supportive of the Spanish-American War in 1898 for its liberation of Cuba from Spain, the easy victory had placed Cuba, Puerto Rico, Guam, and the Philippines in American hands. The United States, flush with national pride and international ambition, spurned Filipino independence and went to war again the following year, determined, in President McKinley's words, "to take [the Filipinos], and to educate [them], and uplift and civilize and Christianize them." Twain spoke out in sharp protest, helping to form the Anti-Imperialist League

FIGURE 2. *Mark Twain is depicted as "The American Lion of St. Mark's" frightening American imperialists, including President William McKinley in the center, in a 1901 cartoon from the humor magazine* Life. *Courtesy Louis J. Budd and the Mark Twain Archive at Elmira College, Elmira, New York.*

along with Jane Addams, Andrew Carnegie, former president Grover Cleveland, and others. A 1901 cartoon (fig. 2) shows the humorist as the stalwart anti-imperialist lion confronting an evil, pusillanimous McKinley. Twain called McKinley "a consciousless thief & traitor" in a private letter, and in December 1900 he publicly attacked what he considered the "snatching" of the Philippine archipelago and Americans' eagerness to join with the British in colonizing as much of the world as possible. When introducing Winston Churchill, a recent hero of England's Boer War in South Africa, he acidly praised the English and Americans for being "kith and kin in war and sin." Advised by friends to temper his vitriol lest he offend the public, Twain shot back: "I have always preached. . . . [I]f the humor came of its accord and uninvited I have allowed it a place in my sermon, but I was not writing the sermon for the sake of the humor. I should have written the sermon just the same whether any humor applied for admission or not."[13]

His scornful opinion of the presidency had replaced one of general admiration and, in the case of one president, total adulation. Early in his career Twain's political loyalties were with the Republican Party, and he briefly served as a private secretary for Republican Nevada senator William M. Stewart in Washington, D.C. Though he had fleetingly served in the Confederate Army (for nearly two weeks), he was awestruck by Civil War legend Ulysses S. Grant and supported his election in 1868 and again in 1872. Indeed Grant has been described as Twain's "public idol," but Twain's deep admiration seems to have grown in spite of Grant's years in the White House rather than because of them. Their friendship continued to blossom even as Twain co-wrote *The Gilded Age*, a satiric indictment of government corruption during Grant's administration; years later he salvaged the impoverished former president's estate by ushering Grant's memoirs through to publication as Grant succumbed to throat cancer. He also advocated the election in 1876 of Republican nominee Rutherford B. Hayes, but Hayes's compromise win over Democrat Samuel J. Tilden, which came at the expense of Reconstruction efforts in the South, disillusioned him. In 1879 he revealed his cynical belief that the presidency could attract only the most depraved and avaricious of men by posing as a candidate himself in an article in the *New York Evening Post*. The best way to get elected, he maintained, was to "own up in advance to all the wickedness I have done," and to that end he admitted that he had once forced his rheumatic grandfather up a tree, buried a dead aunt under a grapevine, and regarded the poor as so much wasted material. "Cut up and properly canned," he said with a satiric flourish reminiscent of Jonathan Swift's "Modest Proposal," the poor "might be made useful to fatten the natives of the cannibal islands." In concluding, he recommended himself for president as "a safe man—a man who starts from the basis of total depravity and proposes to be fiendish to the last."[14]

Late in his life Twain was convinced that the Republican monopoly over the presidency—broken only by Grover Cleveland's Democratic administrations, which he endorsed—was leading the country toward monarchy under Teddy Roosevelt, who ascended to the presidency after McKinley's assassination in 1901, and his political progeny, especially William Howard Taft. "You hear much of the President of the United States," he wrote. "[There is] no such office. There is a President of the Republican party. . . . The party, only, is hereditary now, but the headship of it will be hereditary by and by, in a single family." For Roosevelt and his expansionist foreign policies Twain found it increasingly difficult to express anything but "withering contempt." While he confessed that he fairly loved Roosevelt the man, he was as president "the most formidable disaster that has befallen the country since the Civil War." For Roosevelt's part, the president publicly acknowledged the humorist as a genius and his influence—on both American literature and culture—as powerful. But Twain also could be a "prize idiot," and his comments often infuriated him.[15]

Surprisingly, Twain and Roosevelt maintained a cordial if irregular personal correspondence. The venomous attacks leveled between the comedian and the president occurred mostly in unpublished communications with third parties, only occasionally in print, and never directly from the stage. Although Twain's acknowledged conspicuousness in national affairs made Americans well aware of his opinions (and many criticized him for them), most did not permanently associate the father of Tom Sawyer and Huck Finn with open ridicule of the president. For the most part his reputation—and certainly his memory—stood then as it incompletely stands now: on popular, not political, ground. Similarly, although Teddy Roosevelt's flair for showmanship is rightly legendary, in the long litany of ways he is remembered—as imperialist, conservationist, Rough Rider, teddy bear, wielder of the "big stick"—neither his calculated use of humor per se nor his sparring with Twain is among them, even though he clearly understood the growing potency of popular humor and enjoyed amiable associations with later comedians. This president and this comedian were not often thought of in tandem. Rather, they enjoyed equal if largely separate stature, each a consummate master of his particular craft and as giants of their time. Consequently the national audience came to realize that both comedians and presidents, whose influence had heretofore been dismissed or minimized, could be towering characters on the expanding stage of American cultural and political life.

In 1904, six years before his death, Twain proposed that William Dean Howells, publisher George Harvey, and the popular columnist Finley Peter Dunne, whom Twain admired, join him in forming the "Damned Human Race Luncheon Club." The group met only a few times as Twain's comet dimmed and the darker elements of his mood ultimately overshadowed the lighter facets of his humor. "If I could keep my faculty for humor uppermost I'd laugh the dogs out of the country," he wrote to Dunne. "But I can't. I'm too mad."[16]

• • •

If Mark Twain saw the yawning incongruities of the Great American Joke becoming too wide for humor to bridge, Finley Peter Dunne considered satire and literary burlesque to be perhaps the only sure means for reconciling the booming growth of the country—exemplified by his hometown of Chicago—with the plight of the immigrant working class, those who were fueling this growth without commensurate access to its benefits. Through the sage philosophy of his comic alter ego, bartender Martin Dooley, Dunne expanded on what Charles Browne had intimated and Twain had defined: the role of the humorist as not merely a performer but also a public oracle. Dunne was not a lecturer or entertainer; he was a writer, after all, and he always maintained, in Mr. Dooley's signature Irish brogue, that "th' hand that rocks th' fountain pen is th' hand that rules th' wurruld." Still, for millions of readers who could practically hear the bartender's wise and funny monologues thanks to Dunne's faithful print reproduction of the neighborhood dialect, the Chicago saloon on "Archey Road" became Dunne's theater; Mr. Dooley was its leading player, and a more modern and authentic political show began to be performed there. Examples of Mr. Dooley's "performances" therefore require some discussion, both for their significance in bringing the increasingly diverse American audience into closer proximity with a remote national leadership and for their role in setting the stage for future standup comedians.[17]

Mr. Dooley's creator came by his Irish credentials honestly. Dunne was born in Chicago in 1867 (the year of Charles Browne's death) and was raised in a middle-class parish on the Near West Side in a family that reveled in discussing and participating in the hurly-burly of city politics. He experienced a metamorphosis like those of Browne and Samuel Clemens and went to work at seventeen for one of Chicago's half-dozen daily newspapers, where he quickly made a name for himself covering the sports and police beats. During these years Chicago was likewise being transformed. It and the nation's other large cities were dominated no longer by Anglo-Saxons but increasingly by Irish arrivals, who continued to enter the country along with the millions of "new immigrants" from southern and eastern Europe during the second half of the nineteenth century, and whose numbers mushroomed in the first two decades of the twentieth. Chicago now bore little resemblance to the frontier town it had been at the time of Dunne's birth; it was the country's second largest city and a teeming metropolis of profit and poverty, abuses and opportunities, where immigrants by 1890 constituted a majority of the population of more than 1 million.[18]

Approximately 300,000 of these Chicagoans were Irish American. To reach this audience, *Chicago Post* managing editor Cornelius McAuliff offered to pay Dunne ten dollars apiece for humorous features in Irish dialect that would showcase his already evident wit and help boost circulation. After first introducing his neighborhood saloonkeeper to readers in late 1892, Dunne quickly understood what comedians before him had learned from both the page and the stage: that the guise of Mr. Dooley and the apparent triviality of humor gave him both license to criticize and the chance to endow his ethnically diverse readership vicariously with a measure of cultural and political power through their laughter.[19]

Mr. Dooley was no simpleton. Although his homespun straightforwardness reminded readers of Major Jack Downing, Artemus Ward, and other earlier cracker-barrel humorists, several considerations testified to his special potency as a commentator for the Industrial Age. First, he talked not as a clown on the margins of society but as a spokesman for a vibrant ethnic community that labored hard and debated seriously the issues that affected their daily lives. Dooley's humor served as a conduit mediating between

the democratic principles that appeared to many Americans of long standing to have lost their luster during the Gilded Age and the hopes of a new
generation of Americans freshly arrived, for whom the country seemed full
of possibilities. He gave voice to a new celebration of American ideals even
as he cherished the distinctiveness of the Irish and ridiculed the homog-
enizing prejudices that tended to come with assimilation. In the words of
Mr. Dooley: "I was afraid I wasn't goin' to assimilate with th' airlyer pilgrim
fathers an' th' instichoochins iv th' counthry, but I soon found that a long
swing iv th' pick made me as good as another man . . . , an' befure I was here
a month, I felt enough like a native born American to burn a witch." If Mark
Twain was ready to give up on the capacity of humor to blow "humbug . . .
to atoms at a blast," Dunne was just getting started.[20]

Furthermore, Mr. Dooley's "voice" brought the consciousness of a modern mass culture to political humor. To date, Jack Downing, Artemus Ward,
and Mark Twain, speaking as the American everyman, may have sounded
rural and deceptively unsophisticated, but they were distinctly white and
Anglo-Saxon or Scotch-Irish. Dooley's Irish American dialect augmented
and complemented the generic American vernacular, updating it to reflect
contemporary society more accurately.

With Mr. Dooley's growing popularity, especially after his work was syndicated nationally in 1900, Dunne took on a wider range of topics and abuses.
Increasingly he invited his millions of daily readers to join with him in poking satiric fun at everything from the political comedy of errors being played
out in Chicago to national affairs that often appeared nothing short of farcical, such as the clamor over the free coinage of silver during the heyday
of Populism or the nation's clumsy and inexorable march toward imperialism. These "dissertations," as the philosopher-wit's monologues came to be
known, as well as the nationwide circulation networks that distributed them,
gradually brought Dunne, his audience, and the presidency into closer proximity as news of the nation's affairs and the doings of the president acquired
the same familiarity as discussions over the next aldermanic elections or the
price of beer. It was even possible, according to Mr. Dooley, that the president himself might stop by for a cold one, as he imagined during a visit to
Chicago by William McKinley:

> Th' Presidint is as welcome [here] as anny rayspictable marrid man. I
> will give him a chat an' a dhrink f'r fifteen cints; . . . I'll give . . . two f'r
> twenty-five cints, which is th' standard iv value among civilized nations
> th' wurruld over. Prisidint iv th' United States, says ye? Well, I'm pri-
> sident iv this liquor store, fr'm th' pitcher iv th' Chicago fire above th'
> wash-stand in th' back room to th' dure-step. . . . There's Prisidint Mack

[McKinley] at th' Audjiotoroom, an' here's Prisident Dooley, . . . an' th' len'th iv th' sthreet between thim. Says he, "Come over to th' hotel an' see me." Says I, "If ye find ye'ersilf thrun fr'm a ca-ar in me neighborhood, dhrop in." An' there ye ar-re.[21]

The scene is reminiscent of Jack Downing shaking hands in place of an exhausted Andrew Jackson or Artemus Ward's fanciful "interview" with a harried Abraham Lincoln, but now those images were being updated for a much expanded, more diverse urban working-class America. Although McKinley presumably never arrived for his drink and chat, Mr. Dooley made it appear that he might have at any time, and he would have been received as convivially as any other customer, provided the president had his "fifteen cints" and was not too out of sorts after being "thrun fr'm a ca-ar." Dooley, and vicariously his everyman audience, proclaimed their own personal sovereignty by humorously impeaching the president's.

In 1900 this familiarity extended to Mr. Dooley's deciding to review New York governor Theodore Roosevelt's popular new book, *The Rough Riders*. In it Roosevelt gave a dashing account of the personalities and exploits surrounding his regiment's assault up Kettle Hill in the battle for San Juan Heights in Cuba during the Spanish-American War. The bartender acidly praised Roosevelt for his "Account iv th' Desthruction iv Spanish Power in th' Ant Hills" and for the battle that, by Dooley's reading, TR apparently waged solo:

I haven't time f'r to tell ye th' wurruk Tiddy did in ar-rmin' an' equippin' himsilf, how he fed himsilf, how he steadied himsilf in battle an' encouraged himsilf with a few well-chosen wurruds whin th' sky was darkest. Ye'll have to take a squint into th' book ye'ersilf to larn thim things. . . . But if I was him I'd call th' book "Alone in Cubia."[22]

Dunne's satiric poke at how bravely and conscientiously TR had taken up what Rudyard Kipling called "the white man's burden" did not go unnoticed. Roosevelt good-naturedly wrote Dunne saying, "I regret to state that my family and intimate friends are delighted with your review of my book." After Roosevelt's unexpected rise to the presidency following McKinley's assassination, Dunne—and Mr. Dooley—continued to find humor in the president's larger-than-life persona, whether with regard to his views on trusts, labor, and American imperialism or his perspective on what Roosevelt called "the strenuous life" in general. In 1907 Dunne wrote to tell Roosevelt that he considered him his "most valuable asset," accounting for 75 percent of his inspiration.[23]

Roosevelt's relationship with Dunne also grew. The president had every reason to curry favor with the humorist and his comic bartender; after all, Mr. Dooley's "dissertations" appeared in more than one hundred newspapers as well as magazines including *Harper's Weekly*, *Collier's*, and the *American Magazine*. A popular song, the "Mr. Dooley March," was released in 1901. When Mr. Dooley congratulated TR for his "Anglo-Saxon triumph" at the polls in 1904, the president understood the potent impact that humor—well delivered and now more widely distributed than ever—had on the country, thanks to Dunne as well as Mark Twain. He wrote back in mock protest and admiration, calling Dunne a "laughing philosopher (because you are not only one who laughs, but also a genuine philosopher and because your philosophy has a real effect upon this country)." Even though Dunne never hesitated to criticize Roosevelt's policies, the personal acquaintance between the two men steadily blossomed—much more readily than had that between the president and Twain—and it was based in part on a mutual understanding of the power each had to affect the body politic. The president invited Dunne to the White House often, including the day after Dunne's wedding in 1902 for dinner and a reception in the bride and groom's honor. Dunne said of Roosevelt after TR's death in 1919: "He valued humor on a par with the other qualities which mark the civilized man: intelligence, charity and courage. He even pretended to take as much interest in my work as I took in his." Although the long and deep extent of their relationship makes it plain that there was real friendship between them, Roosevelt clearly understood the political benefits as well.[24]

President Roosevelt's attraction to the comedian Dunne was part of a larger strategy that TR pursued to communicate his policies and his personality to the American public. As the defining occupant of the "bully pulpit," Roosevelt capitalized on both the widening power of the presidency brought on by war and the increasing public exposure of the office caused by the frenetic political climate of the time and the surging growth in print media. Roosevelt, whose exploits as a cowboy, hunter, civil servant, author, governor, and war hero Americans had already been following for years, saw the advantages in placing his formidable persona center stage. While William McKinley's administration—and in particular the president's secretary George Cortelyou—was the first to make accommodation for an enlarged presidential press corps, including an expanded work area for journalists and regular press briefings (although McKinley did not attend these himself), Roosevelt was the first to personalize the modern presidency, imbuing the office with a star power that extended even to the Executive Mansion, which he now rechristened, glamorously enough, the White House. Reporters who were in the president's good graces might even find themselves admitted to an unprecedented brand of presidential performance by being allowed to take part in TR's occasional "shaving hour" press conferences, which journalist Louis Brownlow described as "more fun than a circus." Often the president—freshly lathered and with the razor inches from his neck—would burst out of the chair in response to a question, much to the delighted shock and admiration of the newsmen. With a wink to the barber and always in control of his choreography, Roosevelt would retake his chair only to hop up again a second later. Although it would take other presidents at later times to tap the press conference and its unwitting audience for its fullest comedic potential, Theodore Roosevelt initiated the presidential showmanship that gave them their cue.[25]

·   ·   ·

The auditioning of the president as comedian also continued thanks to the press itself with the advent of the Gridiron Club. Founded in 1885 as a private social and dining club by forty of Washington's most powerful political correspondents, the Gridiron sought, in the words of its own 1915 historical account, to offer comradeship and diversion and, at the same time, to hold up "the mirror to those who sit in the seats of the mighty and [show] them in the reflex, with a touch of humor and satire, that even in the national and international complications which surround them there is a lighter side to the picture." The dinners started modestly, but they occurred more frequently and attracted crowds approaching three hundred by the time of Woodrow Wilson's administration. While the membership was extremely exclusive, guests were invited to attend the rollicking affairs, to eat, drink, be roasted—hence the "gridiron"—and, finally, to defend themselves in remarks of their own. Presidents were on the guest list at the outset, and every one has attended save Grover Cleveland, who was in office when the club was formed and who firmly declined each time he was invited, privately confiding to one reporter "that he 'would not fit in,' and was . . . of the opinion that Presidential dignity would be greatly ruffled by submitting to the 'fun you boys would have with me.'" (Barack Obama made news when he followed Cleveland's precedent and declined to attend the first Gridiron dinner of his administration in March 2009, citing a conflict with a family vacation.) Perhaps Cleveland's decision can be traced to the fact that as a Democrat, he was in more hostile territory in a press establishment that was dominated by Republicans. Certainly his refusals also were influenced by what he considered the intrusive media coverage of his private life and the public heckling he endured concerning charges (never completely denied) of an illegitimate son. One popular chorus was particularly stinging:

Maw, maw, where's my pa?
Gone to the White House, ha, ha, ha.[26]

Others did attend, however, often grudgingly but increasingly aware of the necessity of occasionally joining in the comedic dance in order to create or preserve positive press relations. Benjamin Harrison, no fonder of newsmen than was his predecessor Cleveland and considered stiff and aloof (one visitor described the presidential handshake as rather "like a wilted petunia"), waited until three years into his term before taking part, but when he did, the event became a watershed moment between the conventional perception of the presidency and a new perspective that would become prevalent in the twentieth century and would be made visible through humor. Confronting the unprecedented situation, Gridiron president H. B. F. MacFarland introduced Harrison formally with an implied warning to his fellow members, who were equally nervous and uncertain, that the usual antics must be dispensed with in deference to the president. Harrison, who had addressed a gathering of patent officials a few days earlier, surprised the journalists by joking, "This is the second time that I have been called upon this week to open a congress of American inventors." The presidential icebreaker worked. The few subsequent jokes that followed served not only to endear Harrison to those in attendance—however temporarily—but also to model the expectations for future audiences and presidents alike at Gridiron dinners, all of whom tacitly agreed to join in the lighthearted fun of the occasion. It is significant that while comedy flowed freely at Gridiron affairs, presidential inhibitions were in no real danger. The dinners operated under two standing rules: "ladies are always present," which meant that vulgarity or other unseemly behavior was prohibited (in fact the expression was tongue in cheek; women were not admitted as members of the Gridiron Club until 1974); and "reporters are never present." This second tenet was critical, for it signaled that, while many irregularities may hold sway at Gridiron dinners—presidents cracking jokes among them—none of the goings-on was ever to appear in print or otherwise before the public. Although some details invariably leaked out in this—as in any—Washington function, what happened at the Gridiron was to stay at the Gridiron. Still, after the 1880s the Gridiron Club provided a good crowd and a new venue for presidents occasionally to try out the material and hone the timing they would come to rely on more publicly in the coming decades.[27]

These improvised interactions between presidents and crowds at the Gridiron Club, between Finley Peter Dunne and Theodore Roosevelt, or between Mark Twain and government power in general are illustrative of the diverse ways that Americans began to laugh with, about, and occasionally at their chief executive. As the nineteenth century gave way to the twentieth, developments in the United States—gilded prosperity, unalloyed poverty, industrialized entertainments, and devastating war—made political humor incrementally more prevalent, more caustic, and, for many, more truthful. A larger, more diverse, and more seasoned American audience now encountered this humor more directly, more comfortably, and more often, and caught longer glimpses of celebrity comedians and White House performers. Such meetings still occurred almost exclusively in print, but thanks to the relentless influence of Mark Twain, the monologues of Martin Dooley, and the effervescent antics of Theodore Roosevelt, the stage was set for other, more spontaneous performances. It took the peculiar and momentous exigencies of the twentieth century—and new stars—to bring political humor, the American audience, and the presidency fully into the limelight.

3

cA Presidential Crinoline

WILL ROGERS was unique. At first the arrival in 1904 of the funny, disarming, and oddly enchanting cowboy, whose show business debut coincided with the cresting popularity of vaudeville, did not augur any profound change in the state of the nation's humor or the relationship between the American people and their president. During the next three decades, however, this self-described "ropin' fool" ingeniously mastered the revolution in mass media and the related expansion of the entertainment industry to become not only the country's favorite comedian but also its foremost political commentator and social critic. By the early 1930s, when legendary Hollywood director Cecil B. DeMille described him as "the American who least can be spared," millions of others—from paupers to presidents, Democrats and Republicans, rural folk and urban dwellers, progressives and isolationists—agreed. As such, Will Rogers earned the nation's permission to poke open fun at the chief executive in unprecedented ways, and he convinced much of America that performing political humor was more than merely good entertainment; it served a vital public service. Almost single-handedly, Rogers taught his grateful countrymen and women—sobered by increasingly obvious social disparities, one world war, depression, and what another master of humor named Franklin D. Roosevelt would later call "fear itself"—a decidedly different dance. He called a high-spirited, participatory reel that encouraged Americans to employ humor to do the serious work of democracy, and he challenged the presidency to keep up. Not only did Franklin Roosevelt accept the challenge, but also by 1935, when Rogers was killed in an airplane crash, the president was calling the steps.[1]

As myriad other studies have well established, humor feeds off incongruity and contradiction, using them to wrest power from laughter where there might otherwise be nothing but resignation or despair. Similarly, comedians most often come from the ranks of those most affected by the discrepancies that define the Great American Joke, be they immigrants, minorities, or others whose social, economic, or personal origins relegate them to the margins of mainstream America. Will Rogers's life was thoroughly intertwined with such incongruity. His fame and influence sprang from cultural and geographical borderlands similar to those that produced Artemus Ward, Mark Twain, and Mr. Dooley, although Rogers embodied this dissonance and harnessed it for humorous purposes more completely than anyone else before or since. He was born in 1879 in the Cooweescoowee district of the Cherokee Nation, which had been exiled west of the Mississippi River during the 1830s following the Indian Removal Act to clear much of northern Georgia for white farmers. The Cherokee—inspired to create their own constitution by the founding ideals of presidents George Washington and Thomas Jefferson, then sold out by the presidential betrayals of Andrew Jackson—teetered on the threshold of accommodation and rebellion in a region that made the transition during Will's youth from the Indian and Oklahoma territories into the state of Oklahoma in 1907. During the Civil War the region sat in the pleat between North and South. Many Cherokee were slaveholders, and most—including Will's father—fought for the Confederacy, which offered more freedom and better prospects than the federal government.

Will was the youngest of eight children and the only surviving son of black-haired, broad-faced Mary Rogers, who died in 1890, and fair-haired, blue-eyed Clem, both of whom were products of mixed-blood marriages, which made Will—like them—slightly more than one-quarter Cherokee. Clem was almost frighteningly industrious. Forced to reinvent himself constantly in the face of changing times, he conquered every challenge with a keen sense of innovative pragmatism. As a rancher he controlled a cattle range of some sixty thousand acres within the Cherokee framework of communal land ownership, but the arrival of the Missouri Pacific Railroad in 1889 effectively bisected his property. More significantly, in 1887 the Dawes General Allotment Act began the process of transferring reservation land from communal to individual ownership; as a result Rogers's holdings shrank considerably, and he diversified into other endeavors, managing to maintain his wealth in the process. He energetically embraced political life as well, never losing an election, and served as a district judge for eight years, then in the Cherokee senate. In 1896 he was chosen as one of the Cherokee delegates who met with the Dawes Commission to represent tribal interests, and in 1906, just four years before his death, he was elected a delegate to the constitutional convention for the new state of Oklahoma. Will's home county eventually carried the Rogers name, not because of the humorist son but in honor of the farmer-politician-philanthropist father.[2]

Because of his personality and his many commitments, Clem had plenty of money and no small measure of affection for young Will but little time and, often, little patience. The young boy did not do well in school but was endlessly good-natured, often reckless, and so boisterously talkative that his lifelong friend Jim Hopkins said it seemed as though he had been vaccinated with a gramophone needle. Will lived away from home to attend school, first at the local schoolhouse twelve miles distant and eventually at a military academy in Missouri. He appreciated his father's accomplishments and passionately shared his willingness to take on new challenges, but he did not share Clem's work ethic. He preferred horses and roping to books or the prospect of managing a ranch. In 1898, not long past his eighteenth birthday, he left school and headed back to Indian Territory, passing by his home to work as a ranch hand on the other side of the state. Will Rogers was motherless before he turned eleven, the restless son of a disciplined and accomplished father, a student at six schools but the graduate of none, and the citizen of a disappearing nation within a nation. He was endowed with the same paradoxical combination of mestizo blood, accommodation and rebelliousness, and reverence and mischief that characterized his tradition, his parents, and for that matter the United States as a whole.[3]

Although Rogers ultimately owed his enormous popularity to his humor and his sophisticated yet homespun philosophy, his entrée to celebrity was in his ability to spin not words but lassos. Certainly the rope was an economic lifeline for anyone working around livestock, but Rogers became especially enamored with trick roping after seeing the famous Mexican vaquero Vincente Oropeza throw intricate loops at the World's Columbian Exposition in Chicago in 1893. The lariat became Rogers's constant companion thereafter (and, to his teachers, a constant distraction), and his skills served him well during his short career as a cowboy after he struck out on his own. Following his brief stint as a hired hand, he returned home, entered a steer-roping contest, and won first prize. In 1899 he traveled to the St. Louis Fair for another competition; although he did not do well, he later recalled that the performance "gave me a touch of 'Show business' in a way, so that meant I was ruined for life as far as actual employment was concerned." Rogers never seriously entertained thoughts of leading the life of an Oklahoma rancher after that.[4]

In fact his self-effacing comments concerning the connection between show business and "actual employment" are telling, for they mask the considerable importance of the entertainment industry and the cultural influence it was continuing to wield at the turn of the twentieth century. Conservative objections to the propriety of shows and show people notwithstanding, show business was big business by 1900, and it continued to expand. Two of Thomas Edison's electronic marvels—the phonograph and the motion picture—were just beginning to attract mass audiences to the novel sounds of the gramophone and animated sights of the nickelodeon, where for five cents one could see a short silent film starring Mary Pickford. While these mechanized crazes began to grab headlines, the live show continued to dominate. By the beginning of the new century there were more than five thousand theaters in operation nationwide, offering everything from cheap amusements to lavish spectacle, from opera to legitimate plays to vaudeville. Broadway alone now housed more than twenty theaters, and by 1910 New York City boasted a combined seating capacity of nearly 2 million within its many playhouses and music halls. Other cities saw proportionately the same explosive growth. Performance afforded thousands of show business professionals—like Will Rogers—jobs because it was also becoming an increasingly essential diversion for millions of Americans from theirs. As leisure activity, performance offered working-class audiences glimpses of cultural egalitarianism in a society that was still changing rapidly and was now increasingly segregated. Industrialization continued to construct stark divisions at work between the masses of low-income laborers, the legions of middle-income managers, and the few but fantastically wealthy owners. Immigration infused 25 million people into American life from 1870 to 1914, although most were separated from full access to that life by language and long hours on the job. This, combined with the accelerating migration of African Americans from the Jim Crow South into northern cities, furthered the marginalization of ethnic and racial minorities. Just as profoundly, Americans struggled to reconcile the contrast between their future as a predominantly urban, industrial society and their mythic past as a rural, agrarian one.[5]

All manner of workers, therefore, regardless of race, class, or gender, considered leisure a priority. Rowdier male audiences still imbibed burlesque shows and concert saloons, and middle-class patrons could choose from live dramas, musical comedies, and all manner of revues. But by far the most popular form of live entertainment for mass audiences remained vaudeville, which continued to attract 2 million patrons every day. In 1906 the Keith-Albee circuit of theaters in the East combined with the Orpheum in the West to create a network of venues that catered to much of the nation, thanks to innovative ticket pricing and virtually continuous performances. Young, single working-class women—who constituted a rapidly growing segment of the population as teachers, clerks, and garment workers—developed a voracious appetite for vaudeville and other amusements. Mothers and their children took part; recreation surveys revealed that women and children made up 48 percent of the vaudeville audience in San Francisco in 1912, 45 percent in Milwaukee in 1914, and one-third of the audience in New York City. The theatrical space between these increasingly diverse and receptive audiences and the performers who played to them provided a critical site for freewheeling and experimental behavior that in turn introduced the potential for a new culture—what anthropologist Brian Sutton-Smith calls protoculture. Shows—especially vaudeville—promised freedom *from* the ritualized obligations of work as well as the freedom *to* shape new social configurations and rituals that might reconcile some of the incongruities present in traditional relationships. Just as the blues and then jazz at this time were beginning to mitigate the intractable divides between blacks who created these forms and white music fans who flocked to experience them, Will Rogers similarly used humor to confront the customary gulf between citizen and president. Artemus Ward, Mark Twain, and Mr. Dooley had engaged these same possibilities inherent in performance, but in the smaller performative spheres of their times. Now, given the increasing intricacy of communications and entertainment networks that made shows cheaper and more diverse—and news about them almost ubiquitous in the press and eventually on the air—leisure was becoming the indispensable complement to labor for the working masses of American society.[6]

As if by stealth, Will Rogers came of age as a performer at precisely this moment. His wholesome and self-effacing style masked the potency of his effect on audiences in the same way that the cultural power of performance in general was cloaked in the guise of bright lights and greasepaint. His seamless metamorphosis from working cowboy to working performer was just as innocently surreptitious. After a period of scant success performing in roping and riding contests throughout the Midwest, he journeyed to Argentina in 1902 in search of ranch work but succeeded only in exhausting his (and increasing amounts of his father's) money. Left after a few months without, by his own estimation, "enough dough to make the first payment on a soda cracker," he secured a job helping to tend a shipment of livestock bound for South Africa. Not long after his arrival there he saw an advertisement for one of the many cultural imports from America—Texas Jack's Wild West Show—and paid it a visit, thinking he might help out behind the scenes. The interview led to Rogers's demonstrating a few rope tricks, and he was hired on the spot at twenty dollars a week. Dubbed the "Cherokee Kid," he performed across South Africa with Texas Jack, then with a circus in Australia and New Zealand before returning to the United States in the spring of 1904. His reputation and career were slowly gaining momentum. Adjusting to the contingencies of the age, Will Rogers was thriving as a cowboy the only way it was now profitable to do so in an increasingly urban and indus-trialized society: by playing one onstage.[7]

Rogers was an immediate hit in South Africa. He earned two encores in his first performance before an audience that had never seen such prowess with a rope. Crowds were especially dazzled by his grand finale. Called the "Crinoline," it was a mesmerizing combination of artistry and audacity, and involved Rogers on a horse twirling a horizontal loop around himself, then, as the circle grew in size, around the horse, and finally, with the loop now ninety to one hundred feet in circumference, around a good portion of the delighted—if somewhat anxious—audience. It was a difficult and strenuous trick, but Rogers performed it better than anyone else and seemingly with-out effort, and it became a trademark of his act when he began to perform for American crowds. The rope—particularly the "Crinoline"—remains a metaphor for Rogers's widening and captivating influence over people and presidents, and for his unique ability to pull them into close—if not always synchronized—association. Years later, by the time he replaced his lariat with jokes, it was easy, in both Rogers's mind and those of his fans, to make the move from roping horses to roping presidents.[8]

Later in 1904 Rogers made his vaudeville debut in Chicago as one of several "dumb acts," performers whose novel skills required no verbal in-teraction with the audience. Eager to distinguish his act from others, he brought a horse onstage and roped the cooperative animal with lassos of increasing size and complexity. Rogers named the pony Teddy, after Presi-dent Theodore Roosevelt. Like his namesake, Teddy, according to the press, was intelligent, appreciated applause, and was known to "whinny his disap-proval" when kept waiting. Rogers perpetuated the tacit comparisons with TR by describing the horse as "a lively critter [that] can throw up a little dust when he gets started." It is clear that Teddy's close resemblance in tempera-ment to the rambunctious Roosevelt influenced Rogers's choice of a name. Will Rogers was roping and reining in presidents before he ever said a word onstage. What is more, the audience was delighted, and even the one being roped did not seem to mind.[9]

After touring several states, Rogers traveled east to vaudeville's capital, New York City, on a personal migration that was reminiscent of those of Charles Farrar Browne and Samuel Clemens a half-century before. On the way to perform at New York's Madison Square Garden as part of a Wild West show, he nearly roped not four-legged Teddy but the president himself. According to the *Washington Times*, during a layover in Washington, D.C., Rogers and a fellow cowboy "went to the White House, and did some tricks for the entertainment of the children of the President." Roosevelt was out of town, but the occasion marked the first of Rogers's many invitations to the White House over the next thirty years.[10]

His and Teddy's first appearance on a New York vaudeville stage took place in June 1905. Soon afterward his act ceased to be "dumb," as he began to apologize for the occasional missed rope throw and explain his more difficult tricks. Such off-the-cuff remarks—delivered through his trademark wad of Beechnut chewing gum and distinctive Oklahoma twang—immediately produced laughs, surprising no one but Rogers himself. As with the classroom clown encouraged by his first taste of approval, his comedy career was launched. For the next decade he delighted huge audiences across the country, touring the Keith-Albee, Orpheum, and Poli circuits. The public accepted him and his natural cowboy persona—which was infused with nostalgic frontier simplicity, candor, and a unique blend of rural western naïveté and urban eastern show business savvy, the iconic cowboy turned cosmopolitan sage—as utterly American in both a classic and a wholly innovative sense. Will Rogers the showman was becoming not simply well liked but well trusted.

* * *

Florenz Ziegfeld, New York's best-known promoter, was not among Rogers's growing number of fans. The Oklahoma cowboy's antics and his "aw shucks" appeal were lost on the humorless Broadway impresario. Still, it was impossible for him to deny Rogers's growing popularity among the city's audiences and critics or his sensational reception across the country. Furthermore, he recognized that Rogers's attraction was consistent with the very strategy that had established Ziegfeld as an arbiter of popular culture for more than two decades. He had made a career and a fortune tantalizing Americans with acts that challenged conventional attitudes toward sex even as they appeared to cater to respectable middle- and upper-class tastes. Among his most sensational discoveries was the German-born strongman Eugen Sandow, who reinforced the heroic image of early-twentieth-century masculinity even as Ziegfeld paraded the scantily clad muscleman around the world, encouraging society women to touch his rippling muscles, which many eagerly did. Similarly, he brilliantly promoted the exotic European music hall dancer Anna Held, who transfixed audiences with her combination of high fashion and highbrow propriety mixed with unalloyed sensuality, becoming the first modern American "showgirl." Will Rogers did not exude sex; indeed his wholesome wisdom and hardworking prowess with the rope stood in humorous yet purposeful and reassuring counterpoint to the racier components of Ziegfeld's fare. Nevertheless Rogers, like Sandow and Held, stood on Ziegfeld's stage at the intersection of cultural convention and cultural subversion and entertained receptive Americans even as he jovially challenged their traditional identities with regard not to sex but to politics.[11]

In 1915, after Rogers had sold out the Palace Theatre and virtually every other major vaudeville house in New York, Ziegfeld hired the cowboy comic (by now working without Teddy), first as part of the *Ziegfeld Midnight Frolic*, an innovative cabaret performed on the roof of the New Amsterdam Theatre after the nightly curtain of Ziegfeld's legendary *Follies*. A year later he joined the main attraction downstairs (fig. 3). With the *Follies'* well-heeled clientele and Ziegfeld's sophisticated publicity machine, the two men's initial four-year association further crystallized Rogers's fame and offered the perfect forum for his increasing use of topical humor. Joking had been a transitional device between rope tricks for Rogers, but gradually the rope was becoming subordinate to the wit. His banter grew more frequent, and

FIGURE 3. *Will Rogers in his days with Ziegfeld's* Follies. *Courtesy Will Rogers Memorial Museum, Claremore, Oklahoma.*

he sparred amiably with celebrities in the audience. In an effort to remain current, he followed his wife, Betty's, suggestion that he talk about what he read in the daily papers. It was an epiphany. He found the day's news and newsmakers to be vastly more comical than the more synthetic theater gags he had been repeating night after night. "So I started to reading about Congress," he told a 1919 interviewer for *American Magazine*, "and believe me, I found they are funnier three hundred and sixty-five days a year than anything I ever heard of." Audiences agreed. The national coverage attested to Americans' enthusiastic response to this unlikely star whose "meteoric rise, in four years," the article went on to say, had lofted him "to a place among the few real humorists of the stage."[12]

In the spring of 1916 he was invited to join the all-star cast of the *Friars Frolics*, a production of New York's Friars Club that toured several eastern cities, including Baltimore. President Woodrow Wilson and his new wife, Edith, made the fifty-mile drive to see the comedy show, a surprising effort given not only the president's Presbyterian conservatism but also the abundance of issues and crises at hand. Mexican revolutionary Pancho Villa had recently executed sixteen U.S. citizens and raided Columbus, New Mexico, prompting Wilson to send Brigadier General John "Black Jack" Pershing and several thousand troops in a fruitless bid to capture him. The debate over military preparedness raged on as Wilson's administration struggled to keep the country out of the Great War in Europe despite German submarine aggression against American interests and lives. Wilson also was preoccupied by his impending bid for reelection. Still, the president was an avid fan of vaudeville, and like any working man, he craved the leisurely diversion. It was the first time a president of the United States had traveled so far specifically to see a comedy performance, and Will Rogers was so nervous he nearly walked out and caught the next train back to Oklahoma. He and the show did go on, however, and with his inclusion of several jokes at Wilson's expense, his act marked a defining moment when humor and live performance joined to herald a profound shift in the relationship between the American people and the presidency.[13]

This was not the first time Rogers publicly kidded a president. Since 1911 his stage comments had slowly grown more political as well as topical. Laughing about politics and particularly politicians was natural for Rogers, whose heritage imbued in him the realization that the personal and the political were closely intertwined. After all, the political affairs of the Cherokee Nation affected every life and every family directly, and for Rogers those affairs were as close as his own father and the policies that had kept his ancestors nomads in their own land for more than a century. Furthermore, under such circumstances, politics—and the conflicting feelings of empowerment, bitterness, cynicism, and hope that it engendered—made for something of a spectator sport; it was a natural source of entertainment. What could be more rewarding than getting involved in politics and hence earning the right and the wisdom to joke about it? This ethos permeated Rogers's entire life, and this easy intimacy with political power became formative to his public persona. Politicians from alderman to president may wield enormous power relative to their fellow citizens, but to Rogers, in the end they were just flesh and bones, skills and faults; perhaps they were all the more admirable because of this fallibility and their ability to recognize it. If they lacked such self-recognition, Rogers was more than willing to help them along. Presidents especially, he maintained, were "the most human of our men." This was what Revolutionary jesters, Charles Browne, and others had intimated from the relatively tight confines of earlier print culture and the lecture platform, but Will Rogers began to broadcast it to mass audiences in the most personal—even neighborly—of ways. He modeled for Americans how to negotiate the complex tension between worshipping their leaders and vilifying them, and then how to articulate it. For his audience, Rogers's words not only offered entertainment; they also added to the day's political discourse. He refined his natural acumen for political humor into a studied skill during his vaudeville years, and over time his unique approach endeared him to both the nation at large and politicians who sought to bask in and capitalize on the glow of his contagious goodwill.[14]

Perhaps it was not a coincidence that Rogers's first presidential joke was aimed at kindred spirit Theodore Roosevelt in October 1911, just as Rogers retired the horse Teddy and began working alone. The former president was nearly three years out of office, but, profoundly disappointed with the policies of his successor, fellow Republican William Howard Taft, he was considering another run at the White House. A New York critic thought Rogers's joke at TR's expense significant enough to record, and Rogers evidently agreed, saving the clipping in his scrapbook:

> It was at Hammerstein's [Theatre] where Will Rogers first appeared doing a "single." From that day the managers have never again desired that he should surround himself with a company of men and horses. Rogers and his rope supply enough fun for both the managers and the public. . . . He has some witty talk, too.
>
> "You remember," he asked, "when Teddy Roosevelt came back from a long tour of the West? Or can't you remember that? You must remember Roosevelt, don't you? Well, Teddy was a pretty good fellow, when he had it. I wonder what has become of him?"
>
> After the laugh had subsided he continued:

"You know, they do say that sometimes they come back," and then after this laugh has subsided: "But not often."[15]

Rogers clearly admired Roosevelt. He had tried to enlist in TR's "Rough Riders" regiment as a young man (he was rejected as too young) and first met Roosevelt in 1900 along with other cowboys at a roping contest where the heroes of San Juan Hill were holding a reunion. Both men were products of the western iconography of the day and owed much of their popularity with the American people to its allure, although Rogers ribbed the patrician Roosevelt for not being "a real, sure-enough cowboy, 'cause he had plenty of money all the time, and a sure-enough cowboy never has any money." Their mutual admiration continued to the last years of Roosevelt's life. TR wrote to Rogers while in seclusion following the death in World War I of Roosevelt's youngest son, Quentin, in 1918 to thank the comedian for kind words said about him from the stage, and Rogers was in attendance by personal invitation for Roosevelt's final major speech at Carnegie Hall that October. Years later Rogers wrote that Roosevelt should have been elected president at age fifteen since "he could have run [the office] as good at that age as most men could at 50."[16]

The response to Rogers's onstage jibe at Roosevelt in 1911 was positive. However innocuous by today's measures, it was popular enough that Rogers repeated the joke often; three years later it was still part of his standard act. After all, a mild jest at a president years out of office seemed comfortably within the bounds of propriety, for the comic as well as his audience.[17]

Five years later, in the spring of 1916, with President Wilson very much in office and very much in attendance at the *Friars Frolics*, things were different. Rogers suffered terrible stage fright the night of the performance, teetering between confidence and uncertainty that kidding the president was acceptable, especially with such tension at home and abroad. Later he laughingly recalled that the stage manager knocked on his dressing room door, telling him, "You die in 5 more minutes for kidding your country." Nevertheless, while all the others on the program performed their standard routines, Rogers, in his own words, "gave a great deal of time and thought to an act for [Wilson], most of which would never be used again, and had never been used before." The decision was daring and momentous in the history of American political standup comedy. By teasing the president to his face and in the open public sphere, Rogers was simultaneously heeding his instincts as a political humorist and dancing—warily and for the first time—on new cultural ground. He had no idea whether his audience would dance along. He recounted the incident years later in a column memorializing Wilson:

How was I to know but what the audience would rise up in mass and resent it. I had never heard, and I don't think any one else had ever heard of a president being joked personally in a public theatre about the policies of his administration. . . .

My first remark . . . was, "I am kinder nervous here tonight." Now that is not an especially bright remark, and I don't hope to go down in history on the strength of it, but it was so apparent to the audience that I was speaking the truth that they laughed heartily at it. After all, we all love honesty. . . .

I said, "I see where they have captured [Pancho] Villa. Yes, they got him in the morning [newspapers] and then the afternoon ones let him get away." Now everybody in the house before they would laugh looked at the president, to see how he was going to take it. Well, he started laughing and they all followed suit.

Rogers fired several more shots concerning the controversy over the country's poor military preparedness: "There is some talk of getting a machine gun if we can borrow one. The one we have now they are using to train our army with in Plattsburg [New York], if we go to war we will just about have to go to the trouble of getting another gun."[18]

According to Rogers and the glowing media coverage, Woodrow Wilson enjoyed it all, leading the audience in enthusiastic laughter. Evidently it was one of Rogers's last and most volatile jokes concerning the rapid exchange of diplomatic notes with Germany that the president relished most, given Wilson's highly personal investment in foreign affairs: "President Wilson is getting along fine now to what he was a few months ago. Do you realize, people, that at one time in our negotiations with Germany that he was 5 notes behind." Wilson later repeated this line and quoted Rogers often among friends, in speeches, even at a meeting of his cabinet. Backstage after the show, Rogers's fellow cast member George M. Cohan thanked Wilson for making the long journey from Washington. He later recalled the president's response: "I'd travel ten times that distance to listen to as wise a man as Will Rogers." Rogers performed for Wilson four more times at regularly scheduled performances of the *Follies*, and he allowed that insofar as "we of the stage know that our audiences are our best friends, . . . he was the greatest audience of any public man we ever had." In February 1924, when he wrote a reminiscence of the former president, who had died the week before, Rogers called the Baltimore performance "the proudest and most successful night I ever had on the stage." For his part Wilson, according to his secretary Joseph P. Tumulty, deeply admired Rogers the comedian and the man.[19]

Press coverage of the show—specifically concerning Wilson's response to Rogers's material—was extensive and positive. Nevertheless, the greatest testimony to his popularity and Americans' identification with his comments on events—presidential and otherwise—was the public's growing desire to hear from Rogers directly. In 1922 the McNaught newspaper syndicate commissioned him to write a weekly column, and four years later the *New York Times* began to run daily 150-word missives dispatched from wherever he happened to be. Eventually these "daily telegrams" were also syndicated, and more than six hundred newspapers ran the two columns, which he continued to type out daily until his death and which earned him $2,500 per week by 1930. It was estimated that these columns were read by 40 million Americans daily. A lucrative contract with the *Saturday Evening Post* soon followed the McNaught deals, and in 1927 a trade brochure jointly produced by the *Post* and film production company Pathé Exchange boasted that Rogers was the most publicized man in America. (Pathé had recently been purchased by an up-and-coming motion picture magnate and Wall Street millionaire named Joseph P. Kennedy a decade after the birth of his second son, John F. Kennedy.) Rogers made his first silent film, *Laughing Bill Hyde*, in 1918, and he signed long-term contracts with Goldwyn Pictures Corporation and Fox Film Corporation (later 20th-Century Fox), ultimately becoming known as the "Mark Twain of the Screen" and the top male box office attraction of the late 1920s and early 1930s. Radio stardom also followed. The humorist and his ruminations on all subjects—including the American presidency—were in huge demand, and the blossoming mass media of the day rushed to fill it.[20]

The sober Wilson's somewhat surprising enthusiasm for the showman Rogers in 1916 can be traced in part to his administration's acknowledgment that a more performative presidency was needed to suit the dramatic shifts affecting contemporary life—both at home and abroad—and that the surging growth in entertainment culture and the electronic mass media might be leveraged in the president's favor. By sheer dint of his personality as well as his progressive policies, Theodore Roosevelt initiated much of what would be called the modern American presidency in this regard, but Wilson too could appreciate a performer's command of an audience and the impact that such theatricality could have on public opinion. In March 1913, under adviser Joe Tumulty's direction, the Wilson administration had taken Roosevelt's informal shaving sessions with reporters once step further and initiated regular press conferences with White House reporters as a way of bringing the president and his policies closer to newspaper readers. The following month he broke a century-old precedent and appeared in person before Congress to give a speech on tariff reform, commencing the tradition of presidents delivering their State of the Union addresses live before hundreds and eventually—thanks to radio and television—performing them

before millions of people. In 1916, desiring to exploit the sensational popularity of moving pictures, the Democratic National Committee produced
a silent film, *The President and His Cabinet in Action*, which gave many
Americans their first ever look at a president walking, talking, and laughing.
Although the press conferences were discontinued in 1915—allegedly for
national security reasons after the outbreak of World War I—and Wilson
can hardly be considered a media hound, his administration initiated a new
understanding of the increasingly public and theatrical requirements of
the office. Albeit intermittently, the president and the comedian were on
parallel trajectories, at least where the accessibility afforded by mass media
was concerned.[21]

• • •

Wilson's favorable approach to performance in general, and to Rogers's
humor in particular, was not unanimously shared by presidents during the
first quarter of the twentieth century. In many ways William Howard Taft's
administration resembled those of the late nineteenth century more closely
than others of the early twentieth. He lacked the political astuteness of both
TR and Wilson, and often considered the increasing public demands on
his presidency as intrusive. Rogers was not yet a political humorist during
these early years of his vaudeville career; consequently there was no political standup prominent in mainstream popular culture. Even in later years,
the dearth of references to Taft in Rogers's humor seems to indicate that the
comedian thought the former president, while affable, was just as inconse-
quential as Rogers was unknown to Taft.[22]

In the same way, the lackluster Warren G. Harding's brand of "normalcy"
was not attuned to the Rogers wit. Harding was not a magnetic speaker; William McAdoo, treasury secretary under Wilson, once described a Harding
speech as "an army of pompous phrases moving over the landscape in search
of an idea." Neither did he have an appreciation for Rogers's brand of comedy. In early 1922, when Rogers wrote and performed in a skit for the *Ziegfeld
Frolic* mildly lampooning Harding's penchant for golf, the president asked
him, through an emissary, to desist from making such comments, then continued to snub Rogers even when the comedian quickly complied. Rogers
retaliated a few days later, claiming in a newspaper article that Harding—
carrying a bundle of treaties wrapped in paper as he prepared to address the
Senate—looked as much like a bootlegger as a president. Back onstage that
evening, by now emboldened by his success with Wilson years before, and
no longer as squeamish about assailing presidents in front of a live audience,
Rogers commented on a recent fire at the Treasury Department with a prescient reference to the rumors of fraud that were beginning to swirl around

the Harding administration: "The fire started on the roof and burned down and down until it got to the place where the money ought to be and there it stopped [for lack of fuel]. The Harding administration had beat the fire to it. A fire in the Treasury building is nothing to get excited about during a Republican administration." During that night's curtain call, Rogers felt confident enough in his relationship with his audience to chide Harding indirectly: "I have cracked quite a few jokes on public men here, both Republicans and Democrats. I hope I have not given offense. In fact, I don't believe any big man will take offense." Although Rogers and Harding reportedly cleared up their differences and Rogers later had many kind words for the president, who died suddenly of a heart attack eighteen months later, the scandal-plagued Harding administration clearly had neither real awareness nor use for the jokes of a professional entertainer. It is telling, however, that by 1922—the year of both the public tiff with Harding and Rogers's contract with the McNaught syndicate—the public seemed at least as inclined to accept a joke made at the president's expense as to criticize the comedian for making it. Harding was hardly remembered in the jazzy prosperity of the later 1920s, while Rogers gained increasing fame.[23]

By the mid-1920s Will Rogers's mastery of the burgeoning electronic media and his increasingly ubiquitous presence in American popular culture began to attract presidents into his orbit rather than him into theirs. He knew both Calvin Coolidge and Herbert Hoover comparatively well, and both presidents saw the benefit in associating themselves with the comedian even if they were not always willing or able to do the joking themselves. Coolidge's soporific manner remains his most memorable characteristic; when informed in 1933 that Coolidge was dead, writer and Algonquin Round Table wit Dorothy Parker responded, "How could they tell?" Yet his famous reserve obscured a keen and impish sense of humor that served as a willing foil to Rogers's jokes and indirectly advanced the slowly tightening relationship between mass culture and what had been to this point the traditionally somber and aloof institution of the presidency—Teddy Roosevelt's and Woodrow Wilson's appreciation of humor notwithstanding. In fact Rogers credited "Silent Cal" with "more subtle humor than almost any public man I ever met." Coolidge generally avoided outward displays of it, believing that "it was fatal to show humor in public office; it reacted against you," yet the taciturn New Englander, who, according to one observer, "could be silent in five languages," occasionally let his wit shine, albeit through a deadpan prism. When the hostess at an event told the president, "I made a bet today that I could get more than two words out of you," Coolidge replied, "You lose." Rogers fondly recalled a private moment when he stopped by the White House to invite the president to one of his upcoming performances and happened to add that a popular musical quartet would also be appearing. The expressionless Coolidge, without a moment's hesitation, enthusiastically agreed to attend while wryly dismissing Rogers's comedy: "Yes, I like singing." Rogers's personal relationship with Hoover was similarly cordial; Hoover and other members of his administration enjoyed several of Rogers's shows, and the comic felt secure enough in the president's good graces to ask him for executive clemency for an old school friend who had been convicted on a minor bootlegging charge. It was not their personal relationships, however, but rather the roles that Rogers, Coolidge, and Hoover played in the establishment of radio as a forum for presidential humor that made a lasting difference in how comedians, presidents, and millions of Americans perceived the highest office in the land.[24]

In the early 1920s radio was only the latest light in a dazzling display of technological innovations mesmerizing the country. Americans were still entranced by the idea if not the practice of driving an automobile, using a telephone, and turning on an electric light in November 1920, when Pittsburgh's KDKA, the first commercially licensed radio station, went on the air from a rooftop shack to announce the election of Warren Harding. The thrill of being able to pull "voices from out of the air" was euphoric, although fewer than 5 percent of American families owned a receiver by the time Calvin Coolidge took office three years later; their purchase was most often deferred by cost (about sixty dollars), the confusing nature of the equipment, and uncertainty over just what to make of the new gizmo. By 1924, however, as factory-built sets began to saturate the national market, the number of stations increased, and the listening audience surged past 25 million, radio was rapidly becoming the focal point for a revolutionary new culture of consumption. If industrialized work kept laborers fixated on the rapid production of goods and services, then the rest of existence became increasingly obsessed with consuming them. Public relations, advertising, and other forms of marketing used print and the airwaves with unprecedented polish and sophistication to convince Americans that personal fulfillment—even personal freedom—could be realized by buying everything from Henry Ford's Model T to Listerine mouthwash. Radio personalized the sell by seamlessly bringing the myriad sounds of modern life—music, news, baseball games, comedy shows, and advertisements, all accompanied by the most important element, the human voice—into the home, thus coupling the urgency of consumption to both the growing appetite for entertainment and the natural routines of everyday existence. As a result, listeners formed relationships not just with automobiles and mouthwash but with the personalities they heard on the air, "consuming" them as well, even talking back to them through their receivers. Radio heightened

Americans' already enormous fascination with celebrity by bringing journal-ists, sports heroes, actors, and—increasingly—humorists and presidents into close association with vast numbers of ordinary listeners. Such associations were built on performance, sound, and imagination, which made these re-lationships changeable and highly volatile, as three such celebrities—Will Rogers, Calvin Coolidge, and Herbert Hoover—soon discovered.[25]

Characteristically, Rogers was one of the first national celebrities to be heard on the radio. In February 1922, while on tour in Pittsburgh with the *Ziegfeld Frolic*, he was invited to KDKA. Surrounded by a few close friends and fellow cast members, Rogers presumably joked about the show, cur-rent events, and probably the new medium itself (there were no recording devices in place to capture his monologue), while a captivated regional au-dience tuned in via headphones and crystal receivers. Rogers, too, was fasci-nated by radio, although it took another nine years before his voice became a weekly fixture on the air. He was never completely comfortable with the distance that radio put between him and his live audience; after all, it was hard to make the studio microphone laugh.[26]

Nevertheless, given his popularity, Americans heard his voice regularly on radio during the 1920s, whether as part of occasional solo efforts or in guest appearances on other programs. In January 1928 he was asked to take part in the first broadcast emanating from four locations at once: New York, Chicago, New Orleans (where another stage and screen star, Al Jolson, spoke), and Beverly Hills, where Rogers hosted from his home. In his mono-logue he touched on predictable material then said, "I want to introduce a friend of mine who is here and wishes to speak to you." Tightening his lips and affecting Calvin Coolidge's wiry voice, he impersonated a president—without disclaimer—for the first time in front of a mass audience:

> I am proud to report that the country as a whole is prosperous. I don't mean by that that the whole country is prosperous, but, as a whole it is prosperous. That is, it is prosperous for a whole. A hole is not supposed to be prosperous, and we are certainly in a hole. There is not a whole lot of doubt about that.
>
> Everybody I come in contact with is doing well. They have to be do-ing well or they don't come in contact with me.[27]

The uproar over the broadcast was loud and immediate. V. V. McNitt, co-founder of the McNaught syndicate, which distributed Rogers's daily news-paper column, telegraphed him to report that "millions of people" thought the impersonation "was really Coolidge talking" and suggested strongly that he "might want to explain in a daily dispatch that it was not really Cal but you." Rogers did, in his daily telegram of January 13:

I [have] found . . . that some people [have] censored [sic] me severely for leaving the impression the other night that Mr. Coolidge was on the radio. Well, the idea that any one could imagine it was him uttering the nonsense that I was uttering! It struck me that it would be an insult to any one's sense of humor to announce that it was not him.[28]

Publicly Rogers was dismissive that what he considered mere mimicry had been taken seriously, but in private he was deeply concerned. Almost two years before, Rogers had toured Europe on assignment for the *Saturday Evening Post* and had sent back regular, amusing open dispatches to Coolidge, who had no connection whatsoever to the project. The messages—first published in the *Post* and the *New York Times* and later collected under the title *Letters of a Self-Made Diplomat to His President*—had been enormously popular and had brought the worlds of presidential politics and humor into even closer proximity. The president had even played along, and on Rogers's return to the United States, he jovially continued his custom of inviting returning ambassadors to meet with him for consultation, even though this ambassador was most certainly without portfolio. It was the comedian's first personal invitation to socialize at the White House, and he enjoyed his quiet dinner and overnight stay with the Coolidges immensely.[29]

Now he was horrified that the impersonation had crossed the line, destroying these good feelings and, even more important, his tacit license to poke fun at the presidency. The apologetic letter he sent to the Coolidges after the broadcast echoed the same shock and uncertainty that many of his listeners were experiencing:

My Dear Mr. and Mrs. President,
I find that due to my lack of good taste, or utter stupidity, that I have wounded the feelings of two people who I most admire, and should have been the last to embarrass had I purposely started out to annoy the entire world. . . .

Why, Mr. Coolidge you and your wife have been nicer to me than any one in high public life in America. I was never invited to the White House by any other President, and in dozens of ways you have been kind to me. . . .

If I didn't have sincere admiration for you both . . . this thing wouldn't hurt so bad. But it does hurt me to think that I have to resort to bad taste to make my living from men who have befriended me. I did the little talk in a moment of jest, never for one moment thinking the most stupid of people could ever mistake it for anyone but me.

As the long letter continued, he moved from apology to rationalization, doubting not only himself but also his audience:

I just misjudged the intelligence of the people listening, and I can't lay all the blame to them, for I can see now after due thought that it was not the proper thing to do under any circumstances. . . . I realize now that radio is not the stage, where they can see you, and I also realize that the class of people who would come into a Theatre to see you are above the average of some of the ones who would be listening over a radio. All this I have learned to my sorrow, and if you can see it in your heart, you and that dear wife of yours, to forgive me, I will certainly see that it, or nothing approaching it, will ever happen again.

If there ever was a sad Comedian, I am one. . . .
Yours most respectfully,
Will Rogers[30]

In this astonishing private correspondence with the president of the United States, Rogers—caught between his audience, his humor, and the object of that humor—briefly and uncharacteristically lost both his composure and his comedic bearings. In his desperation to make amends, he lashed out at himself, the medium, and other Americans in class terms without recognizing that he had unwittingly brought himself—and his mass audience—to the precarious brink of new and uncertain, but exciting, cultural territory. His listeners could not be blamed. After all, Americans had begun to cultivate close associations with both celebrities. Coolidge included Bruce Barton and Edward Bernays, two early masters of public relations, among his advisers, and many had heard the president deliver several speeches on the radio, including his 1923 State of the Union message and his acceptance of the Republican nomination in 1924. They knew Rogers—anointed "the most publicized man in America" just the year before—even better. Furthermore, as the host of the broadcast, Rogers carried added cultural authority, so when the comedian introduced the president, his listeners had little reason to doubt him, given the close association that Rogers had cultivated between humor and politics, and especially considering the recent pleasant association between the "self-made diplomat" and this president. The misunderstanding was unavoidable for reasons that Rogers could not have foreseen; that is, he was performing transformative humor on a transformative medium before a profoundly transforming public.[31]

As for this new humor of presidential impersonation, it remained on the cusp between daring comedy and tasteless duplicity, with most Americans seemingly inclined to think it the latter, although the president—who would seem to have been most justified in taking offense—was typically placid about it all. For his part, Coolidge responded to Rogers's letter calmly and dismissively, telling him that he "found the matter of rather small consequence" and that "your work makes it all plain that you had no intention [other than] some harmless amusement." Rogers took great comfort from Coolidge's response, and used it aggressively to validate impersonation as a legitimate tool in the political comic's repertoire. By the time he wrote the column of January 13 in which he initially explained the confusion (which ran below the declarative headline: "HE DIDN'T OFFEND MR. COOLIDGE, ROGERS SAYS; HAS A LETTER FROM THE PRESIDENT TO PROVE IT"), his contrition had evaporated. "I knew my man before I joked about him," wrote Rogers. "It's as I have often said: You can always joke good naturedly [about] a big man, but be sure he is a big man before you joke about him. What I did over the radio on Mr. Coolidge I did an entire year on my tour of every State last season, and I knew it didn't offend good taste."[32]

Rogers continued to raise the issue in the months and years that followed. Even as he continued to chastise some for their lack of humor, he steadfastly moderated Americans' hesitancy about presidential mimicry lest such parody somehow cheapen what was rapidly becoming the most powerful office in the world. The public was still divided when the matter faded away in the glare of that fall's presidential election (in which Coolidge chose not to run). Although Rogers had to readdress the propriety of impersonation six years later with another president, the country did not begin to reach consensus on the issue for another forty years. Nevertheless, it was Will Rogers who initiated the modern debate.

• • •

In October 1931 Rogers was heard on the radio with another presidential voice, this time the real thing. Herbert Hoover enlisted the country's favorite comedian and most trusted personality to help counter the ever-increasing economic effects and psychological gloom of the Great Depression. Hoover knew the power of radio, having overseen its introduction and regulation during much of the 1920s as secretary of commerce under Harding and Coolidge, although his naturally introverted nature and deepening sullenness as the depression worsened did not lend itself to good radio. Rogers, by contrast, had proven his star power on the air as he had everywhere else. After the sporadic appearances of the 1920s, he could now be heard with more regularity. In the spring of 1930 the pharmaceutical company E. R. Squibb and Sons contracted with him to appear on the radio for $77,000, nearly equal to Babe Ruth's annual salary. In return he provided a series of twelve fifteen-minute talks profiling leading figures of the day. Now the president sought to associate himself and his policies with the superstar by asking Rogers to join him on a nationwide broadcast to promote the President's Organization on Unemployment Relief (POUR), Hoover's initiative urging a voluntary response to the unemployment crisis.[33]

Rogers was willing to help. He believed that Coolidge's policies, not Hoover's, had caused the most disastrous economic cataclysm in the nation's history. In fact Rogers had made Hoover the subject of a flattering Squibb profile the previous year, when he joked that it seemed Americans expected the president to fix their problems personally:

> Prosperity—millions of people never had it under nobody and never will have it under anybody, but they all want it under Mr. Hoover.
> . . . If the weather is wrong, we blame it on Hoover. So all in all, I believe he is doing a pretty good job, and I only claim one distinction, and that is that I am the only person that I know of that is not on one of his commissions.[34]

Nevertheless, as the economic situation deteriorated, it was increasingly difficult not to lay blame on the White House. The culture of perpetual consumption collapsed less than a year into Hoover's term when workers' wages ultimately failed to keep pace with continued buying and irrational investor speculation. Banks were among these speculators, and when the stock market lost roughly a third of its value in three weeks in October–November 1929, thousands of banks began to collapse. Between the Crash and the end of Hoover's term in 1933, Americans lost $7 billion in deposits, 600,000 people lost their homes, and 25 percent of the workforce was without a job. Shantytowns were dubbed "Hoovervilles," and citizen comedians began to joke that when the president asked for a nickel to make a telephone call to a friend, an aide gave him a dime and told him to "call them both." When Hoover tried to rally the country by invoking the spirit of Valley Forge, Rogers mustered only backhanded tribute: "He found somebody that was worse off than we are, but he had to go back 150 years in history to do it."[35]

Now, on October 18, 1931, and at Hoover's request, the comedian and the president shared the broadcast. Rogers worked in some kidding near the beginning of his off-the-cuff remarks, humorously predicting that radio favorites Amos and Andy were all washed up and "it will just be Hoover and Rogers from now on," but his overall tone was sobering:

> The only problem that confronts this country today is at least 7,000,000 people are out of work. That's our only problem. There is no other one before us at all. It's to see that every man that wants to is able to work, is allowed to find a place to go to work, and also to arrange some way of getting more equal distribution of the wealth in the country.

He put the current crisis in perspective, contrasting it with Prohibition, one of the most divisive issues of the day:

Now it's Prohibition, we hear a lot about that. Well, that's nothing to
compare to your neighbor's children that are hungry. It's food, it ain't
drink that we are worried about today. Here a few years ago we were so
afraid that the poor people was liable to take a drink that now we've fixed
[it] so that they can't even get something to eat.

As always, he found a trenchant way to make his point:

So here we are in a country with more wheat and more corn and more
money in the bank, more cotton, more everything in the world . . . and
yet we've got people starving. We'll hold the distinction of being the
only nation in the history of the world that ever went to the poor house
in an automobile.

He concluded:

I certainly want to thank Mr. Hoover for the privilege of being allowed
to appear on the same program with him because I know that this subject is very dear to [his] heart. . . . [I]f every town and every city will get
out and raise their quota [of donations to the relief effort], . . . why it
will make him a very happy man, and happiness hasn't been a steady
diet with our president. . . . He's a very human man. I thank you. Good
night.[36]

With this final oblique compliment—a heartfelt but somewhat pathetic
reference to Hoover's humanness—Rogers pointed out for his audience the
tragicomic extreme of the Great American Joke: the obvious frailties of the
president of the United States made him ill equipped—even laughably so—
to lead Americans out of difficulty and toward the realization of their highest
ideals. In stark contrast, the comedian, by virtue of pointing this out and by
introducing warmth, compassion, and the healing tonic of humor into what
growing numbers of Americans saw as a vacuum of political leadership, grew
still more powerful and effective in the eyes of his fellow citizens. Requests
flooded in for printed and recorded copies of his talk. Copies of the newsreel
footage of the address—dubbed the "Bacon and Beans and Limousines"
speech—were distributed across the country. As the days passed, virtually no
one recalled what the president had to say, but the humorist's words—and
his reassuring voice—became even more legendary. The broadcast and its
popular reception illustrate just how completely Will Rogers dominated the
middle ground between the people and the president.[37]

Not long before his death, Theodore Roosevelt prophesied Rogers's dual
influence on American political and popular culture. In 1918 he told advertising executive and Republican strategist Albert D. Lasker that "this man
Rogers has such a keen insight into the American panorama and the Ameri-

can people that I feel he is bound . . . to be a potent factor in the political life of the nation." A decade later TR's prediction was borne out. Rogers legitimized the popular performance of humor at the expense of the presidency, and he did so by sheer dint of his ubiquity in the mass media and his wide knowledge of and acceptance by those inside and outside the political establishment and across the ideological spectrum. He amassed such cultural authority that when he laughed at presidents, Americans for the most part gladly laughed along. He modeled the modern definition of a standup comedian—articulated by anthropologist Stephanie Koziski and others—as one whose verbal facility and charisma bestow social authority and credibility as an "intentional culture critic." Rogers exuded just such authority and became more than a critic; he was a cultural arbiter who shaped Americans' attitudes about themselves and their leaders, and in the process—as Herbert Hoover discovered—he could make or break public perceptions of those leaders, whether intentionally or not. He was still an expert at the "Crinoline," only now he was using his mastery of the joke to encircle the economic and political elite.[38]

For a time during the 1920s and 1930s Rogers brought the spheres of celebrity and politics—and those of humor and the presidency—into such close proximity that their convergence nearly became congruence. In 1860 Artemus Ward had urged Abraham Lincoln to fill his cabinet with showmen; seventy years later Americans seemed ready to accept Rogers's own observation that "politics is the best show in America" and were not so jokingly considering putting a comedian in the White House. Sensing the chance to cash in on Rogers's celebrity and to sell some magazines, *Life* magazine editor, playwright, and future presidential speechwriter Robert E. Sherwood persuaded Rogers in the spring of 1928 to throw his cowboy hat in the ring, if only in the pages of *Life*. It was to be just for laughs, although many seriously thought it a good idea. He ran at the head of his own brand-new Anti-Bunk Party with the motto "He Chews to Run," a "gum-in-cheek" reference to Rogers's penchant for chewing gum and Calvin Coolidge's proclamation the year before that he did not "choose to run" for another term. The faux campaign literature roasted Herbert Hoover and Democratic nominee Alfred E. Smith and declared Rogers's profession as a humorist to be one of his top qualifications for the job; "he would," said the magazine, "be the first President in sixty-two years [since Lincoln] who was funny intentionally." Rogers perpetuated the candidacy-in-jest until Election Day, when, according to *Life*, he was elected "by the Great Silent Vote of this nation." Although he accepted by fulfilling his only campaign promise—to resign if elected—he nevertheless inspired the long popular tradition of mock candidacies that was continued just a few years later by fellow performer Eddie

Cantor, most hilariously by Pat Paulsen on television's *Smothers Brothers Comedy Hour* in 1968, and by Stephen Colbert and other comedians in 2007 and 2008.[39]

Many voters were disappointed, and several had more serious ambitions for Rogers. He was recommended for virtually every level of elected office at one time or another, from city council on up. There were legitimate efforts to get him to run for governor in Oklahoma, Arkansas, and California during the mid-1920s. As early as 1924 there was a serious public call for a Rogers presidency. It would be a startling action, syndicated columnist Heywood Broun admitted, but an imaginative and intelligent one. Describing him as approximating Lincoln "more nearly than any other man now under consideration," he praised the comedian's ability to speak with "equal lucidity to the great city and the small town" and claimed that "Rogers talks more substantial common sense between any two rope tricks than [three-time presidential candidate William Jennings] Bryan has spoken in his whole career." In a nation seemingly adrift as it was being tossed through a period of enormous social and technological change followed by economic catastrophe, Rogers was credited with offering buoyancy and stability while simultaneously proposing radically new perspectives on the place of humor in political discourse. In 1928, even as his joking candidacy proceeded in *Life* magazine, talk of his making a bona fide run continued. Henry Ford was among the loudest proponents; but the talk never came from Rogers. In 1931 he finally tired of the continued speculation and asked his readers, "If you see or hear of anybody proposing my name for any political office will you maim said party and send me the bill?" For his part, he frequently extolled the qualities he saw as most valuable in a president; conviction, energy, and honesty normally topped the list. He frequently invoked the model of Teddy Roosevelt, the president who had forecast great things for Rogers back in 1918 and who had been the object of his first presidential joke. In 1924 Rogers lamented, "We will be lucky . . . if we produce another Roosevelt in the next 100 years." As it turned out, another came along in eight.[40]

• • •

Franklin D. Roosevelt's easy but calculated joviality—particularly his performances before the press—would permanently alter the way the nation interpreted the presidency, but Will Rogers had little way of knowing this before FDR took office. In 1932 it was Rogers who was as well known if not more so than any of the candidates marshaled by the Democratic Party to topple the beleaguered Hoover administration. Although he continued to ridicule both parties until his death, and his independent stands on many issues made him difficult to pin down politically, Rogers freely admitted: "I don't belong to any organized political faith. I am a Democrat." Yet he was quick to point out the reason for this natural attraction between comedians and many Democratic policies: "You've got to be [an] optimist to be a Democrat, and you've got to be a humorist to stay one."[41]

In fact he was once again a candidate himself in 1932, if only briefly and in the wishful thinking of his fellow Oklahomans. Four years after his lark on the self-created Anti-Bunk ticket, the Oklahoma delegation committed its twenty-two electoral votes to its "favorite son" during the Democratic convention in Chicago. By the end of the night, however, the votes had gone to the eventual nominee, and Rogers lamented his fate as just another of the thousands of former Democratic presidential hopefuls.[42]

Rogers might have taken solace from the fact that he was more familiar to much of the electorate than—and possibly preferred over—the nominee who commandeered those twenty-two votes. Politically, Governor Franklin D. Roosevelt of New York was widely perceived as lacking the conviction or fiscal acumen necessary to rescue the nation from its economic woes. Personally he was an unknown quantity to most people outside the party or his New York constituency, despite having shared the unsuccessful 1920 Democratic ticket with presidential nominee James M. Cox. Still, after almost a decade's absence from public life, there was some reason to believe he might be able to exert considerable national appeal. Exiled into private life by polio in 1921, Roosevelt battled back to prominence during his two terms as governor. There seemed to be little remaining of the brash young state senator who, in the 1910s, had initially impressed future secretary of labor Frances Perkins as "not particularly charming" and "artificially serious of face, rarely smiling." Indeed she observed only three years later that it seemed Roosevelt had emerged from his convalescence utterly transformed, "completely warmhearted, with humility of spirit and with a deeper philosophy." What neither Perkins nor anyone else, including Roosevelt, could foresee was how this personal transformation would extend to redefine the presidency and the nation, both similarly afflicted by a crippling depression. Likewise, few could anticipate that the chief executive himself—first in step with the comedian, then as the humorist alone—would permanently alter the role that laughter, both at and with the president, played in the national political dialogue.[43]

By 1932 Will Rogers's singular conflation of popular and political culture had brought him closer to the leadership and machinations of the political establishment than any other American observer. He was so effective at making humor synonymous with politics in the national consciousness that he was hired in 1920 by the Newspaper Enterprise Association to write jokes for the syndicate from both the Republican and Democratic conventions (a precursor of later decades when the presence of standup comics such as

Mort Sahl, Jon Stewart, and others at political conventions became first the vogue, then commonplace). He infused the serious work at hand with playful gags: "Mexico don't know how to get rid of [Pancho] Villa. Loan him to us for a Vice-President. That would get both nations rid of him." Rogers was a fixture at both parties' conventions for the next twelve years. His political savvy allowed him to distinguish bright careers in the making from among what, to him, was the crowded field of mediocrity. His instincts as an entertainer also enabled him to recognize pure star power when he saw it.[44]

Both perspectives—as a political insider and a performer—told him that Franklin Roosevelt was going places as early as the 1924 Democratic convention, when FDR nominated Alfred E. Smith for the presidency. Perhaps Rogers was struck by the inner courage and fortitude that had so impressed Frances Perkins that same year. Certainly Roosevelt seemed to be describing himself as much as Smith in his portrait of the "Happy Warrior," even if Rogers thought he was too wordy in the process. In one of his earliest references to FDR, Rogers revealed his rising admiration for the young Democrat's power to move an audience while poking fun at him in the process:

> Franklin Roosevelt started in early in the morning with the "Man I am about to name." He had the opportunity of a lifetime to make a name for himself comparable with the Republican end of the Roosevelt family. But no, he must say, "Man I am about to name" for ten pages. . . .
> But when he did get to the end and named Al [Smith] you would have thought somebody had thrown a wildcat in your face. The galleries went wild and about ten State delegations marched and hollered for an hour.[45]

Rogers continued to track Roosevelt's rising star through the 1920s. In one of his "daily telegrams," he reported Smith's determined efforts to anoint a reluctant FDR as his handpicked successor in New York's 1928 gubernatorial race. Rogers noted that after years of being remembered as the man who got up and nominated Al Smith for president "any time as many as three persons met," Roosevelt was now the one being nominated. He also offered a prophetic assessment of Roosevelt's potential:

> His nominating days over, he is now going to take up politics seriously. He is a Roosevelt by blood, but a namesake politically. If he had retained his splendid qualities and stayed with the Republican end of the family, he would have been President, but I doubt if he could have retained those qualities and been Republican.

In 1930, when FDR won reelection as governor of New York, Rogers was among the first to predict publicly the event's larger significance: "The Democrats nominated their president yesterday, Franklin D. Roosevelt."[46]

FIGURE 4. *Franklin D. Roosevelt (left) responds to his introduction by Will Rogers (behind microphone) at a Los Angeles rally in 1932. Courtesy Will Rogers Memorial Museum, Claremore, Oklahoma.*

Two years later, after the Democratic Party fulfilled his prophecy at its convention in Chicago, the stage was set for two of the country's most prominent personalities to perform together. On September 24, 1932, FDR appeared at a party rally at Olympic Stadium in Los Angeles, which had just hosted the tenth Olympic Games the month before. This night the festivities were courtesy of the Democratic faithful from the entertainment industry, who mustered an audience of some 100,000 to honor the presidential candidate Roosevelt and to hear him introduced by the showman Rogers (fig. 4). The program would have done Ziegfeld proud; it included a polo game, roping and other rodeo demonstrations, and fifteen floats on parade bedecked with scantily clad women, all before the evening's speakers appeared. The title "Motion Picture Electrical Pageant" befitted not only the spectacle but also the atmosphere, as pure politics met pure theater. Taking center stage with FDR only a few feet away, Rogers stood to introduce him:

> This is the biggest audience in the world that ever paid to see a politician. This stadium was dedicated to art, sports . . . and legitimate enterprises, hence there can be no politics. It was also dedicated to amusement, so politics certainly comes under that head. . . .

Now I don't want you to think I am overwhelmed by being asked to introduce you. I am not. I am broadminded and will introduce anybody. Why if Herbert Hoover was to come, I would even introduce him. . . .

Franklyn [sic] Roosevelt, you are not here tonight as a politician or vote getter. You are here as a guest of people who spend our lives trying to entertain. This great gathering is . . . neither Jew or Gentile, Democrat or Republican. Whether they vote for you or not, and thousands of 'em won't, never mind what they tell you, for there is some terrible liars out here. Every one . . . admire[s] you as a man. Your platform, your policies, your plans may not meet with their approval, but your high type of manhood gains the approval of every person in this audience. . . .

This introduction may have lacked enthusiasm and floweriness, but you must remember you are only a candidate yet. Come back as a president and I will do right by you. I am wasting no oratory on a prospect.[47]

FDR roared with laughter, along with the rest of the crowd and those on the platform. Twenty-one years after he roped FDR's fifth cousin Teddy with his first presidential joke, thrown from the safety of an obscure vaudeville stage at a president three years out of office—and sixteen years after nervously lobbing ridicule at Woodrow Wilson, a sitting president in attendance across the footlights—Will Rogers (and, by extension, his approving public) now effortlessly and without hesitation gibed at the nation's foremost political celebrity, a presidential candidate who sought to share the same stage with him and earn his favor. The rally in Los Angeles is emblematic; it gives confirmation not only of the enormous strength and influence of show business within American culture by the early 1930s but also of its broad intersection with political culture and, further, of the comedian's starring role in forging their union. Political standup comedy had found its voice, its audience, and—at least temporarily—its legitimacy as a salable commodity in the marketplace of popular culture, even if such legitimacy came at the expense of the most venerated office in the land.

When Roosevelt was overwhelmingly elected several weeks later, Rogers privately paid homage in a long and heartfelt personal telegram that continued to offer counsel from the comedian to the president-elect. It seems he was unaware that he was following the precedent set by Charles Browne's "Old Showman" Artemus Ward in his whimsical advice to president-elect Lincoln seventy-two years before. Rogers, the jester-everyman, advised the new chief executive on the bittersweet effects of presidential celebrity in the new media age and—indirectly—on the power of humor:

I didnt wire you on your election for I knew you was too excited to read but now that all the folks that want something are about through congratulating you I thought maby [sic] a wire just wishing that you can do something for the country and not just wishing you could do something for me would be a novelty and not unwelcome. Your health is the main thing. Don't worry too much. A smile in the White House again. Why the last one was Tafts. . . .

Why Governor you can go in there and have a good time. We want our presidents to have some fun. Too many mistake their election as going to a Vatican and not to just a white house. . . .

Work it so that when we see you in person or on the screen we will smile with you and be glad with you. We don't want to [k]ill our presidents but they just seem to want to die for us.

He specifically tutored FDR on the judicious use of the media:

Keep off the radio till you got something to say even if its a year. Be good to the press boys in Washington for they are getting those "merry go rounds" out every few weeks. Now stay off that back lawn with those photographers unless you got a [sports celebrity such as] Helen Wills or your fifth cousin Alice Longworth. Nothing will kill off interest in a president as quick as "weeklys" with chamber of commerces and womens political organizations.[48]

It is not clear to what extent Roosevelt consciously used Rogers's message to inspire the character of his administration, but the telegram is a virtual précis of the Roosevelt style. Specifically, the new president's understanding and manipulation of humor and the media placed him and Rogers in almost perfect alignment as the Roosevelt administration got under way. Eventually the president eclipsed the comic.

• • •

Although an individual's sense of humor may be refined or otherwise altered by contingency and experience, its essence cannot be contrived; it springs naturally from within. Franklin Roosevelt was born with deep reservoirs of humor, although it took a personal crisis to teach him how to tap it and two decades of Rogers's presidential ribbing and parody to prime Americans' acceptance of such humor. Numerous historians and Roosevelt associates have explored FDR's celebrated charm and good humor in general and particularly his use of laughter to facilitate his physical recovery, to evade close personal relationships, and to combat the Great Depression. They have noted along the way the contrast of FDR's warm ebullience with Herbert Hoover's comparative frigidity; nearly anyone might have been considered a comic genius by comparison.

The brilliance of Roosevelt's humor was not so much in its content as in his sophisticated knowledge of how to use it and calculate its effect on an audience. Like Rogers—and much more intimately than either Woodrow Wilson or Calvin Coolidge—Roosevelt knew by instinct and experience both the necessity and potency of laughter, and he understood that he was ideally positioned to exploit it for psychological and political gain at the moment when it was needed most. In comedy, timing is everything, and FDR had it beginning with his entrance on the presidential stage.

Franklin Roosevelt did not hesitate, as Will Rogers counseled, to seek out the "press boys." As a self-avowed student of publicity, he had capitalized on media exposure from his earliest days in public life. He held his first meeting with White House reporters on March 8, 1933. The press conference was a Roosevelt innovation modestly begun by TR three decades before and given some regularity during the Wilson years. Although Coolidge was famously mum (he reportedly claimed, "If you don't say anything, you won't be called on to repeat it"), the enigmatic president held 520 press conferences, more than any other chief executive to that time. The press meeting was alternately dreaded, minimized, or ignored altogether by Taft and Harding. FDR, by contrast, considered it a prime venue for promoting his policies while showcasing his charm, confidence, and humor before a potentially hostile but—he was convinced—eminently winnable audience. Although Roosevelt's skill could manifest itself in any form of presidential communication—letters, speeches, broadcasts—these were almost always heavily scripted and collaborative efforts by numerous aides and writers. "A speech by the President was," as author John Gunther observed, "to put it mildly, almost always a composite phenomenon." Though not as direct a medium as radio, the press conference regularly placed him before the American public by proxy, and Roosevelt was determined to engage the press personally and spontaneously, a feat made possible by ego and a comedic charm that FDR aide General Edwin M. "Pa" Watson claimed could "win the bark off a tree." Roosevelt's last press secretary, Jonathan Daniels, described Roosevelt the performer:

> He [was] the master player. He sat behind his great desk, immobilized by his lameness, yet with the air of a great actor who, in advance of his audience, had entered jauntily from the wings to the klieg lights of a world stage. More remarkable, he took the stage each time with no carefully fashioned lines to recite and little advance knowledge of all the questions which would be flung at him. . . . And in command, he was the almost perfect statesman-showman . . . [the] impressario[sic]-in-chief.[49]

His debut appearance before the press in 1933 was greeted, as scholars John Tebbel and Sarah Miles Watts later observed, as "the most amazing performance the White House has ever seen." Welcoming the assemblage to the first of what he called these "delightful family conferences," Roosevelt proceeded to detail stringent rules for quotation and publication, but with such winning good cheer that only the most astute among the journalists realized he was seizing almost complete presidential control over dissemination of the news. He got his first laugh within the first five minutes when he jauntily delivered a stern caution not to attribute background information to him directly lest he "have to revive the Ananias Club," Theodore Roosevelt's list of reporters and others who TR believed had misrepresented him. Thirty-five minutes later the chuckling, mesmerized, and professionally emasculated journalists gave the president the first ovation ever accorded by the White House press corps.[50]

Roosevelt used humor in a wide variety of ways with the press. Early on he was only too happy to capitalize on the impending end of Prohibition to establish rapport with thirsty fellow men who, like him, looked forward to the legally restored flow of alcohol, even if their wives objected. In March 1933 one reporter, perhaps already somewhat intoxicated by presidential charm, asked:

> May I put in an "if" question? If, as the wire reports say, a Milwaukee brewery sends you the first two cases of beer, will you accept it?
> ROOSEVELT: That *is* an "if" question. [Laughter] Off the record, strictly off the record, I will have to ask my wife.
> REPORTER: We know the answer. [Laughter][51]

Frequently his most effective and disarming humor came in short, buoyant quips designed to set the tone for the press conference and communicate what he hoped would be interpreted to the public as his contagious optimism:

> REPORTER: I wrote a story that you have not lost your old smile. Don't throw me down.
> ROOSEVELT: You bet I haven't. It is working overtime. [Laughter]

In 1934 a frustrated correspondent queried:

> REPORTER: Mr. President, I am writing something, generally, about the New Deal and there are four questions to which nobody has been able to give me answers. [Laughter] Will you kindly give me something? Namely, was America, after all, discovered, manufactured, deducted or invented? [Laughter]

ROOSEVELT: I should say that America is in process of being perfected.[52]

Roosevelt was so adept at infusing levity into the atmosphere that he inspired standup comedy performances from the press itself. He was even willing to play the foil if the newsman was clever and quick enough to catch the set-up line. The result was often an exchange that sounded more like a vaudeville routine than a press conference:

ROOSEVELT: By the way, George McAneny is coming in the morning. We will talk about sewers, I suppose. . . .
REPORTER: Who is Mr. McAneny?
ROOSEVELT: Late of the *New York Times*, now the Commissioner of Sewers in New York. [Laughter]
REPORTER: Well trained, wasn't he? [Laughter][53]

Roosevelt was also a master of the rapid quip, the cheap pun, and the long anecdote employed as subterfuge, to deflect attention from undesirable topics or from his physical disability. One admiring victim observed, "I never met anyone who showed greater capacity for avoiding a direct answer while giving the questioner a feeling he *had* been answered." Eleanor Roosevelt admitted that "Franklin had a way, when he did not want to hear what somebody had to say, of telling stories and talking about something quite different." When one conscientious reporter asked what the president's upcoming fireside chat was going to be about, FDR took a lesson from Calvin Coolidge and answered, "about twenty-two minutes."[54]

For most of his presidency, especially prior to World War II, Roosevelt held two press conferences a week before a crowd of journalists that swelled dramatically during his administration. As word got around, the Roosevelt press conferences became hot tickets, and as every subsequent president discovered—those who successfully emulated them and those who did not—they were tough acts to follow.[55]

The immediate benefits of Roosevelt's merry mastery of the press corps confirmed his awareness—reinforced by Rogers's telegram—that the times, the democratizing power of the electronic mass media, and the presidency's flagging credibility during the Hoover years demanded that the president no longer merely inform the American public of policies and pronouncements, or appear occasionally for an obligatory photo opportunity. The modern era—marked so prominently since the turn of the century by progressive reforms at the national level, world war, depression, and electronic media poised to communicate it all—called for the presidency to recast itself, to acknowledge that the executive branch no longer merely played a supporting role to Congress and the judiciary; it played directly to the people. Extraordinary urgencies and unprecedented media exposure, including the fascination with individual celebrity, were elevating the president to star billing. Roosevelt understood these challenges and believed he was uniquely equipped not to confront them but to positively revel in them, and he saw enormous value in projecting this merry confidence outward. Humor was the means. Certainly he would claim even more power for the office in the face of the depression and a new world war, but levity was the equalizing counterweight. It could at once humanize him and empower the American people by encouraging them to laugh in the face of fear. Such humor— which came naturally to Roosevelt and had been refined and auditioned before the public by Rogers—was not mere frivolity; it was an essential strategic tool. FDR modeled it as foundational to the modern presidency, and in this respect the president Roosevelt and the comedian Rogers became kindred spirits. Both performed humor to great effect, although the stage most obviously belonged to Rogers. Roosevelt was more than happy to let him retain top billing, although he exploited his fellow comedian's star power and got in on the act himself whenever he could.

FDR heeded Rogers's advice in his telegram to "stay off the radio till you got something to say," although that something came eight days after the inauguration instead of the year that Rogers proposed. He broadcast the first of what came to be known as his fireside chats on March 12, 1933, and in addressing the ongoing banking crisis, he built upon the mastery of radio that he had cultivated so successfully on a regional scale during his years as New York governor. Roosevelt was attuned to the personal, even intimate associations that listeners formed with those they heard on the air, and he welcomed such direct interaction. The airwaves wafted over the heads of newspaper publishers and Republican opponents, carrying the presidential agenda and voice—idiosyncratic yet upbeat, personable, and resonant— directly into the homes of the estimated 60 million people whom Roosevelt called "my friends." Far from portraying a dictator, a common charge from his critics, radio allowed Roosevelt to identify with his fellow citizens and to encourage feedback: "not less democracy," as he said later, "but more democracy." Its effectiveness was evidenced by the estimated 15 to 30 million Americans who wrote to FDR during his administration. Roosevelt rarely used humor overtly in the thirty fireside chats, but his conversational manner and liberal use of the first person endeared him to a majority of Americans, and his performance on the radio complemented Rogers's comic observations.[56]

• • •

Franklin Roosevelt could use the radio to personalize the presidency in large part because Will Rogers had already long used it to make Americans laugh at the White House and the frailties of its occupants. Historians Lawrence W. Levine and Cornelia Levine have joined others in crediting FDR with "presiding over . . . a revolution in the pattern of communication between Americans and their chief executive," but Rogers was the point man in this revolution. In 1930, when Governor Roosevelt was still struggling to be heard over unreliable networks a scant fifty miles from New York's capital in Albany, Rogers had his own regular broadcast nationwide. In contrast to FDR's carefully crafted chats, Rogers stood without notes before a bare lectern and an open microphone, and told millions of receptive Americans what was on his mind, taking special aim at the political elite and encouraging his listeners to consider themselves equal to their leaders.[57]

In the spring of 1933 Rogers signed a new radio contract with Gulf Oil Company, which agreed to sponsor a series of half-hour programs on Sunday evenings. The programs proved a huge hit, and Rogers continued them until his death. Coincidentally, this gave him expanded airtime just as Roosevelt took office. On his first program—April 30, seven weeks after Roosevelt's inaugural fireside chat and one week before his second—Rogers took up columnist Walter Winchell's call for a new national holiday, President's Day, and celebrated the new president with a combination of humor and worship that any politician would consider priceless:

> Now this is President's Day. We generally recognize anything by a week. . . . We have Apple Week, and Potato Week, and Don't Murder Your Wife Week, and Smile Week. . . . Winchell says, "Well here, if prunes are worth a week, the president ought to be worth something anyhow." . . .
>
> That bird [Roosevelt] has done more for us in seven weeks than we've done for ourselves in seven years. We elected him because he was a Democrat, and now we honor him because he is a magician. He's the Houdini of Hyde Park. . . .
>
> [H]e's made Christians out of the Republicans. . . . [Y]ou'd be surprised at the hordes of Republicans who are crawling up to this shrine in Washington to pay their respects to this modern messiah.

Rogers's messianic hyperbole continued as he went on to address FDR directly—not only was Roosevelt divine; he was a fellow mortal listening in—as one able to commiserate with the American folk:

> Now I understand Mr. Roosevelt—somebody told me he was listenin' in. Now, Mr. Roosevelt, we've turned everything over to you. . . . [Y]ou take [the country] and run it if you want to, you know, and deflate, or inflate,

or complicate, or, you know, insulate. . . . The whole country's cockeyed anyhow. . . . We don't know what it's all about, but God bless you.[58]

Listeners might have compared and contrasted this broadcast with that of two short years before when Rogers spoke of bacon, beans, and limousines, and of embattled Herbert Hoover as "a very human man." Once again the comedian wielded cultural influence when he passed judgment on the president, though this time not to bury Hoover but to praise Roosevelt. Rogers was still the kingmaker, and he helped to validate the "Houdini of Hyde Park" before a mass audience. He primed the airwaves with humor and accustomed the nation to the easygoing conversational authority that was so critical not only to his own success onstage, in films, and over the air but also to that of the new president, who sought to interact with Americans in similarly direct ways. If propriety and sensitivity to the personal hardships at hand told the president that openly making jokes on the radio was ill advised, he took comfort that he did not need to. The nation's favorite comedian—his political soul mate—did it for him, occasionally on the same night.

The styles of the president and the standup comedian were remarkably complementary. The Sunday following Rogers's President's Day broadcast marked the second of Roosevelt's fireside chats, and it was purposely scheduled to air later in the evening, following Rogers's weekly talk from New York City. Millions listened as the comic gave a pitch for his sponsor and joked about sharing billing with the president:

> Now, tonight, I am on here with President Roosevelt. . . . I am selling Gulf Oil, and he is selling the United States, and both of them are good propositions, and don't sell either one of them short.
>
> I am on ahead of Mr. Roosevelt. He is going to talk later on. Generally, at big affairs, where I have been fortunate enough to speak, I generally follow those big men, because they always have a lot of logic and theories and everything, and somebody has to come along and offset them with facts.
>
> But not with Mr. Roosevelt. There is a plain spoken man. That speech over the radio that night the banks closed, that proved, you know, [that] he is a man, you know, [a] very plain spoken man. . . .
>
> He changed the thought of a nation that night with that one speech.
>
> He changed us from a nation of takers-out to putters-in.
>
> That speech will, when history is written, go down some day as being the detour sign where depression turned back. . . .
>
> Mr. Roosevelt and I tonight are both going to speak to you on depression. I will take it up first, and if there is any loose ends left, he can pick it up where I left off.

I am going to explain depression to you in such a way that he will
have practically nothing to say when he comes on, outside of just coin-
ciding with my opinion. You know what I mean. Of course, he can be
wrong if he wants to and not agree with me.[59]

Rogers moved on to a humorous discussion of economic deflation, commodity prices, and the limits of executive power, all of which were central
to the president's message later; he had clearly been briefed on FDR's chat.
As soon as Rogers went off the air, Roosevelt, who was preparing to deliver
his own talk in Washington, D.C., asked through his staff that a transcript
of the comedian's comments be dictated over the telephone. Roosevelt proceeded to speak of "what we have been doing and what we are planning to
do" in more specific and serious terms than had Rogers, but with the same
easy familiarity that made both men radio stars. Perhaps he even inspired
a few appreciative chuckles when he admitted that Americans could not
simply "bally-ho ourselves back to prosperity," or when he used baseball as
a metaphor for measuring his personal effectiveness: "What I seek is the
highest possible batting average, not only for myself but for the team. Theodore Roosevelt once said to me: 'If I can be right seventy-five per cent of the
time I shall come up to the fullest measure of my hopes.'" Americans found
something comfortably familiar in the president's words. When the evening
was over, several friends wondered to Will Rogers if Roosevelt was writing his
material or vice versa.[60]

Whether it was fully calculated or not, the combination of Rogers and
Roosevelt produced a wave of reassuring goodwill in the first one hundred
days of FDR's administration that equaled—in psychological terms at least—
the surge of legislation passed during that time to address the banking crisis,
ease Prohibition, cut the federal budget, provide some relief, and begin to put
Americans back to work. Battling the pervasive sense of pessimism through a
projection of good-natured buoyancy was an accomplishment Roosevelt considered no less vital to the national recovery. More than any of his six immediate predecessors—all of whom Rogers had captured within his presidential
"Crinoline"—Franklin Roosevelt was keenly aware of everything the comic
meant to the country and the enormous influence his humor and personality wielded to change hearts and minds. Of course there were other political
commentators. Although he was not a performer in the traditional sense,
journalist H. L. Mencken regularly captured the spotlight with words, such
as his description of all presidents as "despots of an almost fabulous ferocity."
Father Charles Coughlin, the fiery Catholic priest, used his radio sermons
first to praise Roosevelt's New Deal policies, then to condemn them harshly
before millions of listeners. Other popular comedians ridiculed politics and

politicians; movie audiences delighted at Groucho Marx's zany portrayals of small men in high places, such as Rufus T. Firefly, president of Freedonia in the wild 1933 Marx Brothers film comedy *Duck Soup*. Rogers, however, carried unique cultural authority to comment on and poke fun at the presidency because of his own political acumen. The comedian who laughed with and at presidents could have been one himself. In the summer of 1932, before he secured the nomination, Roosevelt was already sufficiently convinced of Rogers's potency as a political force that he feared it could fatally split the Democratic Party should the comedian decide to mount a legitimate campaign. In a laudatory note to his friend, Roosevelt urged Rogers not to "get mixed in any fool movement to make the good old [Democratic] Donkey chase his own tail and give the [Republican] Elephant a chance to win the race."[61]

Once the threat of a Rogers candidacy dissipated, Roosevelt did not hesitate to harness the comedian's celebrity, whether to complement his fireside chats or to generate support elsewhere. In 1934 FDR instructed his aide and confidant Louis Howe to enlist Rogers's help to reelect Maine's Democratic governor, Louis Brann. In his letter Howe reminded Rogers that he had already made kind comments about the state and the New Deal's positive effects on Maine's economy. Lest Rogers forget the gist of his own words, Howe provided a word-for-word script for him to read. He was then to "talk this on a phonograph record for the Governor to use in his campaign."[62]

There is no clear indication that Will Rogers made the recording (Brann was reelected), although his close friendship with Roosevelt makes it likely that he did. While he had been invited to the White House by every president in the twentieth century save William McKinley and William Howard Taft, he made seven trips to the FDR White House, often for tea or dinner and several times as an overnight houseguest. The two men maintained a personal correspondence and attended many of the same functions. FDR staffers could routinely be found in the studio audiences for Rogers's broadcasts when they originated from Washington or New York, and they helped to provide friendly—and presumably contagious—laughs for his jokes.[63]

Rogers's general support for most of FDR's policies never gave way to outright boosterism. The cowboy could still throw barbs. A consistent isolationist (who nevertheless loved to travel the world), he was highly critical of the country's proposed entry into the World Court in early 1935. That summer Senator Huey Long, the colorful populist from Louisiana, took great glee from the fact that FDR had co-opted some of Long's plans for the redistribution of wealth, and Rogers seemed to agree. The comedian had quipped, "I sure would have liked to have seen Huey's face when he was woke up in the middle of the night by the President, who said 'Lay over, Huey, I want to get in bed with you.'"[64]

Rogers continued to lampoon Roosevelt, even if mildly. As a strict collec-
tionist who believed that loans to other countries should be repaid quickly,
he found it ironic in November 1933 that the United States was considering
formal recognition of the Soviet Union at a time when the U.S. government
was having difficulty getting other nations to recognize their financial debts
to America. Rogers parodied the ongoing conversations between the two
countries by imitating Roosevelt and Soviet diplomat Maxim M. Litvinov in
mock dialogue on the air, with FDR trying to persuade Litvinov to recognize
and buy American goods:

> ROGERS AS LITVINOFF [sic]: Money! Where is America's money?
> I have been here ten days. I have seen no money.
> ROGERS AS ROOSEVELT: Oh, my good friend, Mr. Litvinoff, we
> haven't got any money now. You see, we've had hard luck and we're
> broke.
> LITVINOFF: You broke? . . . Then why should I recognize you? You
> don't think I care about you personally, do youski?
> ROOSEVELT: Ah, but we got lots of things. We got hogs, cattle, . . .
> tractors, . . . safety razors. We'll sell 'em all to you. . . . We'll sell 'em on
> time.
> LITVINOFF: Is it a long time?
> ROOSEVELT: Sure, it's a long time. We'll give you as long as you
> want.
> LITVINOFF: Is it—is it eternity? [Laughter]
> ROOSEVELT: Sure, eternity, Litvinoff—the same terms as the other
> nations have. [Laughter][65]

The broadcast seemed to go well, with nearly twenty pauses for laughter
from the studio audience. Will Rogers had not lost his touch, but neither had
he lost his concern over the propriety of presidential mimicry, which also remained on the threshold between uneasy acceptance and condemnation as
outright treason in many people's minds. In an almost exact repetition of his
self-deprecation following the imitation of Calvin Coolidge six years earlier,
Rogers wired Roosevelt press secretary Stephen Early almost immediately
asking forgiveness from "the boss" (the only other person Rogers referred to
in this way was his old friend Florenz Ziegfeld). He continued to mediate
what he and perhaps the rest of the country still considered to be the trou-
bling relationship between comedy and the highest office in the land:

> I just guessed wrong and was all haywire Sunday night, so you ask the
> boss to excuse me, won't you? This humor business is more uncertain
> than politics. When you are wrong you are just all wrong. There is

no between with humor. Can offer no alibi. Only the intentions were
good.
Regards to all.
Will[66]

This time the president clearly understood parody and its effects better than
the comedian did. Roosevelt had Early cable back the same day:

The boss said quote tell Will I must have guessed wrong, too, because I
liked it a lot unquote. Regards.
Stephen Early[67]

Roosevelt's reaction echoed that of Calvin Coolidge, although the reason
for FDR's is perhaps more transparent. He had a longtime liking for caricature, which apparently did not diminish when he became its object. He took
great delight in the well-known spoofs of him by *New Yorker* cartoonist Peter
Arno and others. He hilariously defended his dog Fala before a supportive
audience of Teamsters in 1944 after the Republican opposition spread the
rumor that he had sent a navy destroyer to retrieve the Scottish terrier after
it had been left behind on a trip. The president's performance stands as
tongue-in-cheek proof that he did not mind personal attacks, even if the
frugal Scotsman Fala did:

These Republican leaders have not been content with attacks on me, or
on my wife, or on my sons. No, not content with that. They now include
my little dog Fala. [Laughter, sustained applause]
    Well, of course I don't resent attacks, and my family don't resent at-
tacks, but Fala *does* resent them. [Prolonged laughter]. . . .
    I am accustomed to hearing malicious falsehoods about myself . . .
but I think I have a right to resent, to object to libelous statements about
my dog. [Laughter, thunderous applause][68]

Like Abraham Lincoln, Roosevelt tended to bear humorous ridicule
well, out of self-confidence, admiration for the fellow humorist, and a personal lifelong appreciation for the comic tradition. An avid collector from
his youth, he prized an assortment of nearly two dozen editorial cartoons
from the Revolutionary era, which he placed prominently in the entrance
hall of his Hyde Park home, ready to greet every visitor with their mockery
of King George III. Roosevelt considered dissension part of any free society,
and he seems to have harbored special affinity for protest that was creative
and intelligent enough to make its point through laughter. As a master of
sarcasm and satire himself, he often gave no quarter and usually expected
none in return.[69]

If Roosevelt the amateur comedian was comfortable with the humor of Rogers's radio impersonation, Rogers—the professional—remained unconvinced, even though he thanked Roosevelt on his next show for being "the answer to a comedian's prayer," for loving a joke "whether it's on him, or off him, or any other way." He had "no alibi" to offer in his telegram to Stephen Early following the impersonation, no excuse for tangling "this humor business" with politics, thereby assuming that an excuse was needed. Ostensibly he apologized for the execution, not the concept, which he thought was "kind of a good idea." His obsequious response, however, somewhat belied his comedic daring. From his initial reference to Theodore Roosevelt to his jibes at Franklin years later, he struggled, as he believed his countrymen and women did, with the distinction between poking fun at the presidency and ridiculing the man. Rogers blazed the trail for American standup comedy's assault on the office, but he hesitated—nor did he feel the necessity—to test its limits intentionally. He broke radical new ground many times while remaining content to pause at the edge. He joked to suit his times. For all his audacity, he often seemed to observe what anthropologist Victor Turner calls the "golden mean," that is, an ethic that essentially preserved the cultural status quo even as his new expressions of humor danced dangerously around it. Two decades later the comedians who followed him and who more fully realized his legacy largely discarded the golden mean as a luxury of Will Rogers's times.[70]

•   •   •

Rogers embraced risk and adventure in other ways as fully as, if not more than, any other American of the age. Aviation was another of his passions; he flew whenever possible, whether with Charles Lindbergh or another of his many aviator friends, whether in the earliest commercial aircraft or on airmail planes, where he paid the equivalent of his weight in first-class postage. He was on one of his many extended flying excursions promoting passenger aviation, this time looking for new routes across the Bering Strait, when he was killed along with pilot and fellow Oklahoman Wiley Post on August 15, 1935, after Post's experimental plane flipped over just after takeoff and plunged into an icy lagoon near Point Barrow, Alaska. The next morning in Hyde Park, still unaware of the accident, Franklin Roosevelt convened a brief press conference in which he joked about golf and hedged about the content of his upcoming radio address.[71]

The nation mourned as it often has for presidents but never before or since for a comedian. Vice President John Nance Garner adjourned Congress in Rogers's honor. Bells rang in more than one hundred cities, and flags flew at half-mast. Nearly 100,000 people passed Rogers's casket at Forest

Lawn Cemetery in Los Angeles before his final interment in Claremore, Oklahoma. All Hollywood studios closed the day of his funeral. As soon as he learned of the accident, President Roosevelt sent shocked condolences to Rogers's family.[72]

Eight days later, following a radio address by FDR, one listener lamented in a telegram the loss of the interpretive humor with which Will Rogers had so often complemented the president's words:

> The President:
> Again accept our gratitude for clarifying our vision. Regret that Will Rogers cannot call our attention to salient points. Promise to carry on.[73]

Roosevelt did carry on. After the initial wave of shocked eulogies, there was little public presidential reaction. In 1937, with the depression still raging, the Oklahoma legislature asked FDR to support $500,000 in matching federal funds for a Rogers memorial. In a personal memo Roosevelt responded that "to my regret as a very old friend of Will Rogers, it is impossible this year." He and Eleanor Roosevelt did send a personal check for one hundred dollars and instructed that word of the donation be kept from the press. Three years after Rogers's death, with the memorial funded from other sources and newly finished, FDR took to the radio to dedicate it, summarize the humorist's contribution to the nation, and—if unconsciously—try to articulate the essence of what the president and the standup comic had in common:

> I doubt if there is among us a more useful citizen than the one who holds the secret of banishing gloom, of making tears give way to laughter, of supplanting desolation and despair with hope and courage. For hope and courage always go with a light heart.
> There was something infectious about his humor. His appeal went straight to the heart of the nation. Above all things, in a time grown too solemn and somber he brought his countrymen back to a sense of proportion.[74]

Will Rogers and Franklin Roosevelt alone did not bring about the revolutionary changes in American comedy performance and its relationship to presidents and those who laugh at them. Celebrity culture and the new electronic accessibility of radio, film, and recording would have made such change inevitable in some form. These two men merely ensured—by the force of their personalities and their dominance on the American landscape—that the new relationship bore their images. The magnitude of Roosevelt's influence on the presidency is clear. So is that of Rogers's on humor. In 1926 *Time* magazine put a comedian on its cover for the first time.

Rogers's image was accompanied by the single word that defined him for the country: "Funny."[75]

His sudden death in Alaska ensured that Will Rogers's softly cutting, always compassionate style of presidential humor was never tested beyond the requirements of his day. He was not compelled to respond to a second, more cataclysmic world war, systematic wholesale human extermination, or presidential power that tried in vain to keep pace with the world's capacity to blow itself up. Similarly, Roosevelt's tolerance for ridicule was never seriously tried by more audacious comics less sympathetic to his policies. FDR died in April 1945 with the nation on a wartime footing, ill suited to such joking, and with the performance of presidential humor left to memories of Will Rogers and to the president's own jaunty self-assurance.

4

New Frontiers

THE REMARKABLE connection between the most significant political comedian of the twentieth century, Will Rogers, and its most powerful president, Franklin Roosevelt, began to cement the relationship between the presidency and comedy performance in the minds of many Americans. Both men were agents and beneficiaries of the boom in electronic mass media, and both skillfully exploited their new proximity to the public through radio, film, and print to humanize the chief executive in diverse ways. Roosevelt's efforts were calculated to endear the president to the people, and humor figured prominently in his strategy. Rogers opened the presidency to ridicule but with such even-tempered goodwill that millions of Americans were willing to laugh along.

The duo of Rogers and Roosevelt, however, danced a distinctive waltz that, although formative in determining how political standup comedy would play out in future decades, turned out to be both ephemeral and unique. Each man led by modeling fresh ways for the performance of humor to interpret political power for a growing mass audience gripped by the fear and uncertainty of the depression. Each in turn was also willing to follow, either by agreeing to become the object of the joke, as FDR did, or by relinquishing center stage to Roosevelt, as did Rogers. For the most part, the public was eager to participate by buying a ticket or a radio, or by casting a vote for Roosevelt in the elections of 1932, 1936, 1940, and 1944, which he won by large margins. Growing numbers of people even played the comedian role themselves when they repeated the cleverest of Roosevelt's remarks or Rogers's quips to friends and co-workers. Americans were becoming not just enthusiastic consumers but tentative producers in the marketplace of political standup comedy that Rogers created and Roosevelt encouraged.

But with the coming of World War II and the deaths of both partners—
Rogers in 1935 and FDR ten years later—the dance ended, and without
widespread regret. War not only mobilized national energies and put an
end to the depression but also steeled public opinion against the commerce
of political humor in the interests of presenting a united front at home and
abroad. National institutions—whether religious, economic, or political—
were fortified anew as invincible weapons in what Roosevelt called the "great
arsenal of democracy" to fight fascism and Nazism. The Four Freedoms that
the president articulated in 1941—freedom from fear, freedom from want,
freedom of religion, even freedom of speech—did not include the freedom
to ridicule the commander in chief for fun and profit. By the 1940s Will
Rogers was no longer onstage and could not argue for what he had successfully suggested during the 1920s and 1930s: that the power of ridicule can not
only be a formidable weapon for ensuring politicians' accountability, but
also function as an exercise of the free democratic expression that Americans most idealize. Even more significantly, Rogers's national audience was
no longer prepared—given the new climate of international crisis—to entertain the proposition, so widely held in the 1930s, that power in a democracy
is always subject to the scrutiny of humor. Instead, Americans now insisted
that the opposite was true: humor must yield to power. Consequently, in the
absence of both an efficacious supply and any widespread demand during
the war, the bottom dropped out of the market for taking jabs at America's
political leadership, especially the president. Rogers and Roosevelt had
been able to exploit commercial media and performance outlets to purvey
political humor precisely because all the components of the performance
transaction—the media, the audience, political comedy, the presidency, and
the tumultuous backdrop of the irrationally exuberant 1920s followed by the
Great Depression of the 1930s—were transforming and undergoing redefinition simultaneously. By the time the United States entered World War II in
December 1941, this transformative moment had passed. War galvanized the
nation, and the country resolved to enlist all means at its disposal, including the media, entertainment, and the popular humor industries—whose
reach and influence were by now well established—to meet the clear threat.
Political comedy still shared one similarity with democracy in the collective
mind of wartime America: there could be no laughter without consent from
the governed, which in this case was the ticket-buying and radio-listening
public. For the time being, America's citizen consumers were in no mood to
buy whatever political standup comedy might be selling.[1]

Times had changed. On the comparatively rare occasions when humor
and the presidency did meet in popular culture during the war years, it was
often to emphasize the widening gap between the dispensable triviality that

many Americans—including many comics themselves—began to associate with comedy and the weighty concerns facing the leader of the United States. In 1940 Gracie Allen, the enormously popular and scatterbrained half of the vaudeville and radio duo Burns and Allen, followed the precedent set by Rogers and launched her own bid for the presidency. As her husband and partner, George Burns, later recalled: "Gracie and I were spending a quiet evening at home . . . [when she] suddenly remarked, 'I'm tired of knitting this sweater. I think I'll run for president this year.'" Running on the plat-form of the "Surprise Party" (so named because her mother was a Democrat, her father was a Republican, and she was a surprise), Allen appeared on several radio shows and toured the country to explain her stand on the issues of the day. Asked about the Neutrality Bill then before Congress, she was firm—"If we owe [the bill], let's pay it"—and when questioned whether, as president, she would recognize Russia, she replied: "I don't know. I meet so many people." Although several of her jokes brought the office down to size with observations that Rogers, Mark Twain, and Charles Browne might have appreciated ("the president of today is merely the postage stamp of tomor-row"), her whimsical candidacy underscored, even flaunted, her ignorance of the concerns facing the country while much of the rest of the world was already at war. When the public heard her battle cry, "Down with common sense, vote for Gracie," it was clearly understood that such frivolity was com-pletely divorced from legitimate political discourse and was meant merely to delight, never to challenge. Although happy crowds turned out wherever the much-loved Allen appeared, and while she reportedly earned several write-in votes in the popular count that November, no one seriously sug-gested that the flighty comic be nominated, as some had with Rogers only eight years before. The tradition of standup comedy performance was well established by the war years, thanks to the ubiquity of vaudeville and radio in general and Will Rogers's influence in particular, and it played its part well—as the popular antics of Burns and Allen, Bob Hope, Jack Benny, Bud Abbott and Lou Costello, and others attested—but the comedians largely eschewed political concerns and were relegated to the supporting cast, part of the chorus of patriotism that echoed official government policy.[2]

• • •

The war footing that effectively exiled the show business of humor from the serious business of presidential politics not only continued after World War II but actually intensified with the almost immediate onset of the cold war. The United States—and especially the enormously powerful presidency—hastily recast itself as the de facto leader of the Free World against com-munism. Most Americans agreed that the distinction between peace and war was again dangerously thin; it was certainly no laughing matter. "Containment" became the watchword of a jittery nation, including not just the containment of communist expansion around the world but even containment of what many Americans considered the dangerous, radical spread of racial integration propagated by Rosa Parks, Martin Luther King Jr., and others during the 1950s. The intense probing of the House Committee on Un-American Activities (HUAC) into communist influence in the United States and the demagogic and deadly serious performances of another showman—Senator Joseph McCarthy of Wisconsin—deepened the atmosphere of antisubversive hysteria. Americans grew increasingly suspicious of any discordant sound in such sober times, especially the pernicious treachery of laughter, and the country became more willing to silence political humor lest it turn out to be the chuckling vanguard of a "fifth column" seeking to attack the nation from within. If for no other reason in the immediate postwar era, Will Rogers was still remembered for having been able to imbue simple jokes with complex power. The understanding remained that such power was inherently dangerous.[3]

Consequently, for nearly two decades—from 1935 to the early 1950s—no mainstream comic performer took up the tradition of presidential humor that Rogers had initiated. There were numerous iconoclasts joking in the wilderness, but it was print that produced the period's most potent political satirists. Editorial cartoonists Bill Mauldin and Herbert Block (known as Herblock to the millions of Americans who saw his syndicated cartoons in newspapers across the country) furthered Thomas Nast's legacy of attacking social inequities and incompetent or duplicitous politicians. Herblock, for example, drew both admiration and intense criticism for depicting President Dwight D. Eisenhower as a smiling blank-eyed clown who failed to address the urgency of civil rights or the abuses of "McCarthyism," a term Herblock created. Followers of the comic strip "Pogo" by Walt Kelly were treated to more veiled but no less potent jabs at McCarthy and what many considered the red-baiting excesses of Vice President Richard Nixon, while *Mad* magazine, from its debut in 1952, hilariously lampooned icons of cultural authority such as Superman (redubbed "Superduperman"), Elvis Presley ("Elvis Pelvis"), and television's marionette kiddy star Howdy Doody ("Howdy Dooit"). In December 1956, weeks after Eisenhower had already been reelected, the magazine's everyidiot front man, Alfred E. Neuman, appeared on the cover of *Mad* to launch a write-in campaign for president using his trademark slogan, "What—Me Worry?"[4]

On the air, radio comics attracted passionate followings to their biting ridicule of all manner of sacred cows, although their work emphasized social satire more than pokes at the political elite. Fred Allen and Henry Morgan were among the most popular. After getting his start in vaudeville, Allen reinvented himself for radio and produced his own weekly program on NBC from 1932 to 1949. An audience favorite, he was, like Will Rogers, formative in taking the American mass audience from the multisensory vaudeville theater to the exclusively aural experience of radio. He did more than Rogers, in fact, to carry humor beyond the microphone and studio audience into the imaginations of listeners at home. He combined scathing satire of the media, the wealthy, and other authorities with what historian Alan Havig calls a pioneering "verbal slapstick" of sound effects, wordplay, sketches, and memorable dialects to produce a richly textured radio comedy that engaged audiences in vivid performance through sound images. His programs also included a regular segment spoofing the news of the week, a feature that not only resembled Rogers's topical humor but also foreshadowed later parodies of the news, including those on *Saturday Night Live* and *The Daily Show*. Allen rarely referred to Roosevelt's administration and mentioned that of Harry S. Truman only slightly more often, but his acidic treatment of political humbug—most hilariously depicted through the verbal antics of the drawling southern blowhard character Senator Beauregard Claghorn—attuned American ears to postwar satire until ill health and battles with network censors effectively ended Allen's career. Henry Morgan, Allen's friend and a frequent guest on his shows, similarly taunted media censorship as well as racism and McCarthyism on his show, *Here's Morgan*, until he was blacklisted in the early 1950s. His and Allen's satire helped pave the way for later performers who took on the White House more directly, but their continual confrontations with their networks and sponsors made them the exceptions that proved the stifling rule: while these satirists valiantly continued to wage what Mark Twain had called the "assault of laughter" in print and on radio, Americans were generally unwilling to side openly with them in their attacks, and the humorists' jabs were commonly met with wary indifference, deep suspicion, or outright hostility. Well into the 1950s American audiences—or more accurately the watchdogs who governed their access to the nation's airwaves—were in no mood for the funny business of presidential ridicule. Groucho Marx lamented that "if Will Rogers were to come back today, he couldn't make a living. They'd throw him in the clink for being subversive."[5]

Instead of howling away at the absurdity of a cold war culture that considered squelching free expression the best way of protecting it, most Americans preferred to laugh at comedy that reinforced middle-class affluence and stability, or at least the illusion of it. Physical humor, gags, one-liners, or television's most influential contribution to 1950s humor—the situation comedy—could giddily anesthetize a nation fearful of postwar uncertainty or intoxicate it in its celebration of booming prosperity. Pointing to apolitical punch lines and pratfalls as testament, Americans readily congratulated themselves on their sense of humor in contrast with "humorless communists," but such levity clearly had its limits. Americans were generally unprepared to laugh in ways that might provoke suspicion or poke fun at the institutions they considered the bulwarks of their freedom. These institutions—including corporations, organized religion, the military, and government—became increasingly sacrosanct. The observance of their workings assumed unprecedented reverence in mass culture; far from being open to playful criticism, they commanded ritualized tribute designed to reinforce a status quo in which laughter played no critical part. The guardians of these institutions—corporate executives, pastors, military commanders, and especially the president—exuded a sober authority that could afford to be seen as warmly beneficent, perhaps, but never funny.[6]

With the advent of television, this atmosphere ironically heralded mainstream comedy's "Golden Age." Standup comedy in particular had, owing to Rogers and vaudeville's popularity, proven itself to be a highly profitable commodity, but as Fred Allen and Henry Morgan discovered, its profitability was symbiotic with that of the government-licensed media that carried it and the corporate interests that sponsored it. Radio had made stars of comedians, but by the early 1950s television was making *superstars* of Bob Hope, Jack Benny, Sid Caesar, Jackie Gleason, Red Skelton, Milton Berle, and Lucille Ball. Yet their careers, which were rooted mostly in the commercial show business traditions of vaudeville, radio, and Hollywood, depended on maintaining a comfortable (and salable) distance from political content. Each comedian was closely associated with one or more sponsors (Pepsodent was a longtime sponsor of Hope; Berle was on television thanks to Texaco) whose expectation was that listeners would consume their mouthwash, gasoline, cigarettes, or coffee with the same easy good cheer with which they consumed the jokes. The comedy, then, like these other commodities, could contain neither objectionable ingredients nor bitter political aftertaste. Furthermore, several of the most popular comic celebrities, including Benny, Berle, and funnyman Phil Silvers, were Jewish Americans, whose full admission into the national mainstream was still tenuous. Anti-Semitism had, after all, been pervasive during the 1930s and 1940s in places far removed from Nazi Germany, including the United States. Branding American products on television required an "all-American" comedy that retreated to the safety of old vaudeville forms and, like much of society during wartime and the early cold war era, trumpeted openness but in reality had little tolerance for provocative content or ethnic or political difference. Gracie Allen reiterated such "Americanism" and celebrated the divide between popular and political culture with her mock presidential campaign in 1940. In 1952, when Lucille Ball was summoned before HUAC for having registered as a communist in the election of 1936, she explained that she had done so only at the insistence of her ailing grandfather, an eccentric union organizer, and that she had not even voted in that election. Furthermore, she assured the committee, "I have never been too civic-minded and certainly never political-minded in my life." Political ignorance, then, far from being a liability to the postwar comedian, could be a badge of honor, or at least a means of professional survival. It is significant that Ball, who by 1952 was the most popular comedian on television, was quickly cleared of any suspicion. Comedy was indeed acknowledged as wielding enormous influence in consumer culture. Ball and her hit TV show *I Love Lucy* served important functions in the cold war calculus, but it was understood during the 1950s that the comic's role—especially that of a female comic—was as a merry booster of national consensus, not a critic.[7]

Bob Hope became the best-known inheritor of Will Rogers's legacy during and immediately after World War II, thanks to his long career in vaudeville, radio, film, and television in addition to his patriotic tours to entertain troops for the United Services Organization (USO). Hope freely kidded presidents, although he did so in tacit step with them and always from safely within the postwar economic and political establishment. An immigrant from England who became a naturalized citizen in 1920, Hope had a deep love for his new country which quickly became reverence for its institutions of power, especially capitalism, the military, and the presidency, and he used his humor to evangelize for them. Presidents from FDR to Bill Clinton were just as eager to associate themselves with Hope's popularity as those from Teddy Roosevelt to Franklin Roosevelt had been to align themselves with Rogers, but the presidents who curried Hope's favor did so without fear of serious challenge to their authority or their policies. He was even more indebted to the establishment than Jack Benny, Gracie Allen, or Lucille Ball. In fact it was FDR who understood the psychological and propaganda value of bringing humor to the front lines and first suggested that Hope entertain troops overseas. ("He asked me because he said I was popular, talented and expendable," Hope quipped.) The costs of his USO tours were usually paid jointly by the U.S. Defense Department and his sponsors, who expected to sell not only plenty of product but pro-government goodwill as well. He flew overseas on military aircraft, and his material was heavily scripted by an army of writers who continually stockpiled his inventory of 88,000 jokes and often wrote the copy for his sponsors' advertisements. Like Rogers's, Hope's newspaper column—"It Says Here"—appeared across the country, although it too was an industrialized commodity. Unlike Rogers's weekly articles and "daily telegrams," which Rogers composed alone, Hope's column was crafted by his writers, who often chose the topic in addition to writing all the copy before submitting a draft for Hope's approval. As for his presidential jokes, they obliquely continued the tradition of revealing the president's humanity, but they tended to be ephemeral one-liners, bits of light comic staccato that rarely probed into policy or evolved into satiric commentary. Rather they typically took a feathery swing at current events or some innocuous aspect of the president's leisure activities, such as his golf game. (Hope suggested that Dwight Eisenhower decided to give up golf for painting because the latter involved fewer strokes.) While his political allegiances tilted clearly to the right, he did not hesitate to needle whoever was in the White House, but never with anything but the most sanitized and commercialized material. Hope's audience, after all, included millions of American servicemen and women—veterans as well as people on active duty—and he took great care not to jeopardize esprit de corps by ridiculing the commander in chief. As cultural scholar Stephen Wagg has pointed out, he was always careful to commodify patriotism just as carefully as he did comedy. Consequently, Bob Hope's barbs of straw made him a favorite of presidents, including Gerald Ford, who considered his humor "a perfect example of how to poke fun and not cross over that line into ridicule." He was the consummate comedian to the majority of Americans of Ford's generation, those who had just won a righteous war and for whom the institutions of the nation were rock-hard monuments to their sacrifice and were to be celebrated with utmost deference. Hope kept the presidency amiably connected to the performance of humor in American culture, even if his soft, predictable punch lines seemed less in sync with unpredictable times.[8]

Just as the performance of political humor reached its nadir as the performance of comedy overall boomed, perceptions of the presidency also underwent a paradoxical change. Hope's buoyant joking aside, Americans' personal familiarity with the president waned even as cold war contingencies endowed the office with an almost mystical prominence. The result was a reestablishment of the traditional presidential distance that Rogers had so effectively shortened and that Roosevelt—even as he did the most to define the new imperial stature of the office during the depression and war—had at least mitigated through his celebrity, his jovial persona, and the sense of intimacy he achieved on the radio through his fireside chats. Yet even though Americans had little understanding of the new complexities of the office and felt more personally detached from the man who held it, the continuing advances in media technologies and the volatile state of international affairs made the White House the clear focus of the nation's political gaze from FDR forward. Once Harry Truman was catapulted into the presidency by Roosevelt's sudden death in April 1945, his image and daily routine were captured and disseminated by mass media that were growing proportionally with postwar economic expansion, the booming U.S. population, and the powers of the executive branch. By 1950, members of the White House press corps, who only five years before had still been few enough to crowd around Roosevelt's desk like excited first-nighters around a star's dressing room door, were so numerous that news conferences had to be moved to the auditorium at the nearby State Department building, with its fixed seats, stage, and proscenium arch. This of course heightened the spectacle of the performance. So did television, which demanded attention even if it did not command immediate respect from either the president or the traditional press. Fewer than one-half of 1 percent of American homes had a television set in 1948, but one-third of American households did by 1952, and that figure surged to 90 percent by the end of the decade. Truman acknowledged the growing dominance of the electronic media by delivering a speech on radio or television nearly once a month on average and relocating the news conferences, although he stopped short of permitting those to be filmed or broadcast. Nevertheless, Americans long accustomed to hearing the presidential voice were beginning to see as well as hear the chief executive more often, whether on television screens behind the plate glass window of the local department store or on the set in their own homes.[9]

For his part, Truman appreciated humor but had neither the desire nor the motivation to match Roosevelt's ebullient rapport with journalists or the public. He tended to avoid the spotlight, preferring the no-nonsense style that was more in tune with his temperament and truer to the workaday midwestern political culture that had produced him. His weekly news conferences were well received and were considered more substantive—if less flamboyant—than Roosevelt's, especially at the start of his administration. He performed well and earned a warm ovation at the end of his first meeting with journalists, many of whom were grateful for the relief from what one observer called FDR's "charm shows," although Truman said afterward he felt as though he had lived five lifetimes in five days. His personal integrity, diligence, ready smile, and dapper dress were widely admired, and his quick, dry sense of humor was appreciated by those who knew him. (Upon receiving an invitation to his own inauguration in 1949, he responded dryly, "Weather permitting, I hope to be present.") Often, however, his humor reflected the ribaldry of a man's man who loved a joke shared with pals in back rooms, far from the spotlight of political decorum. Such stories—frequently off-color and peppered with profanity fueled by his volatile temper—were inappropriate for public consumption. He once imagined that, had he not been president, he "probably would have ended up a piano player in a bawdy house."

Harry Truman could both give and take a joke, but he used humor more as a private resource than a public tool, a choice that for many increased his political liabilities, especially in contrast with Franklin Roosevelt.[10]

FDR's magnetic personal style made his act almost impossible to follow. Truman suffered in the depths of what historian William Leuchtenburg has called Roosevelt's long and powerful shadow, and it extended to both Truman's capacity for laughter and others' ridicule of the new president. Roosevelt had established humor as a requisite credential for the presidency to the point where it came to be seen not just as a conduit for connecting the American people to their government but an expression of the president's overall leadership skill and authority. To the extent that he failed to harness humor as effectively as FDR, Truman was found lacking as president by his political opponents and even by critics within his own Democratic Party. Soon after Truman took office, David Lilienthal, chairman of the Tennessee Valley Authority, dismissively characterized his jokes as those of the Midwest with "its barbershops and filling stations where men pass the time of day, but can you imagine [FDR] saying [such things]?" He went on to critique Truman's response to humor just as unfavorably. Whereas FDR had laughed, he said, "Truman grins broadly. . . . [His laugh] is hardly a laugh at all—a chuckle, or more the sound effect of a grin." For a while it seemed that everyone was a comedian as the presidential jokes began to proliferate, but now the laughter was not *with* the president as had been so common under Roosevelt but *at* the new chief executive. "I'm just mild about Harry," went one popular barb. Another claimed that the new president often woke up with stiff joints from trying to put his foot in his mouth. "I wonder what Truman would do if he were alive," reflected one joker from Texas, while the wife of Senator Robert Taft of Ohio apparently originated the classic zinger, "To err is Truman."[11]

To many, Franklin Roosevelt, Will Rogers, and their times seemed long gone by the early 1950s; yet for all the chilling influences and disparate personalities, comedians and presidents could not ultimately avoid being direct if mostly unwitting inheritors of the two men's larger and more transcendent legacies. Regardless of the current national mood, Rogers and Roosevelt had established the precedent of the American people laughing loud, long, and in community with others at the expense of their president, both with and occasionally at him. What is more, Americans had shown they were willing to pay for the privilege. Historian Joseph Boskin has observed that humor risks losing its communal purpose and cultural relevance unless it adapts to changing circumstances. Given the historical prominence of political humor performance in American life and the power and profit that

Rogers and Roosevelt had brought to it during the previous generation, its return to popular culture was predictable, if in a necessarily different form. As the 1950s progressed, a new generation of enterprising—and politically and culturally rebellious—comedians emerged and began to reshape political comedy performance in light of unsettling events and issues, ranging from the rise of an affluent but uneasy postwar middle class to the aggressive campaign against communism and the potential for nuclear Armageddon after the Soviet Union acquired the atomic bomb in 1949. As historian Stephen Kercher has written, postwar satirists waged humor not to escape from reality but to expose what they perceived as the creeping *unrealities* of American political and cultural life, among them hypocrisy, banality, empty acquisitiveness, and social injustice. They would also do battle with what social critic Malcolm Muggeridge and others saw as the archenemy of humor: fear, whether it be of communism, the indiscriminate witch-hunts in pursuit of it, or the host of social changes affecting postwar American life. "Fear requires conformity," Muggeridge wrote. "It draws people into a herd, whereas laughter separates them as individuals." These new comics—Mort Sahl, Bob Newhart, and Vaughn Meader among others—reestablished the comedian as an everyman-hero in ways that Seba Smith, Charles Browne, Samuel Clemens, and Will Rogers had pioneered, but using strategies calibrated to new imperatives and utilizing new media. They sought to capitalize on the belief that a modern audience—fearful victims more than self-assured victors in the cold war world order—would respond favorably if given the chance to reassert their power as individual sovereign citizens through laughter, even (or especially) if it came at the expense of those who wielded power from the distance of high office. And audiences began to respond. At a time when, according to sociologist C. Wright Mills, middle-class workers no longer owned any significant aspect of business enterprise but were controlled by massive, impersonal corporate interests, many came to applaud these new comedians as cultural entrepreneurs valiantly crafting humor and cracking wise at the business and political elite. As it turned out, the panicked rumors of the demise of political standup comedy proved to be (to borrow Mark Twain's description of the rumors of his own death) greatly exaggerated. In fact it was approaching its zenith, as everyday Americans, comedians, and presidents gazed at political humor across the threshold of a new set of cultural possibilities.[12]

•   •   •

As the 1950s unfolded, a number of factors combined to bring about a revival of such humor. Television's siren song of consumption and pervasive cold war fears presaged a growing discontent that threatened the status quo and set a gradually increasing percentage of the mass public laughing at the presidency all over again, but in active ways that, while evocative of earlier decades, were wholly original. The interdependent factors of the booming postwar economy, the meteoric rise of television, and the accompanying refinements in mass—then segmented niche—marketing made producers and consumers increasingly selective. Advertisers employed intricate strategies to manipulate purchasing decisions, saturate markets, and maximize profits. Given the vast array of goods before them, Americans were becoming discriminating, even skeptical consumers, and they readily claimed the right to question, accept, reject, and even ridicule anything they were asked to buy. Although its scale was unprecedented, this postwar transaction between sellers and buyers bore a strong resemblance to that between producers and consumers during the 1920s as well as to the improvisational interactions between blackface minstrels and the rowdy audiences projecting their sovereignty as citizens during the first half of the nineteenth century. In the bipolar cold war conflict between democratic capitalism and authoritarian communism, however, the freedom to buy was not simply an ancillary metaphor for citizenship; it came to define citizenship itself. For many, especially in the burgeoning white middle class, whose power to produce had been usurped by the corporation, consumption became the dominant expression of democratic liberty, to the extent that Vice President Nixon boasted to Soviet leader Nikita Khrushchev in their famous 1959 "kitchen debate" at a technology exhibit in Moscow that Americans were more free than their Soviet counterparts because they could purchase more time-saving appliances. The newly constructed suburban shopping center was displacing the traditional town square as the hub of the community across the national landscape. Sovereign citizens began to express themselves first and foremost as sovereign consumers.[13]

By the early 1950s television was undisputedly the primary showcase for this supermarket of patriotic consumption, and in 1952 the presidency was added to its product line. In that year's presidential campaign both Democrats and Republicans initially utilized the new medium with knee-jerk predictability, airing fifteen- or thirty-minute speeches by the candidates that droned on tediously and had a hard time finding viewers. The Republicans, desperate to regain the White House after twenty years of exile under Franklin Roosevelt and Harry Truman, decided to engage advertising firms, including New York's Ted Bates and Company, to help promote its nominee, Dwight Eisenhower. Bates's marketing genius Rosser Reeves, whose direct, no-nonsense ads inspired Americans to buy record quantities of headache tablets, deodorants, and chocolate candies ("M&M's melt in your mouth, not in your hand"), invented the twenty-second campaign "spot," a tightly produced commercial designed to quickly introduce a favorable first impression in the voter's mind. At first Eisenhower eschewed appearing on television, believing it was undignified; nevertheless he agreed to make the ads. One disgusted observer commented to Reeves, "It was selling the president like toothpaste." But it worked. To increase their impact, he scheduled the spots to run adjacent to popular programs, and it turned out that Americans "liked Ike" on TV as everywhere else. The ads subtly shortened once again the distance between the citizenry and the imperial presidency, but not in a substantive and personal way as during FDR's fireside chats. Rather it seemed that the chief executive was taking on the showman's role as whimsically prophesied by Artemus Ward a century before. Increasingly the presidency could be compared with any other product capable of being reduced to a twenty-second sound bite. Americans who were becoming adept at judging the value of products by watching popular new game shows such as *The Price Is Right* and *Let's Make a Deal* could now choose to "buy" the president or not, or perhaps chortle about the shortcomings of his appearance or policies. Most "bought" Eisenhower happily and without question, and he left office eight years later as one of the most popular presidents in history, but that office was increasingly delimited by the twelve-inch, black-and-white, two-dimensional screen. Television brought the president into the home on a regular basis for the first time, but this glass façade of familiarity, no matter how adulatory, eventually helped to breed a kind of merry—then eventually more satiric—contempt.[14]

As the decade waned, pleasing images on television of game shows, sitcoms, and a smiling president belied increasing concerns at home and abroad. The outcome of the battle against communism was very much in doubt. It seemed that the military and political stalemate that followed the suspension of the Korean War in 1953 would be perpetual. The launch of the first manmade satellites by the Soviet Union, beginning with *Sputnik* 1 in 1957, trumpeted the communists' early dominion in space. Meanwhile, intermittent recessions caused unemployment to rise and both the gross national product and fiscal confidence to falter. For all the creature comforts and the smiling mass-consumer rhetoric of middle-class success, an undercurrent of anxiety and restlessness began to quicken. What is more, these menacing signals from overseas and domestic sources—broadcast over television and discussed throughout the public sphere—seemed inconsistent with the consistently placid mood at the White House. The eminently popular Eisenhower, the beloved general, and Vice President Nixon, the sober and self-assured Republican disciple, began to appear less venerable and more vulnerable as their second term wore on. Economist John Kenneth

Galbraith characterized their leadership as "the bland leading the bland," and it seemed to many that the energetic forward progress of the country was stalling. In the 1958 congressional elections American voters gave Democrats a margin of nearly two-to-one in both the House and Senate. For the first time in years political wags saw something funny going on, and Americans were increasingly willing but woefully ill equipped to laugh at it.[15]

A growing number of wits sought to combat this deficiency. With the creeping disillusionment aimed at the White House and the fall of Joseph McCarthy in 1954, comic innovators began to test more openly the limits of political satire during the mid- to late 1950s. Tom Lehrer was a graduate student studying mathematics at Harvard University when he gave in to pressure from fans to record the satiric songs he was writing and performing at local coffeehouses. For fifteen dollars in recording time in a do-it-yourself studio and only a few hundred dollars more in production costs, he produced his own record album in 1953; *Songs by Tom Lehrer* went on to sell 350,000 copies to listeners eager to laugh at what they considered the absurd incongruities of cold war life. The frolicsome tone of his sunny piano ditties cloaked a dark and deeply cutting irony that brilliantly captured these incongruities, among them the contrast between the mythic frontier ideals touted by American culture and policies employed by the federal government in a nuclear age that threatened to blow those ideals—and the country—to smithereens. One song, "The Wild West Is Where I Want to Be," blithely juxtaposed the radioactive fallout of incessant nuclear testing in the Nevada desert with imagery of the pristine western landscape, all set to an easygoing get-along tune:

> 'Mid the sagebrush and the cactus
> I'll watch the fellas practice
> Droppin' bombs through the clean desert breeze. (Yahoo!)
> I'll have on my sombrero, and of course I'll wear a pair o'
> Levis over my lead BVDs.

Lehrer quickly developed a cult following that blossomed into more widespread appeal over the next ten years. His work married music to postwar satire in a style that paved the way for the tuneful political ridicule of comedian Mark Russell, standup folksingers the Smothers Brothers, and the Washington, D.C. troupe the Capitol Steps. Lehrer also modeled the relative ease with which Americans could and would become comedians.[16]

Stan Freberg, who was inspired by the satiric muses Fred Allen and Henry Morgan, achieved an even wider influence. Freberg was already a respected voice actor and writer when CBS Radio put him on the air as a summer replacement for *The Jack Benny Show* in 1957. *The Stan Freberg*

Show built on Allen's verbal slapstick with clever writing, original songs with elaborate orchestrations, a top-notch cast, and the best sound effects men in the business. The thirty-minute program brought to the air on Sunday evenings parody that was both trenchant and polished as it skewered everything from beauty pageants to popular music to politics. In an extended sketch spoofing the decadence of Las Vegas and comparing it to the biblical sin cities of Sodom and Gomorrah, Freberg mated the selling of the presidency to Vegas's gaudy brand of show business excess. In one scene, managers of the Rancho Gomorra casino arrange for the 1960 presidential inauguration to be booked into the ballroom for a two-week run, lavishly repackaged as half inauguration, half variety show. The "Inaugurieties of 1960" promised a chorus line of scantily clad showgirls behind the president swearing the oath right along with him but with their left hands solemnly placed on Nevada telephone books. Such daring antics often caused Freberg and his cast to run afoul of the CBS censors; but though the show never found a major sponsor and lasted only fifteen weeks, Freberg's satire, along with Lehrer's, was finding an audience and meeting a need.[17]

In 1958 the *New York Times* published an article, "The State of the Nation's Humor," which asked a panel of experts to ponder "the question of whether America's sense of comedy is being straitjacketed by conformity." Steve Allen, an inventive young comic who four years before had inaugurated NBC's new late-night television experiment called *Tonight!* (later *The Tonight Show*), applauded Americans' love of laughter but observed in the article that "in recent years we seem to have shown an increasing reluctance to laugh at ourselves." Author and cartoonist James Thurber concurred and lamented the consensus from Europe:

> The nation that complacently and fearfully allows its artists and writers to become suspected rather than respected is no longer regarded as a nation possessed with humor in depth. It is generally felt that a jumpy America—"afflicted with night terrors," as one London critic put it— has lost its right to leadership in the field of political satire.

Thurber offered his prescription for the years ahead. It was one that both rejected political ignorance as a comedic strategy and urged his fellow citizens actively to resume Mark Twain's "assault of laughter": "Political comedy must be grounded in serious knowledge of our nation and of the world. Perhaps Mort Sahl is the answer, or one of the answers. I have not yet heard him or his records. From what I have heard about him, he will not be intimidated."[18]

• • •

By 1958 millions of Americans *had* heard Mort Sahl. Five years before, Sahl had begun to establish himself as the point man for a teeming new generation of comics, all of them instrumental in creating the boom in standup comedy overall, but among whom Sahl was already distinguishing himself as a wisecracking voice in the wilderness of political comedy. Like his contemporaries Lenny Bruce, Jonathan Winters, Bob Newhart, and others, Sahl began his career modestly in the tiny coffeehouses and nightclubs of Chicago, New York, and California that served as the enclaves of political standup comedy's guerrilla underground. He got his first job in December 1953—as the McCarthy hysteria was still reverberating—when the owner of San Francisco's tiny but trendy club the hungry i hired him on the basis of a joke about the Wisconsin senator: Sahl had recommended that the popular Eisenhower military jacket, with its many zippered pockets, be updated. The new McCarthy model should have one extra zipper . . . to go across the mouth. "Joe McCarthy doesn't question what you say," he quipped, "so much as he questions your right to say it." As for HUAC's abuses, he remarked, "Every time the Russians throw an American in jail, the HUAC retaliates—by throwing an American in jail."[19]

News that Sahl had dared give voice to what one journalist called "such audacity at such a time" quickly brought him to the attention of university students, then a regional audience, and then a growing national following. Scarcely a year later Sahl, who had been earning approximately fifty dollars a year as a standup comedian, was making nearly a thousand dollars a week. By the time James Thurber mentioned him in the 1958 *New York Times* article, Sahl was selling out clubs and hotel ballrooms nationwide and appearing as a guest performer regularly on radio and television. That same year he headlined a Broadway revue titled *The Next President*, which, while it closed after only two weeks, earned Sahl more fans and publicity. In its review *Time* magazine praised him for offering satire-starved America a "nice fresh breath of carbon monoxide." In an earlier, seemingly less complicated time, Will Rogers would offer a conciliatory "I hope I have not given offense." Two decades later Mort Sahl, whom *Time* described as "Will Rogers with fangs," routinely closed his act with what became a trademark goad: "Are there any groups I *haven't* offended?"[20]

Praise for Sahl was far from unanimous. To be sure, he tapped into the strong antiauthoritarian impulse harbored by many—especially young people—discontented by cold war conformity and the illusory normality of the Eisenhower era, and he appealed to those who generally sought a return to the political and cultural New Deal liberalism of the Roosevelt and Truman administrations. Although Sahl referred to these fans as "the oppressed majority," his humor was considered radically out of tune by many.

Antipathy to him and his comedic attacks on convention was often strong, and he was occasionally heckled by audience members who threw pennies at him and called him a "Jewish, Communist, nigger-lover." Older and more conservative audiences stayed away from him and other "sick" comedians, so called for their brash irreverence and unflinching willingness to tread on hallowed ground. Some considered *The Next President* too impertinent and too clever by half. Television and film executives, while initially intrigued by Sahl's wit and frenetic energy and attracted by his good looks, put him under contract hoping to translate his novel popularity into commercial profitability, but they ultimately shied away from making long-term commitments. The fear of sponsor backlash or controversy that might jeopardize ratings and profits proved too great.[21]

In addition to Sahl, impetus for a new definition of political comedy came from other culturally daring sources. In 1955 two University of Chicago students named Paul Sills and David Shepherd—whom comedy writer Tony Hendra has called the Romulus and Remus of improvisational humor—founded a performance group called the Compass. Their ambitious intent was to reinvent a populist "people's theater" by experimenting with improvisational games that used a small number of performers, everyday situations, and virtually no sets or props to create dynamic and often hilariously funny scenes. Playing with only the simplest skeleton of a script, the actors organically fleshed out the plot and dialogue onstage, while later scenes sprang creatively from the suggestions from the audience. In producing performances that forced all participants to cope spontaneously with conventional situations, such as buying a used car, trying to survive as a door-to-door salesman, or going on a first date, players and audiences alike discovered that the dynamics inherent in such situations almost always led away from socially constrained expectations and toward more realistic and often highly satiric outcomes. One such scene, titled "Teenagers," involved two young people on a date in the backseat of a car trying to reconcile conventional 1950s morality with the timeless urges of adolescent sexuality. As expected, the young people find their conversation becoming progressively heated until the girl says, "If we went any further, I know you wouldn't respect me," to which the boy blurts: "Oh, I'd respect you like *crazy*! You have no idea how much I'd respect you!"[22]

The sketch, which was one of the most popular in the Compass repertoire, starred Mike Nichols and Elaine May, who, along with fellow Compass alumnus Shelley Berman, went on to become popular comedians in the late 1950s after leaving the troupe. Other Compass theaters began to appear in the Northeast and Midwest. Over time, Compass scenarios challenged other rituals and other subjects, including some drawn from politics and the military. By 1960 many creative components of the Compass experiments, and several of its most popular performers, had coalesced into new improvisational groups, such as the Premise, which debuted in New York's Greenwich Village and enjoyed both popular and critical acclaim, and a troupe in Chicago called the Second City, which in turn became the seedbed from which comedy writer Lorne Michaels would pluck talents such as Dan Aykroyd, Gilda Radner, and John Belushi to create *Saturday Night Live* in 1975. Though set against a backdrop of new national and global challenges, and sporting a stylized sense of irony that would have seemed alien to their predecessors, the ensemble performances of the Compass Players, Second City, and the Premise were not far removed from those of Artemus Ward or Will Rogers, who also served as comic facilitators between their audiences and new forms of political expression and did the hard work of cultural formation in the guise of playful laughter. But these new performers and their audiences went further, constructing improvised networks of community and solidarity—albeit initially on a small scale—that countered the privatizing, alienating tendencies caused by television and so much of the cold war culture of containment.

The swelling chorus of laughter at American culture and politics given voice by Tom Lehrer, Stan Freberg, and the Compass Players and further refined and amplified by Mort Sahl proved contagious. In the transformative moment of the late 1950s Americans were not merely increasingly eager receptors of this more radical improvisational humor; they were producers of it. Inspired by the cumulative impact of the new comics, and utilizing that most stealthy means of mass communication, word of mouth, Americans began actively to join this cultural insurgency by creating and performing "sick" jokes that reflected both growing disillusionment with the forced reverence toward established authority and the observation that such authority seemed to be contributing to postwar fears rather than calming them. The most popular and contagious of these joke cycles—the "child joke" and the "elephant joke"—took aim at two of the most powerful sites of authority: the family and the nation's newfound superpower status. Under the cold war imperative of constructing a united front against communism, the traditional nuclear family was sanctified as a bulwark of ideological stability, yet in the competitive rush to middle-class affluence, the family was actually being buffeted by enormous changes. The hunt for promotion and status was constant, and the growing probability of both parents working, combined with the travails of raising large families during the prolific high tide of the baby boom, meant that maintaining a household bore little resemblance to the ideal portrayed on *Leave It to Beaver* and other television sitcoms. In response to the disconnect between the sugary domestic mythology of these tales and the bitter reality of parental absenteeism, rising alcoholism and divorce rates, and fears of juvenile delinquency, Americans — especially young Americans — exposed these contradictions with a barrage of jokes whose dark punch lines rubbed those contradictions raw. "Child jokes" began to multiply:

Mommy, where's Daddy?
Shut up, and keep digging.

Mommy, I want milk.
Shut up, and drink your beer.

Mommy, Mommy, why am I running around in circles?
Shut up, or I'll nail your other foot to the floor.

What's red and sits in a corner?
A baby chewing razor blades.[23]

The "elephant jokes" that appeared during the early 1960s were less explicit but no less insightful in their ridicule of American might and influence, which were becoming more super-sized by the day. As federal bureaucracy, consumerism, and what President Eisenhower himself called the overly expansive military-industrial complex all grew to gargantuan size, efforts to convince Americans of the beneficent and largely benign nature of these trends contradicted observations that the workings of national life were becoming less nimble and more cumbersome, even threatening. It was impossible not to notice such colossal forces in everyday life and increasingly difficult to negotiate around them, even though Americans did their best to do just that, with curious and absurd results. The elephant became the laughable symbol of this unwieldy and ultraconspicuous force, and the jokes started to proliferate from within the ranks of average citizens:

How can you tell if there's an elephant in the bathtub with you?
The water won't go down.

How do you keep an elephant from charging?
Take away his credit card.

How can you tell if there's an elephant in the refrigerator?
The door won't close.

What looks like an elephant, flies, and is dangerous?
A flying elephant with diarrhea.[24]

As the jokes and laughs (and elephants) began to fly, Americans found that through them they were able to aim a small measure of cultural rebellion at the mammoth forces that governed their lives. In dreaming up these silly but oddly routine encounters between the powerful elephant and the puny everyman, the little man and woman discovered that they too could harness—if not the elephant—at least the humorous moment to their own needs and attract an audience, if only one or two members at a time. From sick jokes about family and parents, and wisecracks about the oafish omnipresence of the state, it would be a relatively small step to take wholesale jabs at the president, who, after all, encapsulated postwar Americans' patriarchal images of both the domestic superparent and the international superpower.

•   •   •

Even as these diverse comedic elements converged during the later 1950s, gradually constituting a brand of political comedy performance that would become a staple of American humor just a few years later, it was still widely agreed that Mort Sahl was, as one journalist proclaimed in 1958, "our hottest comic." As a culture critic and something of a one-man Compass theater who riffed spontaneously off his audiences' reactions, Sahl appealed strongly to this growing segment of the postwar public that recognized the potential of humor for expressing dissatisfaction with the political status quo and society's intractable contradictions, including that between what author Susan Sontag called the two competing destinies of the age: the unremitting banality of seemingly limitless prosperity and consumption, and the inconceivable terror of nuclear destruction. Sahl joked that whenever he saw an unidentified aircraft approaching, he never knew whether it was going to unload a hydrogen bomb or spell out "Pepsi-Cola" in skywriting.[25]

Sahl's comedic style was new and provocative, but at the same time something about him was familiar. His manner was conversational and spontaneous, and he composed his own material, much as Will Rogers had decades before. Just as Rogers refined a specific and unique cowboy persona, Sahl rejected the stock uniform of the 1950s standup comedian—suit, white shirt, and tie—in favor of the sweater and slacks that more closely identified him with his audience. Just as Rogers had reinforced his connection with the American everyman by insisting that, like him, "all I know is just what I read in the papers," often Sahl's only prop during a performance was a rolled-up copy of one of the daily newspapers he read ravenously, and which he claimed offered the best script for comedy. Finally, Mort Sahl drew a crowd for the same reason Will Rogers had: he was funny, and he dared to laugh at—among other targets—the president of the United States.[26]

Sahl never seemed to realize that mocking the presidency was taboo in postwar America. It was part of his repertoire from the beginning, although Sahl's earliest routines jabbed only vaguely at administration policies. Not until Eisenhower's second term did Sahl find his best opportunities to take on the White House directly. In 1957, when Eisenhower hesitated to invoke federal authority in Little Rock, Arkansas, to enforce desegregation as unanimously mandated by the Supreme Court three years earlier in the case of *Brown v. Board of Education of Topeka*, a critic chastised the president by saying that if he were really a man, he would have personally taken the fearful black female students by the hand and walked them into Little Rock's Central High School, the focus of the crisis. Commenting simultaneously on Ike's hands-off approach to the problem and the president's famous passion for golf, Sahl quipped, "That's easy to say if you are not involved, but if you are [Eisenhower], you have a lot of problems of policy, like whether or not to use an overlapping grip."[27]

Sahl got enormous mileage from the Soviet Union's downing of a U-2 surveillance aircraft and the capture of its pilot, Captain Francis Gary Powers, in May 1960. In this part of his act, lasting several minutes, he lampooned the early official pronouncement of the plane's disappearance and Eisenhower's handling of the episode: "One of our aircraft [is] missing . . . and one of our presidents, in the opinion of many." He concluded the section by noting how the embarrassing episode was finally upstaged publicly by the successful return to port of the nuclear submarine *Triton* after its eighty-three-day around-the-world voyage. He cracked, "President Eisenhower gave [commanding officer] Captain Beach a medal for being one of the few officers whose whereabouts he knows."[28]

As some in the press took exception to Sahl's material, most network executives continued to fret, and several club managers vainly urged him to cease and desist, the public's ambivalent response to him reflected a nation increasingly divided in its relationship with the presidency. Deference, even reverence, toward the office was still the norm, but Sahl's popularity placed such traditional assumptions under growing strain and scrutiny. Many of his detractors assumed that his acerbic approach to comedy in general—and his mocking of the president in particular—was a temporary annoyance. Others feared that it was symptomatic of the nation's ethical deterioration and its heightened vulnerability to communism. Even Sahl's growing legion of fans did not know whether he was a passing fancy or a prophet, but they thoroughly enjoyed the moment nonetheless.[29]

Sahl's iconoclasm was not easy to define. As a comedic entrepreneur enamored with success and meteoric personal wealth, he adamantly rebuffed comparisons between him and Beat Generation celebrities such as Allen Ginsberg and Jack Kerouac, even though his ridicule often articulated anti-establishment protest in radical, wholly unpredictable ways reminiscent of the Beats. Yet like Rogers (comparison with whom Sahl also rejected), he employed a style of humor that, although more overtly intellectual than Rogers's, tapped into a common logic and cultural honesty that many could appreciate during an era that seemed increasingly confining. In the wake of World War II and the Korean War, many in Sahl's audience were, like him, veterans, college-educated thanks to the G.I. Bill, and looking to redefine themselves in a rapidly changing and confusing postwar order. Superiors, whether they were commanding officers, white-collar managers, ministers, professors, or presidents, tended to restrict this search for personal identity to an absurdly narrow range of possibilities, often citing the exigencies of the cold war. Sahl's performances seemed to celebrate, however subconsciously, theorist Henri Bergson's observation that laughter erupts whenever a society emphasizes convention, ceremony, or ritual for its own sake or to the exclusion of the more natural aspects of society that the rituals purport to serve. In their zeal to direct and protect the foundational freedoms of society, and in their dutiful attention to ceremony at all costs, Bergson maintained, leaders become mere automatons and their followers begin to resemble puppets, appearing unnatural and therefore funny in their jerky and unmotivated movements. It can be argued that such incongruity is at the root of all humor, especially in a democratic society; it is also consistent with the Great American Joke. Sahl simply articulated these same incongruities for desperate and frightening times. Crowds were increasingly drawn to Sahl's humor precisely because he was able to isolate such automatism and give Americans a chance to subvert it through satiric laughter. Some were not amused, but many were. During the high-stakes postwar era Sahl and his comedic co-conspirators unapologetically helped to define the battle lines in the widening cultural divide of the 1950s and 1960s, and they claimed their share of defectors. Those on his side of the divide seemed to be having more fun.[30]

Sahl never enjoyed the ubiquitous popularity Rogers did, but he did not have to. He and many other comedians whose style, political material, or skin color made them unsuitable for television took full advantage—as had Rogers—of the transformative aspects of media technology to communicate their equally transformative humor. Specifically, the long-playing phonograph record, or LP, offered a lucrative if less widespread and prestigious outlet compared to television, and it allowed comics to reach a broad audience, earn significant celebrity, and provide their recording companies with healthy profits.

Postwar innovation gave these comedians their chance. For years record companies had been trying to improve upon phonograph technology that limited brittle and scratch-prone shellac records to four minutes of playing time per side and required a speed of 78 revolutions per minute. A combination of slower speeds and narrower grooves offered the solution, but accomplishing this while maintaining sound quality proved elusive. In June 1948 industry giant Columbia Records announced that it had found the answer: a record of microgrooves pressed in vinylite, a nonbreakable plastic, which played at a slower speed, 33 1/3 rpm, not only without any measurable loss of quality but also with less noise and a sound reproduction that many listeners found superior. Even more important, an LP could hold an astounding twenty-three minutes of playing time per side. For the first time, records could conveniently reproduce entire performances—collections of popular songs, Broadway musicals, symphonies, or comedy routines—in high fidelity and without the constant interruption of changing discs. LPs began to be consumed in large numbers by an eager American audience.[31]

By the mid-1950s the advent of better and cheaper record players made phonograph technology accessible to the vast majority of the American public, including those who enthusiastically bought Tom Lehrer's and Stan Freberg's early releases. The market also included that new postwar demographic—"teen-agers" as they were anonymously labeled for the first time during World War II—whose purchasing power was $9.5 billion in 1958 and who snatched up recordings of their favorite new rock and roll stars on another innovation: the single-song 45-rpm record. Price wars and competition over distribution of LPs lowered the average price from $5.95 during the late 1940s to $3.98. Even more significantly, their meteoric popularity made LPs available through a wide variety of outlets, including mail-order clubs. To prevent competition from smaller direct-mail retailers, Columbia introduced the Columbia Record Club in 1955. Within two years Columbia and its rivals had sold 12 million LPs by mail alone. Consumers found that they could conveniently and cheaply re-create their own music or comedy performance space at home.[32]

Looking to capitalize on the success of LPs, record companies raced to secure the most popular new talent for their labels. Sahl, whose initial success was perfectly synchronized with this revolution in recording technology, was signed by the hip new jazz label Verve Records. Significantly, his comedy performances and those of other comedians who followed were typically recorded live, which captured not only the jesters in performance but the animated audience as well, thus completing the comedic circuit. The crowd's infectious laughter and applause on the records served to energize listeners, especially those who participated in the popular practice of holding parties in their homes to showcase their audio equipment and introduce others to the latest talent sensation. The prerecorded laughs encouraged them to spread the comic contagion by listening again and again, and by repeating their favorite jokes to friends and co-workers, a passionate enthusiasm Sahl described as evangelistic. Consequently, although these comedians may initially have been relegated to clubs like the claustrophobic hungry i, comics such as Sahl, Bob Newhart, and later Vaughn Meader were quickly able to popularize their new and daring brand of political humor in front of a virtual audience that numbered in the millions. This meant, among other things, that by the time it was ready for a new president in 1960, the country was increasingly prepared to laugh at him.[33]

Through most of the 1950s, spoken records remained a curious novelty, and their sales lagged behind musical offerings. Most were recorded collections of famous events or "how to" primers such as *Bowl Your Best* and *How to Listen to the Heart* (which was also available in Spanish). Novelty approaches also burst onto the scene, such as the craze for LPs that encouraged listeners to emote directly to their audio system. In a postwar society in which loneliness and alienation were often the price paid for mobility, suburbanization, and cold war suspicions, record producers hoped to convince buyers that technology itself could be the perfect substitute for more traditional human interactions. One such offering, the *Co-Star* series of recordings, released appropriately enough by Roulette Records, gambled that listeners could be enticed to perform opposite popular stars in the comfort of their living rooms. One *Co-Star* release promised to "take you out of the audience and [place] you in the center of the stage" opposite "favorite star" "Slapsy Maxie" Rosenbloom, a former boxing champion turned nightclub owner and alleged thespian. With the enclosed twenty-page script, budding actors could test their dramatic chops opposite Rosenbloom in a scene from *Romeo and Juliet* or lesser-known classics such as "It Happened in Schenectady." Although sales figures for the *Co-Star* records are unknown, one incredulous commentator marveled at the very concept of spoken records: "Do people listen . . . more than once?"[34]

Sahl and other standup comedians proved that people did. He earned the first Grammy Award nomination for a comic in 1958 for his debut album, *The Future Lies Ahead*, which steadily climbed the bestseller list. Verve Records issued four more albums in rapid succession. By 1960 popular magazines such as *McCall's* and *Good Housekeeping* were running regular columns about comedy records. One writer declared that "the comedians and wits are taking over." In its 1960 holiday issue, *Good Housekeeping* featured an article advising readers how to wade through the growing mountain of comedy records to find the right gift. Its opening sentence acknowledged that "the humor boom began with . . . then-obscure young satirist Mort Sahl."[35]

The record boom catapulted other comedians to fame as well, including those whose approach to political humor was no less audacious but whose less confrontational onstage style made laughing at the president more palatable and therefore even more popular. Bob Newhart was the most successful of these. By the late 1950s the Chicagoan was fed up with both government and corporate authority, although his diffident personality made it difficult to tell. After graduating from Loyola University and two years' service in the army, he applied to attend law school under the G.I. Bill, only to be told after a long silence that his application had been delayed; evidently the photostat of his marriage license was of insufficient quality. Newhart sensed a snafu; he was not married. A subsequent career as a low-level accountant proved unsatisfying, and he deserted the ranks of the white-collar middle class to try his hand at standup comedy. Representatives of Warner Brothers Records signed him to a contract in late 1959. His first LP, *The Button-Down Mind of Bob Newhart*, was released a few months later and was an instant hit, selling more than 200,000 copies in twelve weeks and becoming the first comedy album to sell more than 1 million copies. By mid-1960 Newhart was earning five thousand dollars a week.[36]

Newhart's barbs were more oblique, perhaps, but still penetrating. His trademark gimmick was to deliver one side of a telephone conversation, often with a famous person on the other end of the line. His long pauses, stammered responses, and deadpan expression—with telephone receiver in hand—made the phone a silent partner, the conduit through which the audience could imagine set-up or punch lines delivered by the legendary but hapless caller. Newhart frequently played the white-collar "organization man," such as an advertising or public relations executive, who was determined to superimpose contemporary publicity and merchandising techniques on some iconic symbol of traditional American identity or a figure from its mythic past. In one sketch he advises the inventive Wright Brothers that the only way to "make any loot" on their new airplane is to begin booking passengers as soon as possible, and to "put a john on it." In another he wondered what it would have been like if the art of presidential marketing and image making had been as sophisticated during the 1860s as it appeared to be in 1960. He imagined a telephone conversation between a slick press agent and a rather befuddled Abraham Lincoln as the president was on his way to deliver the Gettysburg Address:

Hi, Abe, sweetheart. How are you, kid? How's Gettysburg? [Pause] Sort of a drag, huh? Well, Abe, you know them small Pennsylvania towns, you've seen one you've seen them all [laughs]. Right. Listen Abe, I got the note, what's the problem? You're thinking of shaving it off? Uh, Abe, don't you see that's part of the image? Right, with the shawl, the stovepipe, the string tie. Aw, where's the shawl, Abe? You left it in

Washington? Well, what are you wearing Abe? A sort of cardigan? Abe, don't you see that doesn't fit with the string tie and the beard? Abe, would you leave the beard on and get the shawl?[37]

Newhart cleverly juxtaposed the idealized understanding most Americans had long treasured of "Honest Abe" with the late 1950s stereotype of the cynical political advertising machine. Lincoln turns out to have sprung not organically from the heartland but from the drawing board of some advertising firm on Madison Avenue. Neither John F. Kennedy nor Richard M. Nixon—who were to be locked in a tight campaign that year—is mentioned by name, but amid the laughter Newhart's audience was forced to wonder—somewhat uneasily, perhaps—just what sort of political culture it had allowed to assume control, and how much of a favorite candidate in the current contest was legitimate and how much was created by the smoke and mirrors of image projected on television and in other mass media. As the routine proceeded, the audience laughed uproariously yet could not help but wonder whether it or Lincoln was the object of Newhart's satire:

Anything else? You talked to some newspapermen? Abe, I wish you wouldn't talk to newspapermen. Well, you always put your foot in it. No, that's *just* what I mean, Abe. No, no. You were a rail-splitter, *then* an attorney. Abe, it doesn't make any sense [the other] way. You wouldn't give up your law practice to become a rail-splitter, don't you see? Would you stay with the bio I gave you? It would save you a lot of trouble.[38]

This scene is reminiscent of that between Artemus Ward and Abraham Lincoln exactly a century before. As in 1860 the comic and the president are absorbed in a mock conversation that uses jokes and punch lines to reassess relative power between the president and the ordinary citizen. By 1960, however, the prophecy that Ward had uttered in jest had come to pass. Politics *was* filled up with "Showmen" and their handlers, who some thought were devoid of principles and knew only how, in Ward's words, to "cater for the public." In this exchange the comedian as culture critic used laughter to force his audience and—however indirectly—the institution of the presidency to recognize that political celebrity had become not just potent but perhaps predominant in American culture. In a funny, engaging, but effective manner, Bob Newhart demonstrated that, for better or worse, by 1960 the presidential showman had definitely arrived on the scene.

As for the president still in office, Dwight Eisenhower remained aloof at best and was often hostile to this trend. He considered himself no showman, and by all accounts he gave the humor of Sahl and Newhart little thought, although he could not avoid at least passing knowledge of Sahl once the co-

median appeared on the cover of *Time* in August 1960. Eisenhower's detach-
ment was a calculated non-response from a man whose military training, life
experience, and assumptions about leadership were anathema to everything
political comedians represented in such serious times. Warm and clearly
capable of appreciating good humor in private, Eisenhower saw little use in
expressing it in the public sphere save through his famous grin. During the
1952 campaign he chastised his Democratic opponent Adlai E. Stevenson
for using humor as a tactic. The Eisenhower campaign explained his position in the *New York Times*:

> General Eisenhower and his advisers have come to the deliberate con-
> clusion that the witty jibes and the humorous anecdotes with which
> Governor Stevenson is wont to lighten the necessarily serious business
> of discussing grave issues may be turned against him. They hope the
> American people can be brought to resent these as a wisecracking ap-
> proach to weighty affairs and the mark of an essentially frivolous man.[39]

Eisenhower interpreted his clear victory over Stevenson in 1952 as, among
other things, a confirmation of this perspective. Yet times were changing and
the presidency along with them, albeit grudgingly. Will Rogers and Franklin
Roosevelt had catalyzed the acceptance of humor in political discourse as
a way of nourishing democracy at a moment when worldwide cataclysms
and the mounting complexity of modern life threatened to smother it. After
more than a decade when it appeared that humor's exile might prove permanent and most standup comedians sat down politically, Tom Lehrer, the
Compass Players, Mort Sahl, Bob Newhart, and others including the candidate Stevenson were reintroducing the performance of humor onto the political stage in new ways suited to new threats and complexities. Ironically,
Eisenhower contributed to the process when he popularized the twenty-
second television spot, which helped promote the postwar chief executive
as an approachable man capable of good cheer as well as good judgment.
By 1958 the president had reluctantly acquiesced to the belief that FDR had
practiced with conviction: that a sense of humor—publicly celebrated—was
now a vital part of the electoral calculus. "A sense of humor goes hand in
hand with independence of thought and an eternally questioning mind," he
told graduating midshipmen at the U.S. Naval Academy that year, even if
his own mind eternally questioned the value of remarks made by standup
comedians. Certainly Bob Newhart's popular sketch about a hapless Eisenhower showing up—golf putter in hand—to meet Nikita Khrushchev at the
airport during the Soviet premier's visit in 1959 did not ingratiate him to the
administration. Neither did Mort Sahl's ongoing ridicule and his description
of the president's press secretary, James Hagerty, as "Ike's right foot."[40]

• • •

By the summer of 1960, Mort Sahl had integrated his comic's-eye view sufficiently into the popular vogue that he was hired by the Hearst Corporation as a columnist to report from both the Republican and Democratic conventions, something Will Rogers had pioneered forty years earlier. Although he did not meet the Republican nominee, Richard Nixon, until more than two years later, he already had a close relationship with the Democratic candidate. He met Jack Kennedy in 1959 at a political banquet he had been asked to emcee. Sahl was nervous, not about meeting Kennedy but about mistakenly repeating any of the material he had already written for the young senator to deliver that same evening. Earlier that year Joseph P. Kennedy had called Sahl personally asking him to write some jokes for his son. Sahl obliged, although he readily admitted that Kennedy "had a pretty good wit himself." The American electorate soon discovered this as the senator from Massachusetts began to play before a large national audience for the first time.[41]

John F. Kennedy and the political machine around him knew the power of humor as well as any professional comic. He did not inherently assume that there was a clear distinction between politics and show business any more than Sahl did, or Will Rogers, or Franklin Roosevelt for that matter. He had seen the combination work too well, both for Roosevelt in the 1930s and for his father even earlier when the elder Kennedy had first sought to make his way in Boston as an Irish Catholic against the prejudices of the powerful Protestant Brahmins who controlled local business, politics, and society. Joe Kennedy also had owned the production company Pathé Exchange (which helped to make Will Rogers "the most publicized man in America" in the 1920s) and ran his own film studio in Hollywood before venturing into public life. Indeed the public boundary between politics and performance—to the extent that it existed at all—was seamless in John F. Kennedy's mind. Plagued by colitis, Addison's disease, and degenerative back ailments that collectively brought him close to death several times as a younger man, he, like Roosevelt, fought physical hardships and found self-prescribed humor to be foundational to his physical and emotional salvation. He knew—both innately and by hard experience—what Abraham Lincoln knew, that the comedic line could empower both the comedian and the audience even as it could engage, disarm, distract, and compensate for personal or political liabilities. In 1960, despite his good looks and financial advantages, Kennedy's candidacy was still fraught with obstacles (not least a medical profile that had been tenuously stabilized by large doses of medication, and largely kept secret): he was too young, too inexperienced, too rich, and too Catholic in a country that had never elected a president of that faith. Unlike General turned President Eisenhower, Kennedy had to conjure his relationship with the American electorate from scratch. His wit would be fully brought to bear on winning the election—just as fully as his father's money.

Kennedy's sense of humor is justifiably legendary for its calculated precision as well as its organic spontaneity. His extemporaneous wit was liberally employed and was his alone, but like every other postwar candidate for high office, he made extensive use of writers from the earliest hectic days of the 1960 campaign. Mort Sahl was among them, and although some jokes he wrote for Kennedy to deliver about Eisenhower's golf game went unused, JFK did respond with a Sahl line when a reporter asked whether he was worried about going to heaven if he failed to follow all orders from the pope: "It's not the hereafter that's bothering me but November 4th [Election Day] is driving me out of my mind." Ted Sorensen, his primary speechwriter, maintained an extensive file of humor and provided a wealth of material, as did journalists Joseph Kraft and John Bartlow Martin. They preceded Kennedy from stop to stop as "advance men," mining the next town for background material and forwarding to Kennedy possible jokes to customize his stump speech. It was the first time this tactic was used so deliberately in a presidential campaign, and the approach garnered warm-hearted laughter at virtually every stop from audiences that were in this way encouraged to associate the witty young candidate with issues that touched them personally. Thanking an Indiana crowd for "a warm Hoosier welcome," Kennedy acknowledged that the local bank had been robbed that morning, saying he was "confident that [the Republican newspaper] the *Indianapolis Star* [would] say 'Democrats Arrive and Bank Robbed.'" In Pittsburgh he applied humor to local sports news, a tactic he used frequently: "I am glad to be here because I feel a sense of kinship with the Pittsburgh Pirates. Like my candidacy, they were not given much chance in the spring." In October the underdog Pirates beat the Yankees, four games to three, in one of the closest World Series to that time. In November, Kennedy defeated Richard Nixon in what would remain the closest presidential race for the next forty years. Humor played a large part in his victory, and it did more than make people vote for him. Like those who follow sports teams or comedians, it often turned them into zealous fans.[42]

By employing the performance of humor so openly, Kennedy established it as a calculated point of contrast between himself and the Eisenhower-Nixon administration; it was part of his plan to reinvigorate what he considered to be a stagnant and dour nation, and, as he kept repeating in his stump speech, to get "America moving again." He was convinced that humor was one of his greatest assets, in several ways. He seemed to sense instinctively that it empowered him in the minds of the American everyman, just as almanac jesters and comedians had shown since the dawn of the republic. It could signal that under a Kennedy administration, even the nation's most obdurate and complex challenges would be met with intelligence, creativity, and heroic good cheer. By extension and at its most elemental, humor could serve as a comic misdirection, distracting his audiences from his inexperience and his spotty record of accomplishments in Congress. It could even confront his deficiencies head-on, as when he at least temporarily deflected the criticism that his father's fortune was responsible for his political success by reading at the 1958 Gridiron dinner a purported telegram from "my generous Daddy" that read: "Dear Jack: Don't buy a single vote more than necessary. I'll be damned if I'm going to pay for a landslide." Finally, he unapologetically celebrated the fact that jokes connected him and his political fortunes to American popular culture, the culture that Eisenhower and Nixon largely eschewed. This was the crowd—members of the growing postwar liberal consensus—that *did* listen to Mort Sahl, Bob Newhart, and the other standup comics, and Kennedy was determined to play to it.[43]

Once Kennedy was in office, his objectives, personality, and ego allowed him successfully to duplicate and expand upon much of the public relations strategy that had served Franklin Roosevelt so well. His regular news conferences (he gave sixty-four of them, one every two and a half weeks on average) continued to demonstrate his ability to disarm—even seduce—the public and press through wit. Though not as numerous as FDR's, they more than compensated for this in spectacle and stage management. Further contrasting the Eisenhower reserve with Kennedy confidence and exuberance, they were typically broadcast live on television from the State Department auditorium, where they had been moved by Truman. Members of the media filled every seat, reminding one observer of "an audience for the *Tonight Show*." Here Kennedy could play to the American public directly, without an editor or even an anchorman censoring the presidential charm. Kennedy rehearsed answers to possible questions with his aides beforehand and prepared for others he knew had been planted by his press secretary, Pierre Salinger. While no clear evidence points to which questions were specifically placed among the press corps, many offered perfect straight lines for a president thoroughly at ease in his role as showman:

> REPORTER: I wonder if you could tell us whether, if you had it to do over again, if you would work for the presidency and whether you could recommend the job to others.
> KENNEDY: Well, the answer is . . . to the first is yes and [the] second is no, I don't recommend it to others . . . at least for awhile.[44]

Kennedy also could use humor to avoid addressing legitimate concerns about his position on various issues, including his hesitant approach to civil rights. He was asked whether he would accept a change in the Civil Rights Bill to exempt small boardinghouse owners—in this case a Mrs. Murphy— thereby allowing them to refuse lodgers "regardless of her reason." The president avoided the subject, at least temporarily and to tremendous laughter from the assembled media, when he responded, "The question would be, it seems to me . . . whether Mrs. Murphy had a substantial impact on inter- state commerce."[45]

As the architect of the "New Frontier" and the postwar champion of the "new generation of Americans" he had spoken to in his inaugural address, Jack Kennedy knew instinctively that his presidency was the prototype of a new age in American politics, even if he struggled to understand the full scope of what that meant. Where communicating with the electorate was concerned, he—like Roosevelt—appreciated the importance of perception and at least an imagined intimacy in shaping Americans' attitudes toward the White House. He understood the all-important role of the electronic media, especially television, and recognized that frequent images of him smiling and joking played to his intellectual and purported physical strengths and to his image of vigor. Unlike Dwight Eisenhower, Kennedy had no natural reticence toward television or its reductive emphasis on consumption; he reveled in them. He was, as Norman Mailer wrote in *Esquire* magazine just prior to the 1960 election, the superman come to the supermarket, the candidate who perfectly embodied the postwar paradox of mythic, romantic individualism packaged for an electronic mass media market. Kennedy's performance of humor helped to cast him as the American idol of heroic possibility and change for the 1960s, and as such he became the ultimate political consumable in a country obsessed with consumption and which, ironically, had been made more experienced at equating political power with raw purchasing power by the Republicans' pioneering use of television in the 1952 Eisenhower campaign. Kennedy's drive for the White House eight years later refined the marketing strategy to an unprecedented degree. Old Joe Kennedy summarized the family's approach during the campaign when he boasted its intent to "sell Jack like soapflakes."[46]

As a consequence, and despite his administration's impact on cold war policy, the escalating war in Vietnam, and lasting if belated accomplish- ments in civil rights and nuclear testing, Kennedy's most enduring legacy is one of style over substance. If not always intentionally, he defined glam- our and showmanship as the newest political assets, enlisted television and other media as his messengers, and offered humor and charm as the en- dearing gestures of a captivating, inclusive brand of noblesse oblige toward the American people. The public, while almost evenly split on Election Day in 1960, increasingly surrendered to the attraction. Like Mort Sahl in macrocosm, Kennedy smiled and joked, and Americans increasingly smiled and joked back, eager to be associated with his style, his wit, and the hope he symbolized for an uneasy country. He was comfortable in the company of comedians and other show business luminaries; Bob Newhart, Mike Nichols, and Elaine May (and, more famously, Marilyn Monroe) helped him celebrate his birthdays. It was no coincidence that Kennedy's televised, entertaining, and often funny news conferences became the most recognized fixture of his administration. Judith Campbell Exner, one of Kennedy's lovers, later confirmed it: "Everyone in the press really, really loved him and he worked them like an entertainer works a room. . . . [H]e used them every single minute."[47]

It is little wonder, then, that another young standup comic named Vaughn Meader—encouraged by the example of other comedians and inspired by Kennedy's magnetism (and broad Boston accent)—decided to capitalize on what he considered to be a winning combination: the news conference setting, the president himself, and the admiration many—including Meader— had for the office and the man occupying it. Not surprisingly, much of the nation laughed along.

• • •

Vaughn Meader had good models. Will Rogers pioneered presidential impersonation with occasional slapdash spoofs of Calvin Coolidge and Franklin Roosevelt, and Americans had long chuckled at the juxtaposition of vernacular speech and political oratory in the homespun musings of Jack Downing, Artemus Ward, and Mr. Dooley. Even so, Meader permanently established presidential mimicry as part of American mainstream popular culture. His comically precise imitation of Kennedy's voice, as well as his physical resemblance to the president, epitomized a new dimension in presidential humor. When his impersonation combined with an eager audience to produce a national sensation and the best-selling LP of any kind to that time, the debate over the propriety of ribbing the presidency—and the very nature of presidential identity—was forced into prominence. The president, the people, and even the comedian were uncertain how to respond to the revolutionary moment before them.

In 1962 Meader was a twenty-six year-old composer, singer, and standup comic from Waterville, Maine (approximately fifty miles from Seba Smith's and Charles Browne's hometowns), who was looking for both a gimmick and a break while eking out a career from appearances in small nightclubs, just as Mort Sahl had years before. "I was doing a little political standup in

[Greenwich] Village," he recalled, "and one night I threw in a line in Kennedy's voice and everybody fell down [laughing]. So I started doing press conferences as Kennedy with the audience."[48]

Meader had found his gimmick. His real break came when his manager was able to book him on *Talent Scouts*, a summer replacement program on CBS designed to showcase young show business hopefuls with, in the words of its host, the comic actor Jim Backus, "one magic moment that will project them right to the top." Halfway through the July 3, 1962, episode, Meader made his appearance. After self-consciously performing some straight political standup that largely fell flat, he stepped behind a podium and seemed to become John F. Kennedy (figs. 5 and 6). The studio audience was momentarily stunned into silence as the performer—Meader, to be sure, but this seemed unmistakably Kennedy's voice—began to complain about his competition:

> I used to be a top nightclub comedian, but for the past three years there's somebody going around this country imitating *me*. Now I didn't mind

FIGURE 5 (*left*). *John F. Kennedy at a 1962 news conference. Photograph by Abbie Rowe, National Park Service, in the John F. Kennedy Presidential Library and Museum, Boston.*

FIGURE 6 (*right*). *Vaughn Meader in performance as Kennedy. Photograph by Al Fenn/Time & Life Pictures/Getty Images.*

[his doing this] around the New England area. I didn't mind [it] around the Washington, D.C., area, but now it's gone just a little bit too far.

It wouldn't be so bad if this was just another guy—this is *not* just another guy—this fellow is also an entertainer. He's doing my act, he's doing my gestures, and he's using my lines. "Do not ask what this country can do for you": that's one of *my* original lines.

My friends say this is not really an entertainer; I ask you people to make a judgment on that. He gave a speech at the [American Medical Association]. One of his lines brought down the house—they're still laughing. The line was, "Old folks need medical care." Now he's a big TV star. He's got his own program. He calls it "Press Conference."[49]

The live audience's initial shock is audible in the videotape of the program. Gasps of amazement at Meader's precision—and perhaps his audacity—are immediately followed by a swelling wave of laughter and applause. Unlike with Rogers's radio imitation of Coolidge three decades earlier, here people could clearly see that this was not Kennedy but a comedian. Yet the characterization was spot-on, and Meader's ingenious monologue emphasizing the split personalities of the comic/president added to the merry, if unsettling, confusion. Was this an impersonation of the president upset at being upstaged by a comic, or of the comedian Meader lashing out at a comic rival who happened to be president of the United States? It was disconcertingly—and hilariously—unclear. Like Seba Smith and Charles Browne, the comic from Maine was leading the country to the threshold of a new cultural relationship between the presidency and the American people.

The performance mesmerized producer and television writer Earle Doud, who watched the broadcast and found Meader's vocal and physical resemblance to the president uncanny. Within three months he and fellow writers Bob Booker and George Foster secured the necessary financial backing and signed Meader to record a comedy album spoofing America's favorite clan. Others were impersonating Kennedy in theaters and clubs (among them was a young actor with the Compass Players in Massachusetts named Alan Alda, who went on to stardom in the long-running television series *M*A*S*H*), but the Booker-Doud project perfectly aligned Meader's virtuoso skill with inspired writing, the simultaneous popularity of the long-playing record, and fortuitous timing. It also took the cue to joke and laugh that had tacitly been given by the humor-loving president, who, having just emerged triumphant from the Cuban Missile Crisis, rode a high tide of goodwill from a grateful nation craving comic relief.[50]

Finding a record company willing to subsidize ridicule of the president proved difficult. Laughing along with the Kennedy wit was increasingly becoming the accepted fashion, but jokes at the expense of this president, or the office in general, were still suspect regardless of—and to many *because* of—the success of iconoclasts such as Mort Sahl. Many continued to consider such comedy treasonous. When Doud and his associates approached ABC-Paramount after three other record labels turned them down, one of its top executives, James Hagerty—perhaps out of revenge for Sahl's insults when he was Eisenhower's press secretary—stormed out of the meeting. He called the proposed album "degrading to the presidency" and proclaimed that "every communist country in the world would love this record." Finally, tiny Cadence Records in New York City agreed to risk the project.[51]

On October 22, 1962, Meader and a cast of eleven others hired to play myriad roles in support of his John F. Kennedy—assorted cabinet members, NASA astronauts, world leaders, reporters, and of course the rest of the extended first family—gathered before a live invited audience in a converted ballroom at New York City's Great Northern Hotel to record the album. The timing was ominous. It was the night Kennedy addressed the nation about the U.S. response to Cuba's importing Russian ballistic missiles and the real possibility of nuclear conflict with the Soviet Union. Meader recalled: "During rehearsals I snuck out to the hotel bar to watch Kennedy. . . . Thank God he took a strong stand, or our record would have died right there."[52]

Three weeks later, with a price tag of $3.98, typical for the time, *The First Family* made its unassuming appearance on store shelves. Radio stations began to embrace it, and within two weeks it had sold more than 1 million copies and pushed past the debut album by the folk trio Peter, Paul, and Mary. Within one month it had sold 2.5 million, with factories around the country running at full speed trying to keep up with the demand. Vaughn Meader suddenly found himself the star of the most popular record album of any kind in American history. In the afterglow of release and self-congratulation following the apparent victory over the Soviet Cuban threat, the country reveled in the catharsis the album provided as it simultaneously ribbed and celebrated the triumphant president. Americans—Kennedy detractors who were more inclined to laugh *at* the president as well as admirers who laughed *with* him—fairly danced to stores to buy their copy and soon parroted favorite lines to others. Radio stations gave the record seemingly constant airplay for weeks. Even Martin Luther King Jr. and other civil rights leaders in his Southern Christian Leadership Conference, who were beginning to plan the next spring's march on Birmingham, Alabama, against the rabid segregation in that city, noted that the album was making the white world "too happy for civil rights." Eventually *The First Family* won the Grammy Award for Album of the Year and sold in excess of 7 million copies, not only eclipsing *My Fair Lady*, the previous record holder, but also far outselling Mort Sahl's latest effort, *The New Frontier*. Ironically, it took an album memorializing Kennedy two years later to outsell it.[53]

As many critics pointed out, the brand of parody in *The First Family* was not overly intellectual, which helped account for its wide popular appeal. It entertained, according to *Time*, more with "gags" than "wit." In one sketch the White House nanny asks the president to help her figure out which of the assorted bathtub toys—including beach balls, a rubber swan, and eighteen toy PT boats (Kennedy had commanded a small patrol or "PT" boat in World War II)—belong to his daughter Caroline and which to son John Jr. Meader as Kennedy proceeds to apportion the various toys, concluding vehemently that "the rubber swan is mine!"[54]

Such broad jokes, however, were complemented by flashes of political insight and satire. During a lampoon of Jacqueline Kennedy's televised tour of the White House with CBS correspondent Charles Collingwood, she is interrupted by the freshly showered, dripping, and thoroughly lost President Kennedy, who is late for a meeting and therefore anxious to "move ahead toward our bedroom with great vigor." She directs him through the maze of official rooms, among them "the Andrew Jackson Smoking Room . . . the Woodrow Wilson Ping-Pong Room . . . the President Grant Drinking Room [and] past the Richard Nixon Dumbwaiter." During the album's mock press conference the president is asked, "Sir . . . when will we send a man to the Moon?" to which a deadpan Kennedy instantly replies, "Whenever [Republican] Senator [Barry] Goldwater wants to go." Another exchange in this same sketch conjured memories of Kennedy's strategy during the campaign to defuse questions about his Catholicism, this time with a twist:

> REPORTER: Now that you're in office, what do you think the chances are for a Jewish president?
>
> MEADER AS KENNEDY: Well, I think they're pretty good. Now let me say I don't see why a person of the Jewish faith can't be president of the United States. I know, as a Catholic, *I* could never vote for him, but other than that . . .[55]

Audiences reflexively embraced the album. Critics declared *The First Family* "the hit record to end hit records," and its fame began to spread. One Los Angeles customer sent ten copies overseas to illustrate "America's unfettered and freewheeling humor," and diplomats ordered hundreds more. Meader was heard on radio stations across the country, asked for interviews by national publications, and booked at clubs and on *The Ed Sullivan Show*. A novelty photo album of the faux "first family" was released, and a live stage tour featuring Meader and other principal cast members went on the road. The record itself and the attendant appearances earned Meader an estimated $750,000 within one year.[56]

Inside the White House not everyone was amused. The Kennedy administration—used to choreographing the laughter—had less experience being the punch line of the joke. Publicly the president responded cordially to the album during a news conference, although his comments do not reveal the good-natured joviality and appreciation that most observers interpreted at the time. In fact, his first choice of words is instructive, and his statement overall was somewhat contradictory and noncommittal, reflecting the struggle behind closed doors over what to do about those who mimicked the president for fun and profit. Asked whether other recent printed lampoons and The First Family in particular caused "annoyment or enjoyment," he answered: "Annoyment. [Laughter] No, they produce . . . yes, I have read and listened. Actually, I listened to Mr. Meader's record but I thought it sounded more like Teddy than it did me . . . so he's annoyed."[57]

Kennedy handled the question with his signature skills of deflection and humorous distraction. Pierre Salinger, Kennedy's press secretary, insisted years later that the president "took the Meader album in very good humor." It was reported that the White House ordered more than one hundred copies, although Salinger's correspondence apparently contradicts this, and he added to the sense of ambivalence toward the record when he wrote that Kennedy "did not buy any copies for any reason." Behind the scenes the president grappled with his response to a phenomenon that at once humanized and endeared him to the public—which he considered crucial to his success—and yet trivialized the prestige of the imperial presidency, which he staunchly promoted. Prior to his apparently gracious news conference response, Kennedy met with aide Kenneth P. O'Donnell and assistant press secretary Malcolm M. Kilduff. They agreed "that nothing could be done about this particular record. However, . . . it might be useful to get some trade magazine to blast this sort of thing." The following spring Salinger, presumably on orders from the president, contacted Newton Minow, chairman of the Federal Communications Commission, and asked him to "look into" the matter, although it is not clear what if anything was done. Kennedy, as the first president subjected to such hugely popular impersonation, danced around the success of The First Family with surprise, uncertainty, muted resentment, and perhaps private appreciation. After its giddy initial embrace of the album, the nation responded with similar ambivalence.[58]

Public reaction poured into the White House. It adds insight beyond that suggested by the raw sales figures, and reflects the debate inside the Oval Office and among the public at large. Kennedy received numerous letters and telegrams representing the full spectrum of response from delight to disgust. Many correspondents revealed a tentative uncertainty—as if to acknowledge that the controversy itself was unprecedented—and looked to the president for guidance on the advisability of such humor. Several authors, producers, and theater companies, even a Catholic priest—all eager to capitalize on the *First Family* craze—assumed that such satire required presidential approval and wrote to request it. The administration tersely replied that none was needed. In mid-1963 the chairman of the Grand Street Boys' Association, a private philanthropic organization, wrote Kennedy for permission to include *The First Family* in packages being readied for veterans' hospitals and numerous overseas schools and orphanages. The chairman's initial enthusiasm over "the very generous contribution" of the records dimmed when Kennedy aide Lee C. White, fully cognizant of the power of humor and fearful of the possible negative use of the parody overseas, offered "in all frankness that were the decision ours we would limit the distribution to the United States." The man promptly wrote back to report that the album had been removed and to admit for the first time, "Frankly, this is a mutual feeling."[59]

Kennedy also received a large number of letters from young people fascinated by the album and eager to know his response. A junior high school student wrote from Detroit to report that it had sparked lively discussion between him and his classmates. One Cornell University freshman wrote Kennedy to report how popular *The First Family* was on campus even though "many of my friends feel that, since it ridicules your family, it is not very popular with you." He bet his classmates that "if I made a trip to Washington during Christmas vacation, you would take time . . . to autograph the record for me." The president's office dismissed the idea of such a meeting. Nevertheless, in the minds of many, especially many of those in the baby boom generation that he so profoundly inspired—the star-struck young man from Cornell among them—not only was President Kennedy a celebrity whose autograph on a hit LP was something to be coveted, but also he appeared to be a complicit partner in the brave new world of comedic egalitarianism that Mort Sahl, Bob Newhart, Vaughn Meader, and others seemed to be defining. After all, wasn't this simply another expression of the participatory democracy espoused by Kennedy's new brand of liberalism? Certainly the president would not object to but rather champion such humor. In fact the right to laugh at the expense of the presidency was something about which many in the country—including the president—still had serious doubt, despite the record sales. The doubts and the debate continued through November 1963, but so did the laughter, the sales, and the celebrity.[60]

Even Vaughn Meader and the producers of *The First Family* were uncertain about the effects of the record and the ramifications of impersonation in general. Meader never met Kennedy, but in a telling coincidence he sent a telegram to the president after the taping of his debut on *Talent Scouts*. It was hauntingly reminiscent of Will Rogers's messages to Calvin Coolidge and Franklin Roosevelt after his attempts at impersonation:

> Dear Mr. President,
> I respectfully call your attention to the Talent Scouts Show which we taped last night for viewing on CBS Television Tuesday night, July 3, 10:00 PM. I impersonated you but I did it with great affection and respect. Hope it meets with your approval.
> Respectfully,
> Vaughn Meader[61]

Similarly, the dust jacket of *The First Family* included a disclaimer emphatically asserting from the outset: "This album is for fun! . . . No one has more respect for the high offices and the people suggested here than those of us who . . . [put] this together. . . . This album can be played loudly at any time, . . . anywhere people have a right to laugh." The sensational popularity of comedy albums in general and the president's own good humor made Meader and the record's producers reasonably sure that it was safe to take aim at Kennedy this way, but there was no harm in hedging their bets.[62]

Despite the lucrative response to *The First Family*, by the middle of 1963 Meader thought it wise to ease the Kennedy material out of his act. Although the president's chances for reelection in 1964 looked strong, interest in the impersonation certainly would fade, and Meader was determined to broaden his reputation beyond mimicry. In early November 1963 he recorded an album called *Have Some Nuts!!* which parodied communists, the Ku Klux Klan, unions, and the Bay of Pigs invasion but did not mention Kennedy. On November 22, with the new album not yet released, the *New York Post* included an article in its morning edition with the headline, "JFK Record Is Haunting Vaughn Meader."[63]

For the time being, though, the comedian still gladly accepted the bookings that took him and his famous impersonation across the country. That day—the same day Kennedy flew to Dallas to calm internecine battles within his party in advance of the upcoming campaign—Meader flew to Milwaukee to perform at a comedy show. As he stepped into a taxi, the driver turned to him and asked, "Hey, did you hear about Kennedy in Dallas?" Clearly, thought Meader, this was the setup for yet another Kennedy joke, another unsolicited gag from a well-meaning fan. It seemed the entire country still wanted in on the act. The comic obliged. "No, how does it go?"[64]

At a time when the comedians, the president, and the American people were dancing so closely together, Meader's error was absurdly tragic and yet thoroughly understandable. Together with Mort Sahl, Bob Newhart, and others, Meader had become both a producer and a beneficiary of a laughing mass economy whose currency was jokes and whose transactions permanently affected American popular and political culture. Now, however, Kennedy was dead. The president and Meader had risen to national stardom together employing the performance of humor, but in late 1963 the impersonator found himself mimicking Kennedy one last time, unknowingly and unwillingly riding the president's bloody coattails toward oblivion.

5

All Lies and Jest

THE FIRST DAYS and months after John F. Kennedy's assassination were as unkind to political standup comedy as they were to the grieving nation as a whole. *The First Family* was removed from store shelves, as was a sequel, which had been released in the spring of 1963. The horrors in Dallas prompted the albums' producers to call Cadence Records and ask that all unsold copies be returned to warehouses to be destroyed out of respect for the murdered president and his family. They were. Nightclubs were mostly empty the entire weekend of the assassination. On Broadway, where Mort Sahl had assailed the political establishment in *The Next President* more than five years before, theaters and restaurants went dark for days. Even the film industry was shaken. The official preview screening of *Dr. Strangelove, or: How I Learned to Stop Worrying and Love the Bomb*, Stanley Kubrick's dark satirical film about thermonuclear Armageddon, was postponed, and worried film editors hastily dubbed over a coincidental off-color reference to Dallas made by Major T. J. "King" Kong, a B-52 pilot played by actor Slim Pickens, and replaced it with an allusion to Las Vegas instead. American show business deferred almost completely to the tragic spectacle in Texas and Washington, D.C., where the president's state funeral captivated the country. In death as in life, Kennedy drew a crowd and got top billing. *Variety*, the entertainment trade weekly, estimated the cost of the television coverage of the murder and the funeral during the five days following the assassination to be $40 million.[1]

In New York, the only comedian to take the stage on November 22 was Lenny Bruce, who appeared before a muted audience at the Fox Theatre in lower Manhattan. Bob Booker, one of the creators of *The First Family*, caught his act a few days later as Bruce made his entrance, looked at the audience, and said, "Boy, did Vaughn Meader get fucked."[2]

Bruce's remark was prophetic in several ways. Meader was devastated personally and professionally and never imitated Kennedy for profit again. He did attempt a comeback in January 1964 at the same club where he had launched his famous impersonation, but he foundered through an assortment of non-Kennedy material groping for laughs, without much success. "In the end," said the critic from *Time*, "he . . . scored on about 35% of his shots." Similar reviews from *Newsweek* and *Variety* ensured the early close of his act. Alcohol, cocaine, and heroin addictions followed, and although he made sporadic attempts to revive his career with a pair of comedy albums later in the decade and subsequent appearances as a country singer, nothing worked. Meader eventually returned to his home state of Maine, where he died in October 2004, largely forgotten.[3]

Bruce might have said the same thing about Mort Sahl. Sahl's barbs at Dwight Eisenhower helped elect Jack Kennedy, but when he entered the White House, the new president became fair game. Sahl pursued the New Frontier in ways true to his iconoclastic tradition, criticizing policy, attacking the Bay of Pigs invasion, and ridiculing the Kennedys as America's "royal family." In what proved to be a haunting reference, Sahl claimed in 1961 that he could put to rest the rumor that Cubans were out to assassinate the entire Kennedy family: "Castro denied it, claiming they had insufficient ammunition."[4]

As Kennedy's popularity grew, Sahl's began to decline, in large part owing to pressure from the administration, which further demonstrated the president's ambivalent response to being the object of the joke. Although Kennedy had once praised Sahl's "relentless pursuit of everybody," the comic's refusal "to become court jester" to Kennedy ostracized him from the White House and the Democratic Party, which considered him a traitor to the president. After Kennedy's victory, Sahl responded onstage to those who assumed that Kennedy's election was what he wanted, saying, "You didn't have to do it for *me!*" Old Joe Kennedy was incensed. Two years after encouraging Sahl to write material *for* his son, he issued an ultimatum through third parties that he stop performing material *about* him, promising to teach Sahl "the meaning of the word 'loyalty.'" Even Sahl's agent told him he resented the comments about the president, and while Vaughn Meader's sensational imitation was earning him an appearance on *The Ed Sullivan Show* in 1963, Sahl was being dropped from Sullivan's and others' guest lists and had a difficult time finding work. In the early 1960s the comedian's annual income plummeted from $400,000 to $19,000, and he claimed with justification that he was the victim of blacklisting.[5]

In short, the Kennedy assassination killed Meader's career outright and hobbled Sahl's. As the presidential showmen whose material associated them most closely with the showman president, they had the most to lose when the issue of presidential satire turned serious inside the White House, then when the market for presidential humor collapsed altogether—albeit temporarily—following the president's assassination. Kennedy's performance in the office had become so ubiquitously displayed in the mass media that show business and the business of politics became conflated in popular culture in formative ways that resonate clearly to the present day.

The interaction between Kennedy and Meader was the defining watershed. Although the president and the comedian never met, their relationship through laughter was multilayered, even intimate. Kennedy's jokes at news conferences melded fluidly into Meader's parody of the news conference on *The First Family* and then back again as Meader and his album became the topic of conversation, first at Kennedy's news conference in December 1962 and then behind closed doors as comedy performance and response to it became a matter of presidential concern. Humor intertwined the rituals of presidential custom so closely with freewheeling moments of cultural play that many Americans could not always differentiate between the president, the comedian, and the joke. After all, the Cornell freshman who wrote to Kennedy after listening to *The First Family* wanted Kennedy's autograph, not Meader's, as though the president himself had performed on the album. Americans played the LP repeatedly during late 1962 and most of 1963, and even organized social occasions around playing it so that the performance could be experienced again and again with various audiences. Many people committed one-liners or entire sections to memory and then took great delight in becoming comedians themselves by imitating the comic's imitation of the president. Four decades before the term "viral video" entered the vernacular to describe the rapid spread of sensational clips of news, entertainment, or political events among willing hosts on the Internet, Kennedy's wit and Meader's record made the comic performance of the presidency contagious within mass culture.

With *The First Family*, Meader and Kennedy came together in much the same way that Artemus Ward had encountered Abraham Lincoln in 1860. Their encounter also was reminiscent of those between Mr. Dooley and William McKinley then Theodore Roosevelt at the turn of the twentieth century, and Will Rogers's ongoing association with Franklin Roosevelt. Modeling these earlier pioneer comedians, the comic again became the equalizing force between the people and the president, empowering the former through ridicule that simultaneously humanized the latter by poking fun at his vulnerabilities. Meader's record, however, accomplished this on an unprecedented, massive scale, and it did so in specific response to postwar American contingencies.

What is more, mainstream commerce feverishly sought to capitalize on this relationship rather than squelch it, as it had the social and political satire of Fred Allen, Stan Freberg, and even Mort Sahl. Given the public good humor of the president and the phenomenal success of *The First Family*, the media and the sponsors that lubricated mass consumption promoted both the record and the premise behind it: that presidential humor could foster a brand of merry egalitarianism between Americans and their president that, as citizens, most people would condone with easy laughter and, as consumers, pay for with hard cash. Such laughter, it was recognized, could very well be culturally constructive, but even more important, it could be economically profitable. *The First Family*'s sales, the speed with which the sequel reached the market, the meteoric rise of Meader's income and celebrity—including the zeal with which promoters booked him on television and stage—and the proliferation of myriad copycat projects all attested to the appreciating financial value of such humor. Advertisers and entrepreneurs rushed to cash in with performances of their own. In early 1963 Connecticut-based Mars Broadcasting launched local and regional advertising campaigns of "Great Vigah" commercials around the country using an actor mimicking Kennedy's voice—or, more accurately, Meader's impression of Kennedy's voice—to sell a variety of products. In one radio ad, western Pennsylvanians were given "presidential" assurance that local car dealer Vern Staley was "leading the people in Pittsburgh to a new frontier" and "selling Dodges with great 'vigah' [while] passing the savings on to his customers." White House press secretary Pierre Salinger moved quickly to quash the ads, pointing out the longtime "understanding" between the White House and the Better Business Bureau that "the President's voice or imitations of his voice should not be used at any time in commercial advertising." The company quickly complied by recalling the commercials, insisting that no disrespect was intended. Rather it had assumed "that the national vogue recently created by the 'First Family Album' made our creation acceptable." Such a presumption was understandable; linking laughter and the presidency had earned political capital for Kennedy and wealth for *The First Family*'s creators. Where did the profit stream end, and who was entitled to drink from it?[6]

Such questions temporarily evaporated in November 1963. After the surreal events of Dallas, neither the president nor the grieving audience nor even the comic was left unaffected. In time, however, the convergence of forces that led to the wide acceptance of *The First Family* and the political material of other standup performers during the early 1960s proved lasting. The cultural acceptance—then the economic mass production and commodification—of presidential comedy crystallized haltingly but assuredly over the next dozen years. The close proximity of the comedian and the president, and the endorsement of this intimacy by an American public that purchased the album and delighted in performing the parody themselves, consummated the modern relationship between the people, the president, and the standup comic, and gave license to all three to exploit this familiarity to their own purposes. Joking at the expense of the president—which had been a marginal form of political and cultural interaction—gained cultural and economic legitimacy by the mid-1970s.

•   •   •

Nevertheless, Kennedy's death and the remarkable decade that followed affected the trajectory of the process in radical ways. Americans had laughed mostly in concert with the president and the professional political comics, and they joked largely as chorus; but when the leading players were silenced by the assassination and its collateral damage, they began to choreograph the dance of the comedians critically, actively, and organically, readily accepting more caustic humor as in keeping with the times and even performing as comedians themselves. As American society during the 1960s and early 1970s careened through the Vietnam War, urban unrest, economic recession, and seemingly endless violence and assassination, humor directed at the presidency started to emanate more widely from a public sphere increasingly attuned to the potency of such humor, newly prepared to accept its more radical manifestations, and motivated to co-opt them for its own use. Convinced of the close relationship between humor and the presidency by the president himself and comedians such as Mort Sahl, Bob Newhart, and Vaughn Meader, growing numbers of Americans were utilizing political comedy in its many manifestations—satire, impersonation, parody, even slapstick—alternately to deride and celebrate the yawning gulf that had opened between the people and the chief executive. As it turned out, the murder of the president—an act described by more than one comic as "the sickest joke of the century"—proved to be a mere setup for a decade-long tragicomedy in several acts that alienated Americans from their leaders to a degree unprecedented in the country's history. Lyndon B. Johnson's escalation of American involvement in the Vietnam War from 1965 to 1968 and his accompanying pronouncements of imminent victory rang hollow against both the accounts of those fighting the war and the bloody images that splashed across television screens and the pages of newspapers. The result was a widening "credibility gap" between the electorate and the executive branch. This fissure deepened with the ironic contrast between Johnson's rhetoric describing his Great Society—capable of conquering poverty and social inequities through compassionate federal leadership—on the one hand, and events that implicated the president in helping to create a society that was becoming ever more violent and polarized on the other. Richard Nixon's remoteness from the public and his temporary widening of the war with the sudden invasion of Cambodia in 1970 worsened the rift. Finally, constitutional abuse and widespread duplicity associated with the Watergate scandals that forced Nixon to resign in 1974 made the presidency synonymous with criminality.[7]

All of this served to turn many Americans against the White House only a few turbulent years after the comparatively benign humor of the Kennedy era had brought the people and the president toward cultural parity, even intimacy. Many had laughed at the incongruous notion made comically plausible by *The First Family*: that the majestical Kennedy clan was remarkably like the folks next door. By the late 1960s Americans no longer used humor simply to equate themselves with the lofty authority of the presidency. No longer was laughter merely in the service of seeking what Alexis de Tocqueville called in 1831 "a mid-point between the supremacy of all and the absolute power of one." Americans now used ridicule to subordinate the office to depths of inferiority far *below* the electorate, where the president lately proved he rightly belonged. Given the horrors of Vietnam under Johnson and Nixon, and especially in the wake of Nixon's resignation, the "Great American Joke"—referring to Americans' long-standing use of humor to reconcile the discrepancy between national ideals and the human limitations that impede their realization—was turning sour. With his criminal behavior, Nixon cynically implied that the ideals themselves were the joke, while for their part, Americans began to believe that the joke was the presidency. With government turning to farce, Americans reveled in exiling the fools. No lie would go without ridicule; no crime would go without trial by jest.[8]

In this way the performance of presidential humor—like nearly every aspect of American life during the tumultuous period from the mid-1960s to the mid-1970s—became an increasingly desperate zero-sum game. Any power that could be gained by the comics, whether professionals or amateurs, meant not only victory for them but also an equal and welcome loss for the political establishment. This cultural calculus registered with Americans of all ages, but it was particularly clear in the eyes of the enormous baby boom generation. The 78 million Americans born between 1946 and 1964—especially those on the leading edge of the boom—came of age with the cold war and its contradictory messages that safety grew in direct proportion to the size of the nuclear arsenal and that home was where the bomb shelter was. They were fed on television and its sweet promises of a comfortable, homogeneous suburban life pillowed by situation comedies. But these jolly manufactured images—still mostly of white faces in the mid-

1960s—clashed with the spontaneous televised sight of mostly black faces being pummeled by water hoses in Birmingham, Alabama, or clashing with police in the Watts section of Los Angeles and dozens of other cities as the civil rights movement surged on with a frantic and captivating intensity. Baby boomers caused the doubling in U.S. college enrollment during the 1960s by going off to college in unprecedented numbers, ostensibly to learn the discipline and skills essential to obediently joining the hierarchy of corporate production; yet they were already firmly schooled in the conflicting principles of postwar consumer sovereignty that stressed personal choice (at least in economic terms), immediate gratification, and self-expression. Regardless of their political ideology—whether inspired by a youthful Kennedy to ask what they could do for their country, roused to "affirm certain eternal truths" by the conservative Young Americans for Freedom, or called to "participatory democracy" by the New Left ideology of Students for a Democratic Society—many boomers jousted with the political status quo in proactive and often funny ways.[9]

As the political stakes escalated along with the Vietnam War—especially for young men considered ripe for the military draft at eighteen yet too immature for the vote (which was denied to those under twenty-one until 1971)—these contradictions fermented into a passionate activism that moved far beyond the veiled hit-and-run ridicule of the "child" or "elephant" joke cycles. Rigid battle lines were drawn between those who formulated national policy and those who challenged the legitimacy of both the policies and the authorities behind them. The performance of laughter and comedy, much like the acoustic protests of folk music and the electric assaults of rock and roll, became both a defensive strategy and an offensive political weapon. The serrated edges of irony and sarcasm took on a more tactical prominence and became visible in diverse ways. For example, as the nation's military defense policy known as "mutual assured destruction" (MAD) linked the ultimate preservation of national security to total nuclear obliteration, it was no surprise that *Mad* magazine vied with *Life* as the most widely read periodical among young people. Students who scrawled, "Flush twice. Washington is a long way from here," on a bathroom wall at UCLA mocked not so much the geographical distance from the nation's capital as the political and generational separation from those in authority by dumping on them in the same manner they believed political leaders had been dumping on America for years. When radical activists Abbie Hoffman and Jerry Rubin choreographed members of their Youth International Party, or "Yippies," into a parading troupe of comedians to assail the New York Stock Exchange in 1967 and the Democratic National Convention the following year, they performed humor as a guerrilla tactic to counter the rituals of mainstream culture with rebellious play. In waging what satirist Tony Hendra has termed "Boomer humor," Americans aimed antic, anarchic new waves of what Mark Twain had called the exorcising "assault of laughter" at the new host of "colossal humbugs" they saw pervading national government.[10]

The accelerated process by which baby boomers and many older Americans evolved from being tentative *consumers* of political humor toward also becoming more radical *producers* of it continued to absorb influences from the professional performers even as it was fed organically by these deep divisions in American society. Mort Sahl's signature antiauthoritarianism set the tone for modern political standup before recriminations from the Kennedys and Sahl's own obsession with assassination conspiracy theories largely silenced him. Bob Newhart continued to attract fans; so did Tom Lehrer, whose cheerfully grim tunes satirizing postwar culture not only encouraged listeners to sing along but also seemed so simple that anyone might easily turn do-it-yourself comedian. Laughs continued to emanate, too, from the Second City, the Premise, and other performance groups. In San Francisco the Committee (defiantly named after that more infamous committee from the early cold war years, HUAC) was founded in 1963 and engaged in all manner of political theater for the rest of the decade, provocatively ridiculing what it considered lagging, hypocritical, or immoral White House policy on civil rights, the cold war in general, and the Vietnam War in particular. While the Committee and these other groups attracted comparatively small audiences in clubs and theaters, their comedic daring leached throughout the grass roots of the wider counterculture and from there into a redefined cultural mainstream by the end of the sixties. These groups also helped to ignite the careers of members turned comedy stars whose humor later became enormously popular even as it grew decidedly political, including Alan Alda as antiwar army surgeon "Hawkeye" Pierce in *M*A*S*H*, Rob Reiner's outspoken liberal urbanite Mike "Meathead" Stivic in *All in the Family*, Valerie Harper's funny but strong and independent character Rhoda Morgenstern in *The Mary Tyler Moore Show* and then *Rhoda*, and Howard Hesseman as countercultural rock DJ Johnny Fever in *WKRP in Cincinnati*.

Americans also valued network television's fleeting prime time experiment with a more provocative brand of satire during the mid-1960s—more, in fact, than the network valued it. Featuring David Frost, *That Was the Week That Was* (widely known as *TW3*) originated in 1962 on Great Britain's BBC television, offering audiences songs, sketches, and mock news reports that skewered the prime minister, royal family, and virtually all other facets of the British establishment. After two popular but controversial seasons, the weekly satirical review was abruptly canceled in December 1963 in advance of approaching British elections and left the air with a sober finale in tribute to John F. Kennedy a month after the American president's assassination. Eleven days prior to Kennedy's death, NBC television—just as eager as other commercial media to capitalize on the boom in political satire brought about in large part by Mort Sahl, Vaughn Meader, and Kennedy himself—piloted a U.S. version of the show, also starring Frost, to widespread popular acclaim. Although NBC's decision to continue the show was delayed by the chilling effect of the president's death, the network opted to produce *TW3* as a weekly series beginning the following January. The thirty-minute live program closely replicated its British predecessor and earned applause for its satiric observations on all aspects of American society, including civil rights, Hollywood, and even the hands that fed it: advertisers and the media. It showcased Tom Lehrer's music before a mainstream television audience; Gloria Steinem numbered among its writers a few years before the author and feminist co-founded *Ms.* magazine; and Henry Morgan was featured among its cast, temporarily reviving the career of the radio satirist who had been evicted from the airwaves a decade before.[11]

Politicians were *TW3*'s principal targets, particularly the new president, Lyndon Johnson, and conservative Barry Goldwater as it became clear that he would be Johnson's Republican challenger in the 1964 election. Ridicule of Johnson was relatively soft and sparse during the first few months of the new administration, but the show's attacks became more frequent and cutting by May. When Johnson ordered the White House lights turned out at night as a symbol of his efforts to economize, writers came up with a sketch titled "Pennies for the President" that likened the dimmed lighting to diminished presidential brainpower in the wake of the more intellectual Kennedy:

> When they have enough [pennies] then
> They will turn all the lights on again
> Even tho I've heard the absurd remark
> That Lyndon works much better in the dark. . . .
> [Kennedy adviser] Ted Sorensen's gone, past recall.
> And the boys who were so on the ball.
> With the intellects gone
> Your staff carries on
> Can't you stand any brightness at all?

That same month, images of Johnson delivering a speech to a Chamber of Commerce gathering in Washington were accompanied by lyrics that sarcastically cast the president as a comedian selling his hardening approach to Vietnam as so much showbiz razzle-dazzle:

> When they asked about my policy
> On the fighting in Viet Nam

I made 'em laugh
I made 'em laugh.
They said about that war the folks
At home don't really give a damn
Well, I made 'em laugh
I made 'em laugh.
I said, "I've got a fabulous idea that really is uncanny
Let's make the war more popular with Junior and with Granny
Let's call it what it really is
A shootin' Hooten Nanny."
Oh, boy
Well, I made 'em laugh.

Such satire used the joking precedent established by Mort Sahl, the production values of Stan Freberg's work, and the proven acceptance of presidential humor popularized by *The First Family*. Americans were receptive, rewarding the show and NBC with high ratings.[12]

Public reaction was positive through the rest of TW3's first season, even though praise was far from universal. Part of the appeal was its freshness; of necessity the program was produced from scratch every week. Such immediacy inspired eager participation on the part of fans, many of whom wrote in to contribute jokes and ideas for sketches. Over the course of several episodes, producers encouraged viewers to indicate whom they would *least* like to see elected president. A woman from California wrote in saying she could not stand the thought of four more years "of those 'birds' [the Johnsons] in the White House." In addition to the first lady—Lady Bird—and Johnson daughter Lynda—known as "Lynda Bird"—she suspected that "one of Daddy's good friends may become a Jail Bird," a reference to a scandal then making headlines involving Johnson protégé Robert "Bobby" Baker. As for Barry Goldwater, who frightened many with his extreme hawkish support for the use of nuclear weapons in Vietnam, a viewer from Massachusetts hoped he would not become president "because I simply cannot afford a bomb shelter." TW3 encouraged its nationwide audience to play a part, and many did by becoming armchair comedians.[13]

Despite the show's early success, the NBC leadership and sponsors began to squirm even before the first season ended. In a desperate attempt to maintain high ratings and broaden appeal, producers shuffled the writing staff and cast. At the same time, the network feared the alienating effect that such bald political satire might have on the public and advertisers in advance of the 1964 nominating conventions and election. Kennedy—who had given satire the presidential seal of approval and had tacitly mediated its acceptance by the political and broadcast establishment—was gone, and

NBC began to backpedal. First, it moved *TW3* from its Friday night spot-light slot to Tuesday night opposite the broad comedy of *Petticoat Junction* on CBS and the romantic intrigue of *Peyton Place* on ABC. Then it sold the half-hour to Goldwater's campaign, which specifically requested the time slot to squelch the program's ridicule and to counter what it believed to be the dire influence of *TW3*'s satire. The campaign successfully preempted the show for most of October. By the time *TW3* finally reappeared for its sec-ond season in November 1964, its viewers were disoriented. One frustrated fan wrote the show's producers to observe: "*TW3* is our favorite program. So when do we get to see it?" After it was permanently taken off the air in May 1965, NBC received petitions with the signatures of legions of angry fans, in-cluding one cleverly crafted by a "disappointed, deprived, disenchanted, dis-pleased, disgusted, disillusioned, distressed, and otherwise dissident group of television viewers."[14]

NBC came to wage preemptive war against *TW3* for the same reason that the producers of *The First Family* had difficulty finding a record company. Despite the apparent encouragement of the Kennedy years, the institutions of national power still tiptoed very tentatively along the new frontiers of political comedy performance. Jittery executives—including those in the media, corporate boardrooms, and the White House—alternately embraced and feared the influence that such performance might have on the body politic. The public wrestled with this ambivalence as well, but to a lesser extent as the upheavals of subsequent years inspired Americans to enter-tain new and more openly subversive expressions of humorous dissent. As they had done in the days of Artemus Ward, Mark Twain, Will Rogers, and Mort Sahl, many took their cue from the playful audacity of comedians who joked from the fringes of conventional propriety and then, in company with the comedians, redefined convention. Initially hostile, mainstream media and the rest of the national establishment—including the presidency—haltingly struggled to understand the new cultural landscape, then rushed to profit from and manipulate it to their own ends during the coming years. As it turned out, *TW3*, like *The First Family*, heralded this transition. Even though political satire on television died aborning in 1965, it was resurrected in other forms with programs such as *The Smothers Brothers Comedy Hour* just two years later and proliferated further with *Saturday Night Live, Not Necessarily the News, The Daily Show with Jon Stewart, The Colbert Report,* and other programs during the next four decades.

Americans watched, laughed, and learned. Along with taking comedic inspiration from performance groups, *TW3*, and "new" comedians from the later fifties and early sixties (even if the work of some of these comics al-ready seemed naïvely benign), they also were drawn to more radical standup professionals whose work had been considered beyond the pale for various reasons just a year or two before but whose material now began to reverberate with shocking authenticity.

• • •

Lenny Bruce had the greatest influence on this transformation, even though he largely avoided politics and remained unseen and unheard by most Americans. His raw assessment of Vaughn Meader's fate just after Kennedy's murder spoke the brutal truth. Assassination not only killed Kennedy; in the same instant it also blasted the innocent, self-congratulatory depiction of American society that most political humor largely endorsed. With one punch line, Bruce read aloud the dirty writing on the wall: in a new culture of comedic Darwinism that increasingly trumpeted the survival of not merely the funniest but the most cutting, Meader's soft ridicule was becoming extinct. It was gradually replaced by a more corrosive brand of political humor that ate away at the façade of an always beneficent, unimpeachable authority with a ruthlessness more stark than Mort Sahl's or that of any other performer at the time. In a career that lurched from the anonymity of sleazy strip clubs to critical acclaim, then to arrests on obscenity charges, and finally to a drug overdose that killed him in 1966 at the age of forty, Bruce forced the debate over what political humor should sound like in an age of assassination, war, executive deceit, and presidential resignation. Bruce's confrontational style made a mockery of all laughter save that capable of surviving gunfire, and although the country fought against his satiric extremism until well after his death, it ultimately acknowledged his influence in the way it joked and laughed at itself and its leaders.

Born Leonard Schneider in 1925 on Long Island to ill-matched parents who divorced when he was eight, Lenny Bruce absorbed show business life from the start. At the age of twelve Bruce started to accompany his mother, a sometime dance teacher and stripper, to burlesque houses, where she also performed as a comedian and emcee. After serving in the navy during World War II (and being discharged in its waning days when he faked a penchant for cross-dressing), he tried doing impressions and working in film before settling into standup. He slowly graduated from strip joints to roadhouses, then to trendier clubs in Los Angeles, before an appearance in San Francisco in early 1958 introduced him to *Playboy* publisher Hugh Hefner. Hefner, who played midwife to the careers of many comics, including Mort Sahl, booked Bruce into the Cloister, a new club in Chicago. A recording contract with Fantasy Records soon followed.[15]

Bruce's experiences growing up in and surviving "the toilets"—his term for the dives he played early on—bred a comedic style that can best be described as one of shock and awe. He combined what comedian Steve Allen among others acknowledged was the wisdom of a true social philosopher with natural charisma and liberal amounts of confrontation, profanity, and even cruelty to become a lightning rod for controversy. Like Sahl, he reimagined the comedian as jazz artist, blending words and speech rhythms spontaneously into verbal riffs that sometimes lasted a half-hour or more. As he jammed unflinchingly about drugs, sex, corruption, religious hypocrisy, and the harder sides of life, he exuded a kind of hip awareness. Bruce reveled in rebelliously pointing out the disparities between reality and the official *depictions* of reality promulgated by religious, corporate, and civil authorities who reduced it into a neat, rational, and unjustifiably rosy symmetry. In this way he recognized and exposed the "credibility gap" more graphically than any other performer years before the term entered the vernacular during the Vietnam War. His methods ran the gamut from outright cruelty to satire. He would occasionally place a call from the stage to a babysitter to say that her employers, a young suburban couple sitting in the audience, had been killed in a car accident. In one of his most daring routines at the time, titled "How to Relax Your Colored Friends at Parties," he mercilessly satirized the self-righteousness of northern white liberals who pilloried southern racism while barely masking their own bigotry behind grinning pleasantries. The conversation between a white party guest, played by Bruce, and the black pianist hired for the night, played by African American jazz guitarist and friend Eric Miller, included small talk that spoke volumes:

WHITE GUEST: Hey, it's a hell of a spread. They really know how to put out a feast, these people.

BLACK PIANIST: Yes, it's very nice.

WHITE GUEST: Very beautiful. I didn't get your name. . . . Miller? My name's Dennis, Miller.

BLACK PIANIST: Nice to meet you.

WHITE GUEST: I never saw you around this neighborhood. You live around here?

BLACK PIANIST: Yeah, on the other side.

WHITE GUEST: Ah, I was wondering about that. [Pause] That Joe Louis is a hell of a fighter.

BLACK PIANIST: Yeah. . . .

WHITE GUEST: Yeah, there'll never be another Joe Louis. . . . You got a cigarette on you?

BLACK PIANIST: Yeah.

WHITE GUEST: Uh. Oh, the one *you're* smoking? All right, I'll put that out for you. . . . [Pause] That Bojangles. Christ, could he tap-dance.

BLACK PIANIST: Oh . . . yeah.

WHITE GUEST: Oh, you tap-dance a little yourself, huh? All you people can tap-dance, I guess. You people have a natural sense of rhythm. Born right in you, I guess, eh? . . . The way I figure it is, no matter what the hell a guy is, if he stays in his place he's all right. . . . That's what's causing all the trouble in the world. . . . [Pause] Well, here's to Joe Louis. . . . Joe Louis was a guy who . . . knew when to get in there and get out of there, which is more than I can say for a lot of you niggers. . . . [But] you're all right, you're a good boy. Did you have anything to eat yet?

BLACK PIANIST: No, I haven't. I'm not hungry.

WHITE GUEST: I don't know if there's any watermelon left . . . fried chicken. . . . We'll see if we can fix you up with something. Uh, I want to have you over to the house, but I got a bit of a problem. I don't want you to think I'm outta line, but I got a sister, and I hear that you guys . . . you know, my sister . . . and . . . Well, let me put it to you a different way: you wouldn't want no Jew doin' it to *your* sister, would you? That's the way I feel. Well, I don't want no coon doin' it to *my* sister. . . . No offense, you know what I mean?

BLACK PIANIST: Oh, no. Sure.

WHITE GUEST: As far as my sister's concerned, shake hands on it and. . . . You're all right. Hey, listen, I'd like to have you over to the house, like I was tellin' you, but as soon as it gets dark. . . .[16]

To Bruce, "squares"—like the straight-arrow suburban couple with the babysitter—and philanthropic bigots at neighborhood parties were identical in that they lived in fantasy worlds that ultimately perpetuated stereotypes and the unjustified authority of certain people over others. Bruce believed that neither the stereotypes nor the cozy self-deceptions behind them could be tolerated, and that they deserved to be exploded in the most brutal terms. To judge from recordings of his live performances, Bruce's audiences generally tittered, then laughed loudly and knowingly to hide their uncertainty as to whether they were being joked *to* or *about*. Others were left cold. Though hailed by his many fans, most of Bruce's routines were at best considered far out of sync with the middle-class mainstream. At worst they were vociferously condemned as obscene and illegal. Yet as his observations began to ring true against subsequent events and his comedic extremism seemed more fitting to confront abuses of power in general and presidential power in particular, his brand of comedy found increasing appeal. "All my humor is based upon destruction and despair," Bruce once said. "If the world were tranquil, without disease and violence, I'd be standing on the breadline." On the contrary, until Bruce's controversial choice of words began to get in the way during the early 1960s, he was very much in demand.[17]

Bruce's attacks on the presidency usually did not attract denunciation in and of themselves because, unlike Mort Sahl, he rarely focused on the president for long. Part of his political aloofness emanated from his cynical belief that presidents were by definition deceptive and incapable of rehabilitation. In his autobiography he offered an offhand excuse for their behavior— recognizing that to be successful, politicians must be "chameleonlike"— while attacking their essential inhumanity: "I could never visualize Eisenhower even kissing his wife. Not on the mouth, anyway. He didn't even go to the toilet either, he just stood there." His occasional jabs at Eisenhower, Kennedy, and Johnson were typically wrapped in assaults on so many other taboos that it was often hard to know what to take Bruce to task for first. One such routine was "Ike, Sherm, and Nick," a send-up of a 1958 scandal involving Eisenhower's chief of staff, Sherman Adams, whose acceptance from a manufacturer under federal investigation of a vicuña coat and an oriental rug ultimately led to his resignation. In the sketch Ike sends for Richard Nixon ("Hello, Nick sweetie! Sit down, baby") with the idea of dispatching the vice president overseas, thinking that if Nixon were assassinated, it might divert attention from the Adams scandal. The scene takes place not in the White House but "in Ike's apartment," and the president's casual allusions to murder, prostitution, and Nixon's wife Pat's "overdressing"—all while sounding oddly like a stereotypical Jewish mother—compound the effrontery. With Bruce's mockery of so many institutions simultaneously, it was difficult to know how to prioritize offense to the president.[18]

Despite his notoriety (and to some degree because of it), Bruce's comic genius could not be completely ignored by the conventional media. His album *The Sick Humor of Lenny Bruce* earned a Grammy Award nomination, and he appeared on network television a half-dozen times as producers tried to force his round humor into the square hole of TV comedy. One such episode took place in 1959, when Steve Allen booked him on his *Steve Allen Show*. Allen was a comedic visionary who recognized Bruce's prescience even as he acknowledged his raw unpredictability. Allen had pioneered the late-night talk-comedy-variety show format that led to NBC's *Tonight!* (later *The Tonight Show*) in 1954, which he hosted from its premiere until 1957. More than simply understanding the fluid and evolutionary nature of comedy, Allen understood it as performance art. He knew that at the heart of it was an interdependent relationship between the comedian and the audience, and he constantly innovated to nudge this relationship beyond conventional boundaries. He could joke thoughtfully about jazz, history, and philosophy, then deftly turn to broad physical comedy by stripping to the waist, covering himself with peanut butter and jelly, and inviting the audience to attack him with slices of bread. During one 1963 broadcast a pie fight engulfed the entire studio, with the audience (which had thoughtfully been provided with ponchos and caps) getting in some of the best shots. On occasion he would ask his audience if anyone wanted to be a standup comedian, and a few tickled volunteers would be invited onstage to read from cue cards and get laughs they could call their own. Similarly, Allen did not hesitate to introduce his audiences to daring artists like Bruce, who he predicted would make a significant mark on American humor.[19]

Allen also knew, as do all successful comics, that timing is everything. As it turned out, Bruce's appearance in April 1959 was not well timed even though it proved prophetic. Bruce happened to share the bill with those quintessential slapstick artists the Three Stooges, fellow comics but stylistically the "anti-Bruces." Although Allen clearly intended to treat his audience to both extremes of the comedy continuum—Bruce performed first and the Stooges followed as something of a pratfall chaser—the clowns from vaudeville and film brought down the house, while the reputedly shocking new "hip" comedian received polite but rather mystified applause. Having thoroughly sanitized his act to get past the censors, Bruce was out of his element, and the crowd was underwhelmed. With his experiment, however, Allen exercised his cultural authority as a comedian to mediate a new understanding between the American citizenry and a slash-and-burn approach to humor performance that would be increasingly utilized in years to come. Allen's creation of the hugely successful talk-comedy-variety format and the trust he established with his audience enabled him to provide a showcase for all types of performers, including Lenny Bruce, whose brand of cutting-edge iconoclasm slowly gained traction and acceptance. Allen's innovative tenure on late-night television was succeeded by that of Jack Paar—less a comedian than a host and commentator—who helmed *The Tonight Show* from 1957 to 1962 and gave significant television exposure to Mort Sahl (who once substituted for Paar as host), Mike Nichols and Elaine May, the Committee, Bill Cosby, and others at a time when their type of comedy was mostly relegated to clubs and LP records. In 1962 comedian Johnny Carson began his thirty-year reign, not only as the undisputed king of late-night entertainment but also as the most powerful celebrity in America, reestablishing a comedian's authority as an arbiter of popular change on a level unseen since Will Rogers. Over the next decade Carson superimposed his own genius onto Allen's template to become the prime mover behind the country's most popular manifestations of political comedy performance of the late twentieth century, from *Saturday Night Live* to *Late Night with David Letterman* to *The Daily Show with Jon Stewart*, and finally, of course, to Jay Leno's successful iteration of *The Tonight Show* from 1992 to 2009.

Bruce's hollow and mediocre performance on *The Steve Allen Show* in 1959 was hardly transformational in itself, but it foreshadowed the new, more militant brand of humor performance and the medium by which it eventually entered the mass cultural marketplace. If the physicality of the Three Stooges represented the vaudevillian past, and the political satire of Mort Sahl more popularly characterized the trenchant present, Bruce was the herald of the more anarchic and stylized future of satirical showmanship which, for all its originality, still echoed the past.[20]

Although no one — including Lenny Bruce — recognized or acknowledged it at the time, Bruce had much the same transforming effect on Americans' attitudes toward comic performance and its place in the national consciousness as Artemus Ward exactly a century before. He was the Old Showman for a new age. Thanks to his upbringing and ragged climb to stage success through dingy clubs and past abusive hecklers, his perspective on the human condition was thoroughly steeped in what Ward earlier called "the show bizniss," and most of his routines reverberated with the imagery and cool vernacular of stage life. Bob Hope claimed in 1973 that Bruce — for all the controversy surrounding his material and his use of profanity — was his favorite among the younger comedians: "He had so much greasepaint in his blood it came out in his act. That's what I loved about him. He talked our language." What is more, Bruce understood that talking show business was also talking the country's language. The line between performance and reality — between artifice and truth — was effectively nonexistent for Bruce, and he observed that this was largely true for Americans in general. As a result of their obsession with celebrity and the pervasive dominance by the 1960s of entertainment culture, especially television and film, people looked to entertainment as truth and truth as entertainment. They might eye entertainers with moral suspicion or claim to dismiss them outright, but they were in love with show business spectacle and saw much of life through stage-managed illusions, and Bruce thought them hypocrites for not acknowledging as much. Like Artemus Ward before him, Bruce observed that life was blatantly glutted with showmen, whether clad in the costumes of comics, dancers, and clowns or businessmen, religious leaders, and politicians. Like Ward, Bruce performed his own "grate Moral Entertainments" such as the provocative "How to Relax Your Colored Friends at Parties" to expose those leaders' selective morality and tear off the façade of veneration that had been constructed around them. While Ward's tactics were infinitely more subtle and broadly appealing, both he and Bruce attacked their audiences' perceptions of their world and their leaders with satire and laughter. Finally, like Ward, Bruce rarely performed political material overtly, but he modeled the audacity that would mark other comics in the years ahead.[21]

Nothing better illustrated the intertwining of the performance of comedy with the comedy of life than Bruce's very real legal troubles over his act and the words that constituted it. He was first arrested on obscenity charges in San Francisco in October 1961 for using the word "cocksucker" onstage to attack the prejudicial treatment of homosexuals. Although the performance was before a paying audience who appeared untroubled by his language, the arresting police officer, maintaining it was his duty to clean up the neighborhood, claimed that the word and the act it described were fundamentally harmful. "Our society is not geared to it," he told Bruce as he led the comedian to the patrol car. Bruce was acquitted, but the episode was just the first in a series of confrontations that placed him in a legal and cultural tug-of-war with the establishment he so passionately assailed. He was banned from a growing list of cities, states, and foreign countries. The police routinely infiltrated his appearances, and he was arrested nineteen times over the next four years for a variety of offenses ranging from obscenity to making vulgar references to sexual acts and to the Catholic Church. Simple harassment seemed to be the objective in most instances; either charges were dropped or Bruce was ultimately acquitted in all cases until his infamous obscenity trial in New York City in 1964. Arrested for using more than one hundred obscene words and, among other things, making demeaning references to Eleanor Roosevelt's breasts and Jackie Kennedy's "hauling ass" out of the limousine in Dallas "to save [her] ass" after her husband was shot, Bruce was conspicuously brought to trial. The proceeding became a referendum on artistic free speech that held the nation's attention for weeks. He was convicted late that year in a decision that not only effectively ended his career—already crippled by the many earlier trials—but also rendered a verdict on tolerance in America's performance culture, especially toward the more radical forms of satire and ridicule. Between Bruce's extremism onstage and the prosecutions against him, Americans found scant middle ground. Forced to choose, they generally sided against the comedian in a culture war opposing what they were convinced was a legitimate threat to the nation's foundational institutions. Although New York governor George Pataki granted Bruce a posthumous pardon in 2003, the wider conflict over comedy and language raged on, most notably with George Carlin's many arrests during the early 1970s for uttering "the seven words you can never say on television." Despite the popular repudiation of him in 1964, Bruce introduced a radically acidic comedic form that proved transformative and gained currency even by the time of his death two years later from an overdose of morphine. If American society was not, in the words of the arresting officer in San Francisco, "geared to" Bruce's humor in 1961, by the last years of the decade it had become the modus operandi for many in a new legion of comedians—professional and amateur, white and minority—who used it to get the last laugh at a political establishment they considered guilty of performing consummate obscenities from, among other stages, the Oval Office.[22]

Less than a year before his death, Bruce performed through the fog of his deepening drug abuse and legal problems at a community theater in Berkeley, California. In one of his few direct assaults on a president, he mocked Lyndon Johnson by imitating what he considered a speech defect that revealed the president to be no less bigoted than the suburban liberals he had ridiculed five years before:

> No matter how profound a speech that Lyndon Johnson ever would make, he could never make it. . . . They didn't let him *talk* for the first six months. It took him six months to learn how to say "Negro." [He would say] "Nigger-row." [Advisers would say,] okay . . . ah, let's hear it one more time, Lyndon, now. . . . [Bruce as Johnson,] "Nigger. Oh! Oh! Nigger-oh. I can't help it! I can't say it, that's all! I can't say 'Niggra.' . . . Nee-gerr-oh . . . Na-gra . . . Nee-gra-oh. . . . Lemme show you my scar!

To the end, Bruce comically exposed artifice through the elemental components of language and sound. In fact Johnson's natural speech patterns— saturated as they were in the drawl of rural central Texas—did occasionally cause him embarrassing problems with the word "Negro," the commonly accepted appellation for African Americans at the time. Bruce capitalized on this peculiarity to indict the president, who seemed to find it comparatively easy to lift his shirt and publicly reveal his scar from gall bladder surgery— which he had proudly shown off to reporters and photographers earlier that year—yet was unable to confront directly the nagging contradictions of race in America. Johnson's signing of the landmark Civil Rights Act of 1964 had been followed only weeks later by his refusal to recognize the integrated delegation from the Mississippi Freedom Democratic Party in favor of that state's traditional all-white representatives at the Democratic National Convention which nominated him for president. Furthermore, while the Voting Rights Act of 1965 offered real hope to disenfranchised blacks in the rural South, such promises from the Johnson White House did little to address the persistent, crushing discrimination in urban America. Less than a week after the Voting Rights Act was signed, a black neighborhood in Los Angeles— Watts—erupted in five days of rioting that took thirty-four lives. To many, these and other contradictions proved that Johnson's good intentions were irrelevant. They were thin cover for entrenched national attitudes and official policies that perpetuated chronic racism. Although by this time Bruce was considered a cultural pariah by mainstream America and his comments about Johnson were discounted by most people as the ramblings of a self-absorbed tragic fool, his ability to speak truth to power—explosively through satire and laughter—was widely co-opted by comics who followed, including a growing number of Americans who believed that through telling jokes and getting laughs, a measure of power and psychological liberation might be realized by those long denied it.[23]

• • •

Dick Gregory was one of those performers. The young black comic was impressed by Bruce's agile and authentic use of hip vernacular, his spontaneity, and his unapologetic honesty. Gregory considered Bruce "the eighth wonder of the world" and, marveling at his boldness, commented that if authorities "don't kill him or throw him in jail he's liable to shake up this whole fuckin' country." During Gregory's brief reign as one of the country's most talked-about standup comedians, he moved from more conventional strategies for getting laughs toward a heightened political militancy that echoed Bruce's even as it paralleled the growing radicalism within the civil rights movement.[24]

The dominant definition of what it meant to be "American" remained uncompromisingly white, Anglo-Saxon, and heterosexual until well after World War II, but by the early 1960s the intensifying struggle by African Americans for civil rights made the full meaning of Americanism hotly contested, and humor played an important role in the debate. During the three centuries of bondage and discrimination that had legally and culturally disenfranchised them from the privileges of American liberty, African Americans engendered a rich and complex tradition of humor as a means of survival, hope, and veiled rebellion. Capitalizing on this tradition and the gains made through the more direct strategies of court action and civil disobedience executed during the 1950s and early 1960s—including the Supreme Court's 1954 *Brown v. Board of Education* decision, the Montgomery bus boycott in 1955–56, and the hard-won successes of the sit-in movement and Freedom Rides during the early 1960s—African American comedians not only joined the cultural insurgency waged by Mort Sahl, the Second City, Lenny Bruce, and others but also started to effect attitudinal change by successfully utilizing performance to ridicule the tenacious and absurd disparities they observed throughout the country. Riding the new wave of popularity of standup comedy and satire, these artists began to break away from the poorly paying all-black "chitlin' circuit" of clubs and integrate into white venues with a delicate balance between cautious pragmatism and fearless conviction.

Styles varied among these comedians, but the results they achieved could be equally effective. Bill Cosby used laughter disarmingly; his hilarious but nonconfrontational stories of growing up in urban North Philadelphia heightened national consciousness concerning ghetto life even as the exploits of his characters Fat Albert and Weird Harold tickled funny bones. Gregory was likewise careful to meet his audiences across the common ground of laughter, but he confronted discrimination with a more deliberate and trenchant brand of satire that, for him, more accurately matched the fierce racism he had experienced growing up in the slums of St. Louis. Initially his humor also was limited to clubs in the chitlin' circuit, but in January 1961 he became the first African American to achieve significant success with large white audiences when he was asked to stand in for the resident comic at Chicago's Playboy Club. The show, which was performed before a crowd of frozen-food conventioneers from the South, appeared doomed when he took the stage to ice-cold stares and insulting remarks. Then he began to speak:

> Good evening, ladies and gentlemen. I understand there are a good many Southerners in the room tonight. I know the South very well. I spent twenty years there one night. . . .
>
> It's dangerous for me to go back South. You see, when I drink, I think I'm Polish. One night I got so drunk, I moved out of my own neighborhood. . . .
>
> Last time I was down South, I walked into this restaurant. This white waitress came up to me and said: "We don't serve colored people here."
>
> I said, "That's all right, I don't eat colored people, no way! Bring me a whole fried chicken."
>
> About that time, these three cousins came in. You know the ones I mean—Ku, Klux, and Klan. They said, "Boy, we're givin' you fair warnin'. Anything you do to that chicken, we're gonna do to you." About then, the waitress brought me my whole chicken and the cousins said, "Remember, boy, anything you do to that chicken, we're gonna do to you." So I put down my knife and fork, picked up that chicken, and kissed it![25]

Gregory won over the mostly southern audience. His comic misdirection and self-deprecation managed to create a bond with his listeners despite an attack on bigotry that easily could have alienated them, and the scheduled fifty-minute performance went on for twice that long. Several in the audience tipped him as they went out, and Hugh Hefner, who caught that night's second show, launched Gregory's career as he had Bruce's by signing him to a three-year contract. Other offers followed, including recording deals from the Vee-Jay and Colpix record labels and appearances on television with Jack Paar and others. By the following year Gregory could remark: "When

I left St. Louis, I was making five dollars a night. Now I'm getting $5,000 a week—for saying the same things out loud I used to say under my breath."[26]

In fact Gregory was fully aware what sorts of jokes he could and could not make to a white audience, no matter how outwardly encouraging the crowd. As his debut at the Playboy Club demonstrated, his routines were carefully designed to establish rapport across the middle ground of shared laughter, not to exploit racial sympathy that could come and go in an instant depending on the crowd or even the day's news. He knew he had to, in his words, "go up there as an individual first, a Negro second. I've got to be a colored funny man, not a funny colored man." Consequently his material regularly included light jabs at himself and the civil rights movement, such as the joke in which, asked to buy a lifetime membership in the National Association for the Advancement of Colored People (NAACP), he said he'd rather pay a week at a time. "Hell of a thing to buy a lifetime membership, wake up one morning and find the country's been integrated." Once trust had been established, he was freer to aim barbs at his audience: "Wouldn't it be a hell of a thing if all this was burnt cork [blackface makeup] and you people were being tolerant for nothing?"[27]

Using this strategy Gregory was able to reach a level of acceptance that permitted him to join the likes of Mort Sahl and Lenny Bruce and—unlike most black comedians—take on topical subjects and politics directly, including the presidency. Other African American comics had used the president as the basis for self-deprecating humor but not as the punch line of the joke. During the 1950s Timmie Rogers enjoyed great success among mostly black audiences with a routine titled "If I Were President." A typical joke combined dependable mother-in-law humor with self-insult:

> ROGERS AS THE PRESIDENT: Now, Momma, you can't talk to me like that, I am the President of the United States.
> MOTHER-IN-LAW: Yeah, another one of your temporary jobs. In four years, you'll be back on the street again.

By contrast, Gregory was able to elicit laughter at the expense of the presidency from the beginning with an easy confidence. On one of his first albums, *East and West*, he made frequent references to John F. Kennedy's foreign policy troubles in the wake of the Bay of Pigs debacle and his frustration at the Soviet Union's renewed testing of nuclear weapons. Following the second successful flight of a Soviet cosmonaut when Americans were still struggling to get an astronaut into orbit for the first time, he speculated that the frustrated president "probably went downstairs and kicked Caroline." It was a daring joke, especially from a black comedian in 1961, but the intimate gathering at San Francisco's hungry i—where the second side of the album was recorded—laughed appreciatively. Such jokes became commonplace, and in time Gregory's assaults grew even more biting. During the 1964 presidential election he compared the choice between Lyndon Johnson and Barry Goldwater to being forced to choose between a full-time prostitute and a weekend prostitute, saying, "If you choose the lesser of two evils and marry the weekend prostitute, you're only fooling yourself if you don't think you're marrying a whore."[28]

Like Timmie Rogers, Gregory often used the device of imagining himself president for the purpose of gaining laughs, but his popularity among white as well as black audiences and the wider public discourse over racial equality made the effect of Gregory's humor on the national consciousness more potent. It was reminiscent of earlier political comedians, including Seba Smith during the first third of the nineteenth century and Will Rogers one hundred years later. Wielding the cultural authority he earned as a comedian, Gregory comically reduced the status of the presidency while simultaneously elevating everyday Americans. In a 1961 performance he responded to the prediction by Kennedy's brother Attorney General Robert F. Kennedy that a black man would be elected president before the end of the century by placing himself in the Oval Office:

> You heard what Bobby Kennedy said: thirty years from this year a Negro can become president? Treat me right or I'll get in there and raise taxes on you. If I was president, you talkin' about good livin'? Everybody would be swingers! That's right, the first thing I'd do is repeal the [1910] Mann Act [outlawing the transporting of prostitutes across state lines] and anything else that discouraged travel in this country. I think I'd grab [jazz great Louis Armstrong] and make him my secretary of state; [jazz performer] Dizzy Gillespie would be my vice president, and I'll give you [whites] a job just so they won't say I'm prejudiced. That's what I would do my first day in office. My second day I'd take Georgia, North Carolina, Mississippi, Louisiana, Alabama and make it a H-bomb testing area.

By whimsically wielding executive privilege to fill his cabinet with jazz musicians, obliterate the Jim Crow South, and show magnanimity toward the newly subjugated white majority, Gregory commandeered imaginary control from that quintessential symbol of American political power, the White House, and put it in the hands not of the conventional American everyman as had Seba Smith or Will Rogers but of black Americans, the constituency traditionally understood to be society's lowliest and utterly discounted previously from mainstream discussions of power. Gregory's word picture is clearly a comic fantasy. He knew the notion of a black president was not close to being realized, and he could not resist the temptation to get a big laugh by exploiting the stereotype of black sexual licentiousness. Yet just as Mr. Dooley bridged the gaping distance between President William McKinley and the Irish Americans of Chicago by fancifully imagining the president at his bar six decades before the election of an Irish American named Kennedy, Gregory was the first to do the same for African Americans from within the spotlight of mainstream popular culture. As a celebrity he could perform fleeting glimpses of black empowerment before large audiences by using the beguiling triviality of humor. Such images offered encouragement to African Americans, for whom the very presence of a black comic in a white club was a hopeful sign. The scenario was more disconcerting for white audiences, whose enthusiastic response signaled a complex cultural transaction. Their laughter could be simultaneously interpreted as expressing communal solidarity with Gregory's ambition for political equality, good-naturedly dismissing the preposterous absurdity of a black president, and attempting to obscure the serious discomfort many harbored concerning such a prospect. Robert Kennedy's prediction proved to be overly optimistic by a decade and a half—it took forty-seven years from 1961, not thirty, for America to elect an African American president—but Gregory's jokes put the country on notice that the audacity of all Americans laying claim to the presidency now extended beyond class and ethnicity to include race.[29]

Co-opting the presidency was part of Dick Gregory's evolution as an increasingly abrasive and confrontational comedian. Although he would frequently give up performing for years or decades at a time to pursue social issues and various activist causes more deliberately (he ran a write-in campaign for president in 1968 touting his credentials as an activist, not a comic), he consistently presented a satirist's view of institutional power. Along with the work of other comedians, his more consistently humorous material during the early and mid-1960s provided a liberating if symbolic measure of resistance to a presidency that seemed obsessed with both the accumulation of power and the elimination of accountability.

• • •

For most of the twentieth century, the executive branch—citing the imperatives of the Great Depression, World War II, and the cold war—ballooned steadily to produce what historian Arthur M. Schlesinger Jr. termed an "imperial presidency" that many believed finally exceeded its constitutional authority with the escalation of American involvement in the Vietnam War in 1965. Claiming the mantle of commander in chief and invoking their oath to "preserve, protect, and defend the Constitution of the United States," presidents declared the right to make unilateral and secret decisions, bypass the normal checks and balances by Congress and the Supreme Court, and in effect become, argued Schlesinger, "the most absolute monarch among the great powers of the world." Americans generally accepted this gradual concentration of authority during the twenty years after World War II because they acknowledged the concept of a pervasive, monolithic threat posed by international communism; they maintained a high level of confidence in the abiding truthfulness of the president; and they enjoyed — at least to some degree — an emotional bond with their leader based on respect, admiration, and increasingly a sense of humor.[30]

Public acceptance of all three of these tenets began to collapse during the administration of Lyndon Johnson. Unlike the attack on Pearl Harbor that precipitated American involvement in World War II, the United Nations resolution that gave legitimacy to the Korean War, and the imminent threat to American security posed by the Cuban Missile Crisis, the Gulf of Tonkin resolution which authorized Johnson to take any steps he chose in Vietnam soon seemed suspect. Quickly introduced by Johnson and passed just as rapidly by an acquiescent Congress in August 1964, it gave the president sweeping power to conduct combat operations yet was based on dubious reports of attacks by North Vietnamese gunboats on American destroyers that caused no casualties. As the war dragged on, the connection between the Vietnam conflict and a worldwide communist menace that could easily jump from Southeast Asia to the beaches of California became more difficult to sustain. Even more profoundly, the Gulf of Tonkin crisis initiated a litany of calculated deceptions by Johnson designed to maintain popular and congressional support for the war. After the repeated lies predicting imminent victory were exposed by a coordinated series of surprise enemy attacks in early 1968 known as the Tet Offensive, Johnson's presidency suffered widely from a credibility gap that had already begun to permeate other priorities of his administration, including civil rights and the promotion of his Great Society programs.

Other presidents — most notably Franklin Roosevelt and John F. Kennedy — were able to mitigate their use of widening executive power by forging a deliberate personal connection with the electorate, and their use of humor toward this end was masterly. Lyndon Johnson proved incapable of doing the same. Despite his sincere desire to perfect American life and end poverty and racial injustice, and his hatred of the Vietnam War in human terms, the duplicity surrounding his policies cost him dearly with the American people. More fundamentally, he was painfully insecure and sensitive; Barry Goldwater maintained, "His skin is a millionth of an inch thick." Whereas Roosevelt and Kennedy projected a humor that most Americans accepted as a sign of humanity, strength, and self-assurance, Johnson's needs for affection and reassurance were so urgent, especially toward the end of his administration, that they precluded his using humor patiently or strategically. Johnson could be funny among small groups and was often praised for his sense of humor during the 1964 campaign. *New York Times* contributor Alvin Shuster claimed that he had "forgotten more kneeslappers than most people [had ever] heard," but he was referring to Johnson's penchant for hackneyed anecdotes and one-liners, many of them off-color, that had little positive impact and often contributed negatively to his reputation for boorishness compared to the urbane Kennedy.[31]

In addition, while Johnson's personal style was completely given over to politics—the next election or the next congressional vote—for all his genius as a campaigner and persuader, he had little understanding of the interdependence of politics and the wider culture, and he never appreciated the way humor could be used to insinuate his policies favorably over the heads of his critics and into popular opinion through the mass media. Rather than command the performance at news conferences, for example, Johnson attempted to avoid it altogether by announcing the briefings at the last minute, holding them on weekends, or monopolizing them with opening statements that consumed much of the allotted time. This failure to capitalize more constructively on the media's powerful role in modern culture was particularly ironic, given that much of Johnson's and his wife, Lady Bird's, personal fortune came from their shrewd purchase and management of several radio and television stations in Texas. Nevertheless, this strategy—or lack of one—left him ill-equipped either to disarm attacks with public good humor or to retaliate with stinging wit of his own. Whereas Kennedy worked news conferences like an entertainer in the midst of cold war tensions, Franklin Roosevelt confronted deep adversity by displaying a buoyant jocularity to journalists and the public, and Abraham Lincoln countered criticism with an instinctive and self-effacing use of humor during the Civil War, Johnson could bring no such talent to bear to help alleviate the horrific crises caused by the war in Vietnam. In the end, despite the combination of flattery, relentlessness, intimidation, and scheming—the very strengths defining "the Johnson treatment" which made him extraordinarily effective as Senate majority leader during the 1950s—he was incapable of communicating honestly with the American people, humorously or otherwise. When humorists struck—whether with the pen, as in the work of columnists such as Art Buchwald and the cartoons of Jules Feiffer; from the theater, as playwright Barbara Garson did with her scathing 1967 satire *MacBird!*, a send-up of *Macbeth* depicting the political combat between Johnson and the Kennedy brothers; or in the satiric sketches that were beginning to gain a tenuous foothold on network television thanks to *TW3* and, later, *The Smothers Brothers Comedy Hour*—he could respond to the jokes and sardonic laughs with only vindictiveness or the stunned shock of deep personal injury.[32]

With Johnson defenseless against mockery, and despite most Americans' continued approval of the involvement in Vietnam if not his handling of it, a growing minority—especially among baby boomers of draft age—gleefully attacked. Emboldened by the contradictions of the times, the array of print satire from *Mad* to the irreverent ridicule of other popular magazines such as the *Realist*, and the trenchant performances of Mort Sahl, Tom Lehrer, Lenny Bruce, and Dick Gregory, Americans increasingly reveled in taking on the role of comedian. Amateurs, professionals, and a legion of would-be stars went on the offensive to reduce the inflated imperial presidency to its comedic nadir with barbs that ranged from clever one-liners, to unoriginal lighthearted parody, to cutting assaults on the president himself that were unprecedented in American entertainment culture.

Jabs at authority emerged more commonly from the grass roots as comedy seeped, according to a 1966 article in *Time* magazine, "into every corner of American life," with "spreading hipness and . . . general joking" established as the newest common currency of popular culture. The creative and stealthy "people's humor" that was expressed through elephant jokes a few years before continued to bloom in new ways, as diverse groups, including middle-class office workers and the rising counterculture, engaged in comedy performance as a form of revolt against the status quo. Through casual dialogue in the workplace or innovative print media such as graffiti or underground newspapers, people improvised comical responses to what they perceived as the absurd contradictions between the preachings of authority and practices that reeked of deceit and hypocrisy. The president was included as the butt of jokes that often started out as graffiti or bumper stickers but then got laughs from ad hoc audiences when they were repeated in the workplace, at demonstrations, or other gatherings. One popular example, reiterated as Johnson committed growing numbers of troops to the war, urged Americans to "Commit LBJ, Not the U.S.A." Another softly and wishfully kidded, "LBJ Loves Ho Chi Minh," while still another offered counsel on the president's Vietnam policy with a scathing sexual reference that would have done Lenny Bruce proud: "LBJ—Pull Out Like Your Old Man Should Have."[33]

Americans also consumed full-length treatments of Johnson on LP. A rash of comedy albums proliferated in a shotgun approach to presidential humor as producers hoped to duplicate the success of *The First Family* with titles such as *LBJ Menagerie*, *LBJ in the Catskills*, *Here Comes the Bird*, and *Meet the Great Society*. While these LPs found an audience, their humor was uneven, often seemed forced, and rang hollow in the absence of consistent writing and the communal goodwill that had surrounded Vaughn Meader's 1962 hit, when all those involved—the people, the president, and the comedian—at least seemed complicit in the merriment. Now, amid the antagonism and cynicism of the later 1960s, fewer people enjoyed quaint lampoons of the president and his family or were willing to laugh at a formula that seemed as distant and irrelevant as vaudeville, even though it had made a star of Meader only a few years before. Part of the problem, too, according to playwright and director George Abbott, was that with Johnson, the object of the satire was too absurd to be funny. "Humor is exaggeration," he said, "and President Johnson is his own exaggeration."[34]

Other performances cut much deeper. One album, produced by Lew Irwin and the Credibility Gap in 1968, titled *An Album of Political Pornography*, viewed the Washington establishment and the electoral process as a prostitution of democracy. Set in June to September of that year—from the assassination of Robert F. Kennedy to the violent demonstrations at the Democratic National Convention in Chicago—the album (which came with a "political sickness bag" tucked in the liner) is a collage of interviews, speeches, mock news reports, and commentary, with dark satire and blatant sexual imagery running throughout. In the album's opening scene the narrator describes America as a sullied temptress while a crowd sings "America the Beautiful" in the background:

> I hear America singing. A rousing, arousing tune. Turning on in 1968 for the act of '69. . . . We have unlocked history's chastity belt, exposed the vulnerable softness, and displayed the piece to anyone who would look. America the beautiful, 1968. A piece of her. . . . A femme fatale, *very* fatale. Could there be a spot on her marked "fraud"?

The album includes clips of speeches by Robert Kennedy and Johnson (described provocatively as among the "lovers of the body politic") debating Vietnam, urban violence, and other issues. But in the end, following Kennedy's murder and the other events of that traumatic year, Americans are resigned to "casting votes in vain." The act of voters punching their ballots with pointed styluses is described as ritualized fornication: "millions of people, standing behind curtains, pushing their shafts into the holes." By equating democratic authority—that of the voter as well as the chief executive—with forced or at least futile sexual intercourse, the album underscored a mordant and explicit cynicism in American political humor that, while hardly new in the decades since World War II, was gaining deeper popular traction. The Credibility Gap never became a household name, but they did enjoy success for the next eight years and went on to produce subsequent albums for the mainstream record labels Capitol and Warner Brothers. The group served as a launching pad for many who would reach stardom in other media, including Michael McKean and David Lander, who portrayed the off-center greasers Lenny and Squiggy on the popular 1970s television sitcom *Laverne and Shirley*, and Harry Shearer, whose voice is a regular feature on *The Simpsons* and who appeared with McKean on *Saturday Night Live* and in the film "mockumentaries" *This Is Spinal Tap* and *A Mighty Wind. An Album of Political Pornography* was not a best-seller, but only five years after the violent death of a president temporarily paralyzed American humor, comedians rearmed themselves with a ready response—dark, fatalistic, and more radical—to the needs of the age, and audiences began to laugh with the shock of recognition.[35]

One of the most vitriolic assaults came from the Committee. By the late 1960s the California-based performance troupe had become a focal point for the emerging counterculture and the venue for many of its more satirical expressions. Folksinger Arlo Guthrie first sang his antiwar classic "Alice's Restaurant" while a guest performer at its San Francisco theater. In late January 1968, just days before the start of the surprise attacks by Vietnamese communists in the Tet Offensive, the group responded to Lyndon Johnson's State of the Union speech and his plans to continue aggressive bombing with a live sketch that demonized the president to new extremes. While a fellow cast member wearing a cowboy hat sat behind an artificial television screen and imitated Johnson's delivery, Howard Hesseman—a future star of *WKRP in Cincinnati*—listened in frustration and finally grew furious enough to turn off the television set. Johnson's image remained, however, as the president taunted Hesseman, saying, "You can't turn me off—I'm you." Enraged, Hesseman turned to the audience:

> That man made me crazy. . . . I've spent most of my consciousness… trying to get rid of hate, . . . [but when] I watched Lyndon Johnson I discovered that I had been completely unsuccessful and that all that rage and all that desire to kill was brought out by him. And you know something—IT FELT GOOD!
>
> It felt good to have someone as hateful as LBJ to hate. And I know that everyone here in the audience also hates him. We've all experienced hate for him and you may not have admitted it as I have . . . but you all hate this motherfucker.

Hesseman and the cast then took up the chant, "It's fun to hate, it's fun to hate," and the audience yelled back, some calling out their objections, others laughing and carrying the chant to crescendo. As the actor playing Johnson continued to drone, "You can't turn me off—I'm you," Hesseman turned back to the crowd: "There. Didn't that feel good? But obviously hate doesn't work. . . . But maybe, just maybe if we try hard enough we can love the bastard to death." At this the cast, then the audience, began to act out spontaneous expressions of love, kissing, hugging, and laughing, again to a climax. Then, on cue, the theater was suddenly plunged into darkness and a female cast member screamed in a high-pitched voice: "VIETNAM!" The crowd was stunned. In the swirl of mixed signals and emotional extremes, the audience was uncertain how to react. Eventually the participants slowly left the theater, all discussing what had happened and their reactions to it.[36]

As they engaged in an improvisation of tribal play, this tiny ensemble of Americans lashed out in unrestrained hostility against the presidency using an extreme form of satire that danced dangerously on—and, many would argue, well beyond—the fringe of humor and ridicule. Some comedians were urging Americans to attack the presidency, or at least keep their distance from it, claiming that as John F. Kennedy and Lyndon Johnson demonstrated, presidents were either being shot or making a good case why they should be. Such open expressions were rare, but as the undercurrent of distrust in established authority quickened, it was articulated in increasingly confrontational ways. One sign at an antiwar demonstration pointedly asked, "Lee Harvey Oswald, where are you now?" Such blatant tactics were not adopted by mainstream society; still, the wider strategy of assaulting authority more openly through derision began to permeate the broader culture in other ways. By the late 1960s most traces had been obliterated of what Will Rogers and other comic stars earlier recognized as a "golden mean" in humor, an ethical boundary that prevented comedy intended to *strengthen* an established culture from *subverting* it instead. Rather, countercultural impulses now incited precisely such revolutionary subversion. As American humor became more definitively political in all respects, it developed a penchant for exploding taboos on-site, with the hope of forging a new culture from the ashes.[37]

Even as the performance of political humor became more militant, some tapped into comedy's less strident—if no less flamboyant—forms to produce antic expressions of street theater that drew crowds and headlines. Boxing champion Muhammad Ali was a naturally gifted humorist whose wide appeal extended beyond his extraordinary talent in the ring to include a quick and sophisticated wit. After winning the heavyweight boxing championship and joining the Nation of Islam, Ali was drafted but refused to be inducted into the army on religious grounds and—more controversially—cited the persistent racial injustice in the country when he famously declared: "I ain't got no quarrel with those Vietcong. They never called me 'nigger.'" He was convicted of draft evasion, sentenced to five years in prison, and stripped of his title; but when he appealed the verdict (which was unanimously overturned by the Supreme Court in 1971), his became an outspoken voice against the Johnson administration's war policies and for black empowerment. He was able to delight large audiences at lectures and rallies with improvisational scats that landed punches on America's color-coded assumptions about goodness and power, including the power of the presidency:

> Everything of authority was made white. We look at Jesus. We see a white with blond hair and blue eyes. We look at all the angels. We see white [figures] with blond hair and blue eyes. Now I'm sure if there's a heaven in the sky and the colored folks die and go to heaven, [you might ask] where are all the colored angels? They must be in the kitchen pre-parin' the milk and honey!
>
> We were taught when we were little children that Mary had a little lamb whose feet were white as snow. Then we were taught about Snow White. . . .
>
> Angel food cake is the white cake, but the devil's food cake is the chocolate cake.
>
> All the good cowboys ride the *white* horses and wear *white* hats. [Pause] The *White* House.[38]

As Ali's lyric humor drew thunderous applause and laughter, the hippie counterculture employed the spectacle of physical comedy to win converts and draw attention. Abbie Hoffman was by far the movement's most creative and anarchistic jester. Attuned to several muses—his drive for social revolution, a comedic genius, and hallucinogenic drugs—Hoffman created not "guerrilla" humor but what he preferred to call "monkey" humor, aimed at joining the hippie lifestyle to antiwar politics. The Worcester, Massachusetts, native was an early civil rights activist before teaming up with fellow radical Jerry Rubin in 1967 to stage some of the decade's most memorable impractical jokes. That August he scattered dollar bills onto the floor of the New York Stock Exchange, briefly tripping up the capitalist juggernaut when business temporarily came to a halt while traders scrambled for the cash. Two months later he led the effort in Washington, D.C., to exorcise the Pentagon of its war demons by encircling the five-sided bastion of the U.S. military with hippies and attempting to levitate it. While that particular effort failed to get off the ground, despite the ruling of an amused judge who permitted raising the building to "a maximum of ten feet," the two-day demonstration reverberated with other acts, such as stuffing flowers into the rifle barrels of soldiers protecting the Pentagon, as well as rumors of plans, including one reported by *Time* magazine, to kidnap Johnson by "wrestling him to the ground and pulling his pants off." In the aftermath Hoffman encouraged followers to prepare for the following year's Democratic convention in Chicago by making thousands of "Vote for Me" buttons and planning to rush the podium to nominate themselves.[39]

While this particular scheme did not materialize, Chicago in 1968 still afforded Hoffman and his comrades their greatest stage. On New Year's Eve he joined with Rubin and others—including Dick Gregory—to declare themselves Yippies: committed to mobilizing hippie youth (the Y) internationally (the I), and, according to their founding manifesto, to add "meaning, fun, [and] ecstasy in their lives—a party" (the P). Some 2,500 strong, this "Youth International Party" congregated in Chicago late that August for the Democratic National Convention. In opposition to the 6,500 delegates and more than twice that many police, army troops, and national guardsmen marshaled by Mayor Richard Daley to enforce peace, the Yippies looked to perform a Festival of Life to ridicule what they considered a convention of death inside the hall. Most famously they nominated "Pigasus," a pig, for president in the streets outside the convention, reasoning that in a society where all representatives of established authority were "pigs," this was the most honest choice. "They nominate a president and he eats the people," claimed the campaign slogan. "We nominate a president and the people eat him."[40]

The Yippies' antics were short-lived—owing in large part to Hoffman's and Rubin's indictment and trial on charges of conspiracy and incitement to riot as members of the "Chicago 8"—yet their extremist capers contributed to the transformation of entertainment culture during the late 1960s. The mass media, especially television, had a field day with the Yippies, much to the satisfaction of Hoffman, for whom such attention was a prime objective—all publicity was good publicity—and to the disgust of many in the movement who considered the mainstream media part of the corrupt establishment. Hoffman projected the seductive smile and boundless energy of a carnival barker, and his ability to orchestrate memorable images and churn out convenient sound bites proved irresistible to editors and producers. Recognizing Yippie high jinks for what Hoffman said they were—"part vaudeville, part insurrection, part communal recreation"—the media capitalized on his showmanship to broadcast the exotic sights and sounds of "real subversion" to a captivated national audience hooked on entertainment. As a result, the psychedelic spectacle of the Yippies—combined with the broader kaleidoscope of images from the counterculture in general—became increasingly absorbed into the national consciousness alongside the bloody images of war and riots. Stylistically Hoffman and his fellow performers were directly inspired by the show business anarchy of Lenny Bruce, but strategically they absorbed the lessons of Franklin Roosevelt and Jack Kennedy. Just as these presidents used charismatic humor to shape perceptions of themselves and their policies at news conferences and before the general public, Hoffman and his co-comedians became adept at manipulating the media into playing their brand of rebellion to a mass audience. Simultaneously, as the rebellion attracted viewers—supporters and critics equally—radicalism took on a measure of economic legitimacy, and the comedic trappings of antiauthoritarian protest gained consumer appeal. For the first time since collective laughter united Kennedy, Meader, and an eager buying public in 1962 and 1963, media executives and sponsors began seriously to reassess the value of political humor to their balance sheets.[41]

• • •

The force motivating this reassessment was the baby boom generation. The cohort most responsible for producing this new brand of comedy was also most likely to consume it. Born alongside television, baby boomers grew up addicted to popular culture purveyed by the electronic media, and as eighteen- to twenty-four-year-olds became the largest and most lucrative demographic target for advertisers, the media were increasingly addicted to them. Many young people's heightened skepticism, then deepening cynicism, about authority coincided neatly with the rise of humorous iconoclasm in advertising that already was proving enormously effective with all ages. In 1966 the long cigarettes manufactured by Benson and Hedges grew popular by literally not fitting in; rather, in TV and print ads they tended to get stuck in elevator doors or jut out from standard-size cigarette cases. The Vern Staley Dodge dealership in Pittsburgh, which had briefly sold cars by imitating Kennedy's voice in 1963, two years later echoed Chrysler's national advertising campaign that urged Americans to "Join the Dodge Rebellion." Perhaps most successfully, the soft drink 7-Up did battle with established giants Coca-Cola and Pepsi by proclaiming itself "the Uncola" beginning in 1968. Insurgent nonconformity was in vogue, and broadcasters complemented advertisers' rejection of traditional power relationships by producing programs that likewise challenged standard television formats, particularly the variety show and the situation comedy. These decisions were usually calculated; CBS's *All in the Family, Maude, M*A*S*H,* and the *Mary Tyler Moore Show* pioneered this shift toward topical, provocative sitcoms in the early 1970s. Others were inadvertent. A pair of folk-singing comedians—the Smothers Brothers—had revolted against traditional variety show expectations several years earlier by taking ridicule of the political establishment into the sacred zone of prime time television orthodoxy: 9 o'clock on Sunday evenings.[42]

Tom and Dick Smothers were clean-cut California college dropouts who parlayed their folk music abilities and comic timing into a successful career built on nightclub engagements and—after appearing on *The Jack Paar Show* in 1961 and as regulars on *The Steve Allen Show*—a string of popular comedy albums. In February 1967 CBS put them on the air in its latest attempt to dethrone NBC's ratings juggernaut, the family western drama *Bonanza*, and to everyone's amazement, *The Smothers Brothers Comedy Hour* vaulted to instant success. The combination of offbeat comedy sketches, an eclectic assortment of guests, and the brothers' guise of youthful innocence attracted audiences of all ages. Young people delighted in the smart writing, irreverent send-ups of popular folksongs, and appearances by top music acts such as The Doors and Janis Joplin, while older audiences were reassured by their fresh-faced wholesomeness, clean vocal harmonies, and traditional comedy credentials, validated by guests such as George Burns and Jack Benny. CBS rewarded the duo with a long-term contract and, given the show's apparently harmless content, continued to grant them creative control over the program.[43]

The Smothers Brothers were not politically active initially; they achieved fame with material which echoed that of their mentors from mainstream comedy's golden age: Benny, Bob Hope, and classic teams including Laurel and Hardy. This was what CBS had bargained for. As the Vietnam War waxed and the decade waned, however, they turned toward topical satire, influenced both by their more radical contemporaries and by the daily headlines from the war and the civil rights struggle. Further awakened into political consciousness by the show's collection of writers—including head writer Mason Williams, Rob Reiner, and an aspiring comic named Steve Martin— Tom Smothers exercised his creative license to lead the hour-long variety format into uncharted territory worlds away from variety's origins in vaudeville. While still relying on a wide array of performers and content, the show became increasingly mischievous and socially provocative. The brothers attracted Compass veteran and pioneer satirist Elaine May as a guest and enlisted Carl Gottlieb, a member of the Committee, as a writer. Another Committee alumna named Leigh French appeared regularly as a joyful flower child from the mellow marijuana-clouded reaches of the counterculture. Her recurring segment, titled "Share a Little Tea with Goldie," offered helpful advice and plenty of double entendre, such as her salutation in one episode: "I'd like to greet all you ladies as I usually do . . . hi." Censors could not be certain if she was saying hello or describing an elevated state of consciousness, but younger viewers were sure, and they were delighted. So were programming executives, who were thrilled with the show's ratings, especially among baby boomers. Early on, they were inclined to overlook the cheeky cultural references and even the nebulous pokes at authority. In the fourth episode Tom told Dick he had made a correlation between political power and the amount of clothing people wore: more clothing meant more authority. Ordinary Americans, he said, were "the less-ons." Then who's running the country?" asked Dick. "The morons."[44]

Such mild impertinence soon gave way to more radical performances satirizing the Vietnam War and presidential leadership. In the fall of 1967 the show booked folk music icon Pete Seeger, who had been blacklisted from network television for nearly two decades as a result of HUAC's anticommunist crusade. He agreed to perform his latest song, "Waist Deep in the Big Muddy," which referred indirectly with mocking revulsion to Lyndon Johnson as "the big fool" who says to "push on" despite the deepening quagmire of America's combat involvement in Vietnam. The song concluded with a final cutting indictment of the president and a prophecy of impending disaster:

> Waist deep in the Big Muddy, and the big fool says to push on.
> Waist deep in the Big Muddy, and the big fool says to push on.
> Waist deep! Neck deep! Soon even a tall man'll be over his head, we're
> Waist deep in the Big Muddy! And the big fool says to push on!

Fearing retribution from local network affiliates, sponsors, and the White House, CBS balked and initially censored the song from the broadcast. Only after Tom Smothers took the battle over censorship to the wider media did the network ultimately relent and allow Seeger to sing the song unedited on the air several months later. The brothers won, but the episode deepened the friction between the network and the show. Confrontations flared almost weekly with CBS's Department of Program Practices over single phrases, entire sketches, and the choice of guests. In early April 1969 the network, claiming that a videotape of that week's program had been delivered late for preview, used the excuse to cancel the program despite its ongoing popularity and ratings success. It was replaced by the safe cornpone comedy of another variety show, Hee Haw.[45]

The Smothers Brothers Comedy Hour marked a significant transformative step in the final shift of political comedy performance from the tentative fringes of American popular culture to center stage. Spotlighted at 9 pm on Sundays, it occupied the prime of prime-time television and became "must-see TV" for millions of viewers of all ages a generation before that phrase entered the popular lexicon. CBS executive Michael Dann credited it with being the first variety show to deal with social issues. Dick Smothers agreed but made the same point from the opposite perspective, maintaining that even at the controversial end of its brief run, the program was still essentially about entertainment, not social commentary. Indeed, even as the show booked political lightning rods such as Seeger and antiwar folksinger Joan Baez, it continued to welcome crowd pleasers like Jimmy Durante, Liberace, and Kate Smith, who was famous for her rousing performance of "God Bless America."[46]

In the end this deep ambivalence over the show's identity and its potential effect on American culture was most disconcerting for CBS. Like NBC with its hand-wringing over TW3, and even civil authorities with their quandaries over what to do about the utterings of Lenny Bruce, CBS was uncertain what explosive power the combustible mix of show business, social concerns, and politics—ignited by satire—could loose onto the cultural landscape, and therefore took preventive action against it. The show's tenure coincided with that of other volatile comic spectacles such as the Yippies' efforts to levitate the Pentagon and to elect a pig president. Could such humor move the nation, if not buildings? Such were the questions soberly pondered not only by CBS but also by Lyndon Johnson. The president watched *The Smothers Brothers Comedy Hour* and occasionally did so with CBS president Frank Stanton, who was eager to keep the network in favor with the White House. Johnson was well aware of the spotlight cast on humor by JFK, and Kennedy's ability to manipulate the limelight to his own ends. This president—haunted by the war, acutely sensitive to criticism, and, unlike Kennedy, ill-equipped personally to control the performance of humor in any constructive way—could only let his displeasure be known, and Stanton relayed it down his chain of command. Presidents and network programmers alike struggled to gauge the balance between playful entertainment and political discourse as expressed through humor. The program was popular among older audiences mostly because of the variety format and its big-name guests, yet it thrived among baby boomers largely owing to its topical and irreverent satire. For a time the CBS brass believed they could have it both ways. At the height of the show's popularity a network executive told the Smothers Brothers, "We want you to be controversial but at the same time we want everyone to agree with you." Ultimately it was impossible to maintain such a paradox, although everyone involved—the network, the audience, and the Smothers Brothers—debated it openly and humorously for more than two years. With the inauguration of Richard Nixon in January 1969, CBS sensed even less tolerance from the White House and moved to eliminate the forum, although it could do nothing to silence the debate. Like TW3, *The Smothers Brothers Comedy Hour* was muzzled not so much for its *proven* ability to subvert the political authority of the establishment as for its *presumed* impact, and for having the temerity to ridicule in serious times. Viewers at home and in the show's live audience laughed loud and long to the last, but judging the significance of this hilarity—whether trivial or diabolical—remained elusive. Americans continued to grapple with the mercurial meaning of humor aimed at serious targets in high places, but producers, performers, and consumers alike welcomed its more acidic forms into the mass cultural marketplace. *The Smothers Brothers Comedy Hour* stands prominently between the tentative experiment of *TW3*, which lasted barely a year, and the institution that is *Saturday Night Live*, which debuted five years later and remains enormously popular after four decades on the air.[47]

•   •   •

One of the regular features of *The Smothers Brothers Comedy Hour* that delighted audiences and confounded the show's political critics was the appearance of a diminutive, droopy-eyed Norwegian American comic and former Fuller Brush salesman named Pat Paulsen. Tom Smothers included Paulsen in the show's cast from the start, and his regular "editorials" on the divisive issues of the day became a hilarious staple of the show. On the subject of the military draft, the stone-faced Paulsen dismissed critics of the draft who thought it was unfair and immoral and ruined young men's lives. "Picky, picky, picky," he retorted before suggesting that men be drafted according to their hat size; the fatheads, he reasoned, would go into government. Likewise, he could not understand the hubbub over censorship: "Censors have a right to censor what you hear. The Bill of Rights says nothing about Freedom of Hearing." CBS censors, of course, constantly tried to edit his monologues, but Tom Smothers instructed Paulsen to fidget constantly, not only to make him resemble a shifty politician but also to render it all but impossible to cut an offending passage cleanly. The popularity of these brief segments led to a larger comic phenomenon that grew to rival the cultural significance of the Smothers Brothers' show itself.[48]

In early 1968 the brothers approached Paulsen with the idea of running for president. "Why not," he reportedly replied. "I can't dance—besides, the job has a good pension and I'll get a lot of money when I retire." His rationale echoed Gracie Allen's justification for her comic run in 1940 and others' in the years since. Ever since Will Rogers's faux campaign in 1928, celebrities have confirmed the conflation of politics and entertainment by running for president. Publicity is usually the sole objective; ego enhancement or profit from merchandise or higher ratings is typically the motive. Alvin, the front "man" of Alvin and the Chipmunks, ran in 1960 to further the career of the popular cartoon trio, prompting Jack Kennedy to joke, "I'm glad to know that I have at least one worthy opponent." Likewise Paulsen's candidacy made money for all producers of the enterprise and helped to

FIGURE 7. *Pat Paulsen gives an electrifying speech during his 1968 run for president. Photograph CBS Photo Archive/Hulton Archive/Getty Images.*

promote the Smothers Brothers, but like Rogers's campaign, it went beyond novelty to a satirical critique of the campaign process and invited Americans to reevaluate the rhetoric and machinations of those who run for the presidency (fig. 7). In further contrast to the efforts of Allen and others, including Dick Gregory, who waged a serious write-in campaign in 1968 to draw attention to a number of social issues, Paulsen's mock campaign was thoroughly intertwined with a wider social and political context that welcomed this reevaluation and was beginning to champion political satire and iconoclasm rather than suppress it, as the mass media had previously done. Just as important, Paulsen's candidacy balanced its satire with at least as much pure comic relief for a nation besieged by war, violence, and division. Somewhere in the fog of Paulsen's sincere, hardworking, and honest ineptitude, Americans found both a comic candidate they could believe in and a common reason to laugh.[49]

As with Will Rogers's run on the whimsical Anti-Bunk ticket exactly forty years before, much of the therapeutic resonance of Paulsen's bid for the White House (on the platform of the Straight Talking American Government or STAG Party) came from its humor and longevity. "Paulsen for President" was a running gag that the candidate insisted all along was no joke. He announced his intentions on *The Smothers Brothers Comedy Hour* by using deadpan political double-speak to—like most candidates—initially deny that he was running. "I will not run if nominated," he declared to Tom Smothers, "and if I'm elected I will not serve." He then left the stage and waded into the audience, shaking hands with everyone in the first row to thank them for their support. As the next days passed, he earnestly maintained his non-candidacy at a campaign stop:

> The radio and press have once again chewed off more than they can bite. . . . They seem to assume that I am lying when I state that I am not a candidate for the presidency. True, all the present candidates once denied they had any intention of running. But the fact that I am also a liar doesn't make me a candidate.[50]

Voters recognized truth in Paulsen's lies, and his movement took on a populist fervor, demonstrated by the enthusiastic crowds that turned out to see him. They came from all corners of American life. He was warmly welcomed by the Xenia, Ohio, fire department, which made him an honorary member and presented him with a ceremonial hose nozzle. Executives at a Ford parts facility in Michigan hosted him on his "fact-finding tour" of American manufacturing sites by showing him around. They looked on with glee as Paulsen cagily began to plant "Paulsen for President" bumper stickers on hundreds of Ford bumpers stacked on pallets. Crowds at shopping centers cheered him amid confetti and marching bands, carrying signs proclaiming the campaign slogan that presaged Barack Obama's 2008 call for "change" from the status quo, even if Paulsen's wording seemed less carefully thought through: "WE CAN'T STAND PAT."[51]

Politicians jumped on the bandwagon in scenes reminiscent of the days when politicos clamored to be associated with Will Rogers. The Michigan state legislature gave Paulsen a standing ovation when he entered the senate chamber to address the assembly. He was similarly welcomed in his native state of Washington, the nation's largest producer of apples, even as he voiced concern over the apparent economic crisis raging there: "The depression was over a long time ago for most people. Why does the State of Washington have to continue to sell apples?" In Columbus, Ohio, Governor James Rhodes introduced him on the steps of the statehouse by likening Paulsen to Will Rogers, but with the twist befitting his leadership of the STAG Party: "[He] never met a *woman* [he] didn't like." For his part, Paulsen questioned whether he was worthy of the voters' trust by wondering aloud if he was enough of a showman to be president: "Although I am a professional comedian, some of my critics maintain that this alone is not enough. I cannot deny that I stand before you untested and inexperienced. I only spent two years in television, [and] never as a romantic lead or a song and dance man."[52]

Inserted as it was among the traumas of 1968, including the student takeover of Columbia University, the murders of Martin Luther King Jr. and Robert F. Kennedy, and the mayhem at the Democratic convention in Chicago, the candidacy of Pat Paulsen was both a welcome diversion from the darker truths of American life and a satiric interrogation of American leadership. It stood as a communal joke whose boundaries were unclear. Paulsen, like Will Rogers, earned endorsements. Paulsen stickers appeared not just at bumper factories but on moving vehicles nationwide, alongside cars promoting Richard Nixon, Hubert Humphrey, and third-party candidate George Wallace, the segregationist governor of Alabama. This was comedic democracy, where everyone could take part, cast a vote, tell a joke, have a laugh. If everyone could be a comedian, a comedian could be president. Significantly, Paulsen steadfastly played his part, never dropping the straight-faced sincerity of his quest. This forced observers to decide for themselves the distinction between a standup comedian and a candidate on the stump. Which was in earnest and which was the put-on? Was it a president's use of exaggeration, double-talk, and shameless mendacity to get votes and advance disastrous policies, or the comic's use of these same strategies to get laughs? Paulsen inspired such questions, occasionally overtly, as when he was asked to compare himself with Johnson: "Do I consider myself a better comedian than LBJ? Yes, but I couldn't run the country as funny."[53]

Conspicuously absent from this collective performance were Paulsen's rivals for the presidency. The only major candidate to acknowledge the campaign deliberately was Robert Kennedy, who paid Paulsen the ultimate tongue-in-cheek tribute of reflexively attacking his policies just as opponents are expected to do, claiming Paulsen was, among other things, too liberal and a carpetbagger, the very things of which Kennedy was accused. Otherwise the absence of response from Nixon, Humphrey, and Wallace actually served to enhance the effect. At a time when many Americans felt far removed from the imperial presidency, it seemed natural that the "serious contenders" were not in on the joke but instead remained conspicuously below the comedic fray. Much had changed since 1962, when much of the nation—the president included—was laughing in concert.[54]

As a final punch line, the television special *Pat Paulsen for President* aired during the normal time slot for *The Smothers Brothers Comedy Hour* two weeks before Election Day. The show chronicled Paulsen's barnstorming across the country and his many campaign events, including a Paulsen for President eighty-nine-cents-a-plate dinner at a cafeteria on Rodeo Drive in Beverly Hills, where a cast of celebrities—comedy luminaries Steve Allen and Groucho Marx among them—gathered to eat spaghetti, tell jokes, and hear from their candidate. At the close of the TV special, narrator Henry

Fonda summarized Paulsen's popular appeal in poignant terms: "There are those who insist that it's all a joke . . . [, but] in a land marked by political division, even those who [dismiss Pat] must admit that laughter is a better alternative." Fonda's words accompanied images of a solitary Paulsen walking in the Washington, D.C., dusk, contemplating the Washington Monument and Lincoln Memorial, and—too preoccupied with the grandeur to watch where he is going—stepping in something. Thus brought down to earth, he moved to the edge of the long rectangular reflecting pool between the monuments to scrape his shoe, only to lose his balance and, with a deft, deadpan subtlety reminiscent of silent film star Buster Keaton, slip one foot into the pool as Fonda orated on his "testing the waters of leadership." These were cheap laughs, to be sure, but they seemed equal to the man and the moment. The joke also illustrated the incongruous irony inherent in American democracy: attainment of the nation's highest aspirations is constantly distracted by the dirty business of daily life.[55]

Paradoxically, such satire was quickly appreciating in value. Pat Paulsen's campaign on *The Smothers Brothers Comedy Hour*, like Will Rogers's in *Life* magazine in 1928, was a consumer product. It was professionally produced and, although much of its humor sprang from Paulsen's considerable talent, including his expert ability to adlib, a small corps of writers was behind him. His performances and their supporting enterprise found a ready market among citizen consumers eager to lay low both the electoral process and the president in terms not as blatantly extreme as those of the Credibility Gap, the Committee, or Abbie Hoffman's Yippies, but no less vehement. Terrorized by war abroad and discord at home, Americans bought laughter as both a vote of no confidence in the present and a hopeful restorative for the future. By resurrecting Rogers's model of the mock candidacy, latter-day satirists and their audiences achieved for their time what Abraham Lincoln sought in his by reading Artemus Ward during the dark days of the Civil War. When challenged by his cabinet to explain his irreverent pursuit of levity in the face of such horror, Lincoln responded: "With the fearful strain that is upon me night and day, if I did not laugh I should die." In the fall of 1968 it was the humorists and the electorate who recognized the value of this laughing commodity, while it was the president who was not buying.[56]

On Election Day, Pat Paulsen earned more than 100,000 write-in votes—hardly enough to make the comedian president, but the total represented nearly one-fourth of Richard Nixon's 500,000-vote margin of victory. In the following week's episode of *The Smothers Brothers Comedy Hour*, Paulsen generously conceded to "Mr. Nixton." (He consistently mispronounced both Nixon's and Johnson's names throughout the campaign, referring to the president as "Mr. Johnston.") He concluded his remarks with a conciliatory coda to the campaign: "Although I lost, I harbor no resentment toward the voter, for in the long run, he is the real loser."[57]

• • •

Richard Nixon's reappearance on the presidential stage was something of a miracle. After losing in his run for the presidency to John F. Kennedy in 1960 and his California gubernatorial bid in 1962, he famously informed reporters that he had given his last press conference and they would not "have Nixon to kick around anymore." Americans assumed they had seen the last of the former vice president, whose fervent anticommunism and ruthless campaign tactics earned him a reputation among his critics for being mean, artificial, and unscrupulous, and the moniker "Tricky Dick" from Helen Gahagan Douglas, whom Nixon had defeated in their 1950 Senate race. His heavy facial features and overall wooden physical appearance were the stuff of easy caricature. During the 1950s, editorial cartoonists Herblock and Robert Osborn accentuated his dark eyebrows, sloping nose, and five o'clock shadow, adding to a negative image Nixon himself reinforced in the televised debates with Kennedy in 1960, where perspiration under the studio lights and his darting glances made him look ill at ease and less trustworthy than the calm and collected Kennedy. Nixon was easy to laugh at, even for his supporters. Roger Ailes, Nixon's lead television consultant, admitted: "He's a funny-looking guy. He looks like somebody hung him in a closet overnight and he jumps out in the morning with his suit all bunched up and starts running around saying, 'I want to be President.'" Add to this his discomfort with crowds and brooding temperament, and Nixon seemed to embody perfectly what philosopher Henri Bergson defined as the essentially comic side of humanity: that part of a person which shows "peculiar inelasticity [or] conveys the impression . . . of automatism, of movement without life." Nixon appeared uncomfortable in his own skin and seemed eager to mask his humanity behind the machinations of hard work and political calculation. Such mechanical "imperfection," maintained Bergson, requires the immediate corrective of laughter, and Americans generally were happy to supply it, especially given Nixon's apparent lack of humor and his track record as a political loser during most of the 1960s.[58]

By 1968 it appeared that Nixon had changed. As the nation careened through the events of mid-decade, observers began to speak of a "new Nixon": more mature, mellow, firm but compassionate, even more humorous. In 1963 he appeared on *The Jack Paar Show*, where he played one of his own compositions on the piano and engaged his host in easy conversation. "Can Kennedy be defeated in '64?" asked Paar. "Which one?" joked Nixon, to the delight of the crowd. He hired one of Paar's writers, Paul Keyes, to craft material for him, and he got tremendous mileage before student audiences from Keyes's one-liner about being a dropout from the electoral college in 1960. "I flunked debate," he admitted. The humor, combined with other strategies, had its desired effect. As strife over the Vietnam War worsened and the Democratic Party, which most Americans blamed for it, spiraled into disarray, the Republican Nixon seemed composed and statesmanlike. He appeared ready to listen to what he called the "great, quite forgotten majority . . . [of] nonshouters," and part of his appeal to this "silent majority" emanated from his ability to poke fun at himself as had Lincoln, Roosevelt, and Kennedy. Even Norman Mailer, one of Nixon's staunchest critics, said that by 1968 Nixon seemed "less phony."[59]

In fact whatever his innate joviality, and notwithstanding occasional genuine flashes of it, Nixon's sense of humor was utterly suffocated in the vacuum of his approach to politics. Whereas Franklin Roosevelt and Jack Kennedy saw laughter as both an integral component and an authentic reflection of their relationship with the American people, Nixon—like Lyndon Johnson—was unable to exude such warmth. Unlike Johnson, Nixon was capable of delivering a joke effectively, but he distrusted humor and considered it a dangerous sign of vulnerability and unpredictability. Comedians generally revel in their interaction with their audience; Nixon considered his audience to be full of latent hecklers. "People react to fear, not love," he once told an aide. Humor was perilous because its playful and volatile spontaneity was in fundamental opposition to a core Nixon trait: control. He was determined, therefore, that humor be harnessed in the campaign of 1968—not as a threat to this sense of control and discipline but as a subservient expression of it. Humor became a meticulously regulated illusion performed as a means to a foreseeable end—winning the election—rather than a vehicle for honest communication with the American people. If he had lost the presidency in 1960 because of his inability to control his image before the electorate, he left nothing to chance in 1968. He worked tirelessly to manufacture all aspects of his campaign, including his role as the self-assured, smiling, joking candidate. It is telling that Nixon, years after his disastrous physical appearance in the first presidential debate in 1960, hired the makeup man from *The Tonight Show* to paint his image before television cameras in 1968. A sense of humor to him was so much greasepaint.[60]

It was out of such strategic calculation during the campaign that Nixon acknowledged the intersection of political and entertainment culture, and the powerful role that humor played in bringing the two together. The earlier performances of presidents and comics proved that laughs could win support and earn votes; whether or not such performances were heartfelt was immaterial. Nixon saw his opportunity in *Rowan and Martin's Laugh-In.*

In January 1968 NBC opted to replace the action series *The Man from U.N.C.L.E.* with a new variety show that combined the ageless attractions of vaudeville and burlesque with broad-based satire, all infused with a disarming zaniness that simultaneously ridiculed and reveled in the allure of the pop counterculture. Even if the country was bitterly divided across the generation gap, it was hooked on the psychedelic theatrics of flower power and youthful irreverence. During its six seasons, *Rowan and Martin's Laugh-In* popularized poking fun at the president by chasing down its small doses of political humor with large measures of slapstick, sexuality, and lightning-fast pacing. The show became an instant hit in the ratings and earned critical praise as well. "Rowan and Martin," wrote television critic Jack Gould in the *New York Times*, "may be the instrument for bringing TV into the mainstream of modern concern." While this overstated *Laugh-In's* sociological value, the program became famous for introducing slang favorites into popular usage, such as "You bet your sweet bippy" and "Here come de judge" and for its split-second celebrity cameos. For the debut of the show's second season that September, both the Republican and Democratic candidates were invited to make such appearances. Hubert Humphrey turned down the offer, claiming it would be beneath his dignity; he later gave this decision a large part of the blame for his loss in November. To the surprise of many, Nixon agreed. Persuaded by his joke consultant and now *Laugh-In* head writer Paul Keyes that the cameo would counter his image as the ultimate "square" and further the branding of the "new Nixon," the candidate went to the show's studios and worked diligently to record his one line, although it reportedly took six takes before he could deliver it without sounding angry or offended. He was paid $210, the standard rate for a cameo appearance according to the pay scale of the American Federation of Television and Radio Artists (AFTRA). On September 16, 1968, a stunned and surprisingly delighted television audience watched as Richard Nixon appeared on their TV screens for a few fleeting seconds and incredulously exclaimed the show's most popular running punch line, "Sock it to *me*?"[61]

Nixon's appearance was arguably the single most famous moment in *Laugh-In's* history, in large part because it marked another defining moment in the commercialization of comedy performance aimed at the presidency. For the first time since 1963, the president (or in this case the candidate), the comic, and the object of the joke became one and the same. Nixon cashed in the gag for its immediate political value rather than building on it to create rapport or goodwill. Still, set against the tragically absurd backdrop of profound national discord and juxtaposed with the cathartic candidacy of Pat Paulsen that was going on simultaneously, the *Laugh-In* appearance, in combination with his tactically launched one-liners, helped to ingratiate

Nixon with much of the American electorate by portraying him as an ev-eryman who could both give and take in the world of humor, and even engage in good fun despite sober times. Two months later Nixon was elected president of the United States, apparently having acquitted himself of the charge that had dogged him for nearly two decades: that he was a ruthless, deceptive, and even dangerous pretender to presidential greatness. Nixon helped himself by design—if, as it turned out, only fleetingly—by turning comedian. Unwittingly, he also helped to cultivate the widespread demand for presidential ridicule and satire as he proceeded to prove the charge true after all.

First impressions of the new president's wit and his tolerance for it in others were ambivalent. *Time* magazine commented enthusiastically on "Nixon's New-Found Humor" shortly after his inauguration in 1969, report-ing his wry comment that one of the first things he had done to reduce crime in Washington was to turn on the White House lights that Lyndon Johnson had turned off to save money five years earlier. That same year saw the publication of *The Wit and Humor of Richard Nixon* in keeping with the brand-new tradition of celebrating—and marketing—presidential joviality, begun by an anthology titled *The Kennedy Wit* memorializing the late president in 1964. The Nixon volume, *Time* noted, was quite thin in contrast with the Kennedy book and included the complete text of Nixon's speech accepting the Republican nomination the year before, "which con-tained not a scintilla of wit." Over at CBS, the interpretations of signals from the new administration soon led to the cancellation of *The Smothers Broth-ers Comedy Hour*. These and other early assessments reflected uncertainty, even low expectations, regarding the place of humor in the Nixon White House. They were accompanied, however, by the wishful anticipation that the "new Nixon" of the campaign might endure and return a measure of credibility by restoring the president's ability to laugh, however modestly, in community with his fellow Americans.[62]

Ultimately, however, paranoia, duplicity, and the relentless pursuit of his personal concept of the imperial presidency permeated every aspect of Nixon's administration, leaving no room for humor and turning the no-tion of such community into a laughingstock. His profound secretiveness threatened his credibility on a multitude of issues. Nixon's orders during the summer and fall of 1969 to withdraw sixty thousand troops from Vietnam— marking the beginning of his "Vietnamization" policy deescalating U.S. combat involvement—were widely hailed, only to be countered by revela-tions that he had widened the war that March by secretly bombing neigh-boring Cambodia, a neutral country. His subsequent order in April 1970 to invade Cambodia spawned renewed antiwar demonstrations that resulted in the shooting deaths of four students at Kent State University in Ohio and two at Jackson State University in Mississippi by national guardsmen and police. On civil rights, Nixon established a cabinet-level committee that successfully accelerated school desegregation in the South, but his wider "southern strategy" to woo back white voters slowed progress and, along with efforts such as his administration's attempt to prevent renewal of the 1965 Voting Rights Act, even sought to reverse civil rights gains. Most profoundly, Americans' cheering of Nixon's bold initiatives to reframe U.S. foreign policy by reaching out to the People's Republic of China and the Soviet Union in 1972 turned to howling derision as the details of the president's illegal involvement in the tragic farce known as Watergate began to surface.[63]

The culture of criminality surrounding the break-in at the offices of the Democratic National Committee in Washington, D.C.'s, Watergate office complex in June 1972 opened the floodgates of presidential ridicule. As the scope of the investigation widened to reveal the range of abuses — from "dirty tricks" against political opponents to burglary to obstruction of justice — committed at all levels of the executive branch, including campaign officials and former attorney general John Mitchell right up to the president, a cascade of satire and other forms of mockery crashed around the White House. Syndicated columnists such as Art Buchwald and editorial cartoonists Herblock, Paul Conrad at the *Los Angeles Times*, Pat Oliphant at the *Denver Post*, and, most famously, Garry Trudeau with his comic strip "Doonesbury" all became stars for their print portrayals of the Watergate farce and its leading players. On television, *All in the Family*'s bigoted patriarch Archie Bunker, played by actor Carroll O'Connor, helped to convict Nixon in popular opinion even as Archie hilariously tried to defend him against his nemesis son-in-law Mike Stivic. The comedy came from all corners and in all guises, from simple puns to elaborate lampoons to outright profanity.

Watergate inspired unprecedented quantities of laughter at the presidency, and Richard Nixon's was the face that launched a thousand punch lines, but the humor they produced from 1972 through Nixon's resignation in August 1974 rose from wellsprings already discovered and tapped during the preceding decade. "Nineteen seventy-three was the year America became a comedy," reflected humorist and *New York Times* columnist Russell Baker at the end of that year, but the performance of the comedy resonated with earlier influences. Archie Bunker's tirades over TV taboos on *All in the Family* survived the censors at CBS in large part because of the battles waged earlier between the network and the Smothers Brothers. Workers, students, and other Americans joked ferociously and without quarter; calls to "Impeach with Honor" and "Dick Nixon before He Dicks You" circulated around offices and dormitories, echoing previous sentiments leveled at Lyndon Johnson. Even more obscene one-liners utilized the guerrilla tactics of Abbie Hoffman and earlier antiwar demonstrators. The words "Lick Dick" scrawled in a women's restroom on a New York City campus urged Nixon's defeat at the polls in 1972 in graphic terms that got laughs. Vice President Spiro Agnew, who resigned in 1973 amid corruption charges unrelated to Watergate, earned ridicule in tandem with Nixon. "Dick and Spiro add up to zero" went one refrain, while another popular joke was more intricate and comprehensive: "Nixon is the first president to have an asshole for a vice president." "No," went the reply, "Eisenhower was." These attacks gained wide currency in a culture hardened by both the audacity of comedians and the duplicity of presidents. For all the adamant disapproval cast at Lenny Bruce for his use of obscenities, such language now seemed fitting to describe the president, who did not hesitate to use expletives liberally from the Oval Office to describe Mexicans, blacks, and other minorities, and who ordered that investigations of "rich Jews" who contributed to the Democratic Party be pursued "like a son of a bitch." Although these utterances were made in private and such language was not unique to Richard Nixon, their revelation in connection with his wider criminality shocked a nation unaccustomed to hearing such barefaced profanity from the most venerated political official in the nation. More pointedly, Dick Gregory's comparison of the presidency with prostitution years earlier now seemed apt, given Nixon's willingness to sell ambassadorships for campaign contributions and his conspiring to derail investigations, pay hush money, and perpetrate other illegal acts from the Oval Office. Schooled by comics and moved by presidential deception and malfeasance, Americans were equipped by the mid-1970s to joke brazenly and for profit, in short, to fit the comedy to the crime.[64]

•   •   •

Presidential impersonation also returned with increased ferocity during Watergate with David Frye. A virtuoso impressionist whose bipartisan cast of targets included Lyndon Johnson, the Reverend Billy Graham, liberal senator George McGovern, and conservative icon William F. Buckley Jr., Frye seemed to bring the two-dimensional Nixon cartoons drawn by Paul Conrad and Pat Oliphant to eerie life, complete with the dark, brooding scowl, shifty eyes, and quivering jowls. There were other popular Nixon mimics, including Rich Little and James La Roe (who performed as Richard M. Dixon), but Frye—like Vaughn Meader with his Kennedy impression—was able to complement his technical proficiency at mimicking the president's voice and mannerisms with high-quality writing. But Frye went even further. He probed his subject's personal psychology and his relationships with others, including his family, in revealing ways. For many, Frye's mastery of Nixon's automatism, combined with withering satire of the president's megalomania, captured the essence of the man, especially once the Watergate scandal gained momentum.

Frye made frequent appearances on television, including *The Ed Sullivan Show*, but it was through his four LPs during the late 1960s and early 1970s that he found his true following and his satire came into full bloom. *Richard Nixon: A Fantasy*—released in 1973, more than a year before Nixon's resignation and prior to many of the most dramatic Watergate developments— framed the scandal as a gangster film with Nixon as a comical public enemy number one. Gone were any vestiges of Meader's benign obsequiousness toward the presidency. Rather, Frye savagely lampooned, among other things, Nixon's speech that April when he accepted the forced resignations of his chief of staff, H. R. "Bob" Haldeman, and special assistant John Ehrlichman (whom he referred to as "two of the finest public servants it has been my privilege to know") while struggling to deflect all guilt away from himself:

> My fellow Americans, I come before you tonight to tell you the truth. I first learned of the Watergate break-in when I read newspaper reports the following morning. I was appalled at this senseless, illegal action. Therefore, I have the following announcement to make. Today I have regretfully been forced to accept the resignations of 1,541 of the finest public servants it has been my privilege to know. As the man in charge, I of course accept full responsibility . . . but not the blame. Let me explain the difference: people who are to blame lose their jobs; people who are responsible do not.

When it is suggested that he resign, Frye's Nixon rejects the possibility as doing "the cowardly thing":

> Rather, I have decided to take the more difficult course: the only way I'm going to leave the White House is to be dragged screaming and kicking. Because, my fellow Americans, I love America. And you always hurt the one that you really love.[65]

Frye was performing comedy, but the comedian's mocking representation of Nixon's blatant self-serving abuse of the office while callously claiming he was courageously upholding the nation's highest ideals struck many as ironically close to reality. The public humorously identified with Frye's trademark declaration of Nixonian imperiousness—"I *am* the president"— and laughed away the distinction between the chief executive and the impressionist as they came to the realization, along with economist John

Kenneth Galbraith, that the nation had "passed from the age of the common man to the common crook." Frye accomplished what Meader had: his impersonation capered along the threshold between fact and fancy in the popular imagination. But whereas Meader and Kennedy had established the modern precedent of using laughing intimacy between the people and the president as a basis for kidding endearment, Nixon's crimes and Frye's satire exploited that intimacy to opposite ends. Such intimacy now exposed naked abhorrence and—far from mourning—celebrated the alienation created by Lyndon Johnson's lack of credibility and crystallized by Nixon's abject betrayal. Americans who were once entranced by the goings-on inside the White House were now repulsed by them. They moved from the pleasant proposition in *The First Family* that Kennedy and the rest of the presidential clan could be just like them to laughing in the desperate hope that neither they nor their families nor the nation would be tainted by the felonious actions of the president. Furthermore, while Kennedy commanded a large measure of tangible control over the presidential joke by being its object but also a sympathetic comedian in his own right, Nixon could exert no such influence; he could only play the fool.[66]

On Frye's album, Nixon is ultimately convicted by an incriminating "jowl print" left at the site of the Watergate break-in and is sentenced to death. Americans—prevented from seeing Nixon tried in court thanks to his pardon by Gerald Ford in September 1974—prosecuted him using the few means left to them, including the humor crafted and performed by comedians who enjoyed increasing cultural influence and projected it in diverse ways. Lenny Bruce and Abbie Hoffman modeled an antic extremism that estranged them from most of the country, but ultimately their obscene language and dirty tricks merely proved equal to the president's. Bob Hope endured; his appeal within the establishment was emblematic of the conservative brand of comedy that struggled to preserve the traditional deference accorded the president even as the relevance of such boosterism began to fade. His USO Christmas visits to Vietnam were carefully stage-managed but continued to lift morale to the end; his last tour was in 1972. He was even able to parlay his influence into a meeting with North Vietnamese officials in a bold but failed attempt to effect the release of POWs being held in Hanoi. Yet his unequivocal support for Nixon, even to the last, proved a liability once Nixon resigned in disgrace. Though he remained a national institution, Hope became more negatively identified with the establishment he endorsed, and his popularity became rooted in nostalgia. As for Dick Gregory and the Smothers Brothers, they joked at first from the middle ground between conservatism and extremism, reined in initially by the practical imperative of commercial survival before giving full-throated expression to their political activism against the imperial presidencies of Johnson and Nixon.[67]

By 1974 another comedian had established himself as the most powerful cultural arbiter in America, and he became the gatekeeper who sanctioned the final acceptance then outright embrace of presidential ridicule as a bankable commodity. Johnny Carson was Iowa-born and Nebraska-raised, and endowed with a rare mix of rural forthrightness, urban sophistication, and instinctive comedic brilliance. He succeeded Jack Paar as host of *The Tonight Show* in 1962, and by the time he reached the height of his career during the mid-1970s, between 10 and 15 million people ended their day watching *The Tonight Show with Johnny Carson*, which accounted for 17 percent of NBC's total profits. Building on Steve Allen's innovations in booking performers and interacting with the audience, Carson continued to offer a showcase for up-and-coming comics for three decades. Initially Carson danced gingerly around political humor. He considered himself first and foremost an old-school entertainer, and his monologues and sketches were designed to be diversions rather than provocations—topical but not overtly political—befitting a program that people watched, according to Carson, in bed from between their toes. Still, when Carson sensed a sea change in Americans' attitudes toward political humor, he simultaneously reflected and shaped them with material that poked fun at Lyndon Johnson and subsequent presidents with escalating frequency. When he began to inject his monologues with jibes at Nixon as the Watergate scandals deepened (Nixon, he observed, was indifferent to the gasoline shortages of 1973 because "of course, everything's downhill for him"), the laughter aimed at the White House intensified from all quarters of the country, including the working class and Middle America, which had been the most hesitant to poke fun. Just as significantly, Carson's *Tonight Show* provided the license and often the platform for ridicule by others. In 1972 Dan Rowan and Dick Martin of *Laugh-In* regaled Carson and his audience with a routine about President Nixon during a prime-time special celebrating the tenth anniversary of *The Tonight Show with Johnny Carson*:

> ROWAN: I don't care what your politics are, you don't call the president of the United States Old Dick. He's the president.
> MARTIN: We've known him for twenty years.
> ROWAN: I don't care how long we've known him, you don't call the president Old Dick.
> MARTIN: He was a regular on our show.
> ROWAN: That doesn't make any difference. When you talk to him it's Mr. President.

MARTIN: How about Mr. Dick?

ROWAN: Mr.—from the minute a man is elected to that office he is called Mr. President. His most intimate friends, Mr. President. Never anything else. From the day he's elected till the day he dies. If Harry Truman takes a walk around the block, "Good morning, Mr. President." Same thing with Johnson: "Good morning, Mr. President."

MARTIN: Hmmm. Late at night, upstairs?

ROWAN: Well, I don't know—I suppose Mrs. Nixon calls him whatever she used to call him, I don't know.

MARTIN: Tricky Dick![68]

Four years after Richard Nixon's appearance on *Laugh-In*, the ringmasters of this playful comedic circus "socked it to him" before a laughing audience within Carson's immensely lucrative sphere of influence. By finally bringing together network television, an increasingly receptive audience, and daring performances that confronted the historical veneration of the presidency in more sardonic and personal terms—and by giving the union his sanction—Carson catalyzed the process that certified the cultural and economic legitimacy of such humor and therefore brought about its mass production. As it turned out, he was a rather reluctant agent for this cultural change, but once it had begun, even he could not slow the institutionalization of a relationship between the people, the president, and the performance of political comedy that had been forming since the founding of the republic. As consumers, Americans were asserting their willingness to laugh publicly in ways that previously were considered tantamount to treason but now articulated a revolutionary, even patriotic liberation from an imperial presidency. As producers, they became prolific comedians who were equipped to joke with passion and ferocity. More significantly, they became convinced of the widespread marketability of this more acerbic strain of political comedy, and they began to manufacture it wholesale.

6

Rebellion by the Pound

"**I** HEAR THAT whenever someone in the White House tells a lie, Nixon gets a royalty." By the fall of 1973 Johnny Carson's jabs at the president of the United States were becoming more constant and merciless as the deepening Watergate investigation pointed decidedly toward Richard Nixon's personal criminal involvement. In one monologue that autumn Carson remarked, "Did you know that Richard Nixon is the only president whose formal portrait was painted by a police sketch artist?" His audience — numbering five hundred in NBC's Burbank, California, studio, 12 million in front of television sets nationwide, and legions of network executives and sponsors — savored every punch line. Then, during the rancorous summer of 1974, when Nixon's disgrace seemed all but sealed, Carson turned abruptly to his longtime sidekick Ed McMahon before a broadcast and declared: "I've got to let up on Nixon, now. He's going down the tubes and I feel sorry for him." Carson's jabs at Nixon stopped. Others joked on — the market for presidential ridicule having been established and a steady supply being required to meet demand — but Carson, after rendering judgment and dispensing his measure of punishment, was the first to decree compassion. Few questioned the undisputed king of late-night television — either his decision to attack the president with comedy or the wisdom of his merciful withdrawal. Carson the comedian reigned supreme; his authority seemed absolute.[1]

The power of the presidency, by contrast, was laid low. When Gerald R. Ford took the oath of office following Nixon's resignation on August 9, 1974, he became president without ever having earned a single vote from the national electorate. A popular and well-respected congressman elected thirteen times to the House of Representatives by the people of Grand Rapids, Michigan, Ford served eight years as House minority leader before being nominated by Nixon in 1973 to be vice president after Spiro Agnew ignominiously resigned amid his own corruption scandal. When he entered the White House a year later, Ford inherited a host of national crises that included impending defeat in Vietnam, the decline of the country's manufacturing economy, runaway inflation measuring 12 percent annually, and an assessment of the chief executive by an American public so cynical about the president's ability to lead or inspire that its inclination was to laugh first and listen later, if at all. Awash in low expectations, Americans recalled Ford's words from the previous year, after he was sworn in as vice president. He pleasantly surprised many in a country that knew nothing about him with a self-effacing pun drawn from the automotive heritage of his native Michigan: "I am a Ford," he humbly admitted, "not a Lincoln." Americans could only nod in resignation.[2]

The gap seemed irreconcilable between the power of performers such as Johnny Carson to control the dance of the comedians and the president's utter relegation to being always and only the butt of the joke. Although Ronald Reagan is understandably credited with once again empowering the office with joviality beginning in 1981—even as he has garnered both credit and scorn for restoring the imperial presidency—the significance of Ford and his administration's effect on the nation's humor is usually minimized or overlooked entirely. Although he was the victim of continual jokes and scathing parody impugning his legitimacy as president, his judgment, his intellect, and even his physical coordination, he was also an unlikely mediator and modest comedian who was surprisingly effective at rehabilitating people's attitudes toward the presidency while simultaneously redefining the president's calculated use of laughter to advance policy and reestablish a sense of national community and credibility. During his thirty months in office Ford projected an unassuming simplicity consistent with another comment he made during the same speech in which he accepted the vice presidency: "I am proud—very proud—to be one of the two hundred million Americans." By defining himself first and foremost as a fellow citizen, he began the process of recalibrating the equilibrium between the people and their highest elected official, a balance that had been thrown far out of kilter during the previous decade. To the extent that Americans could once again imagine someone sufficiently like their best selves in the White House, capable of tempering personal imperfections with lofty ideals, they could begin to laugh, not only with scorn but also now with a semblance of identification and appreciation. Ford showed that the presidency might be redeemed from exile and reinitiated into the circle of national life, and he did so with surprising good cheer.[3]

Ford's popular image, however, seemed hopelessly blemished by the early fall of 1974. While he enjoyed the approval of 71 percent of those surveyed by the Gallup Poll shortly after he replaced Nixon that August, the soaring endorsement plummeted a month later when he granted Nixon a full pardon for any crimes he might have committed in office. Although Ford maintained that the decision was his alone, that there was no corrupt bargain between the former and current presidents, and that the pardon was needed if the country was to move beyond Watergate—what Ford referred to as "our long national nightmare"—much of the nation was infuriated. The *New York Times* editorialized that in pardoning Nixon, Ford himself had "affronted the Constitution" and that his premature "blundering intervention" had delivered "a body blow to the President's own credibility and to the public's reviving confidence in the integrity of its Government." Many were convinced that the presidency had been doubly damaged, first by a president who had abused his power, then by a pretender who presumed it. Americans may have been willing to accept Johnny Carson's comedic grant of clemency for Nixon, but the new president enjoyed no such authority.[4]

Things did not get any better over the next several months. In addition to the fallout after the pardon, accusations that Ford had flip-flopped on various issues and the failure of his commonsensical but simplistic initiative to curb the nation's runaway inflation led *New York* magazine to portray the president as Bozo the Clown on its November 1974 cover. The following May, while on a European trip, Ford stumbled in front of the international media while descending rain-slicked steps from *Air Force One* in Salzburg, Austria, only to trip again later that day on an equally slippery staircase in the Residenz Palace. Lyndon Johnson's old insult that "Ford is so dumb that he can't fart and chew gum at the same time" began to gain traction. Editorial cartoonist Pat Oliphant began drawing Ford with a bandage pasted across his forehead after the six-foot president bumped his head on the doorframes of various airplanes and helicopters. Despite having starred as a football player at the University of Michigan (and having been offered professional contracts by the Detroit Lions and Green Bay Packers) and a continuing athleticism that included considerable prowess as a skier, Gerald Ford started to earn a reputation as an inept bungler not smart enough to be president and apparently incapable of so much as walking in a straight line.[5]

•   •   •

While the Ford administration wallowed at the nadir of popular opinion, America's top comedian was still riding high. By the end of 1974, as the country grappled with the reality that the former president was a crook and the current president might well be a clown, Johnny Carson was, according to *New York Times* cultural correspondent John Leonard, the primary "legitimizing agency" for the national culture. Few thought Leonard guilty of overstatement when he declared that Carson "alone presides over our consciousness," especially since the ratings and NBC's balance sheet bore him out. *The Tonight Show's* popularity made it the biggest single moneymaker in television history, and Carson likewise became the highest-salaried performer in the history of the medium. Not since Will Rogers's omnipresence during the 1920s and 1930s had a comedian so dominated popular culture, and sponsors scurried to associate their products with his punch lines just as they had basked in the profitable glow of Rogers's aura. Carson's material was not remotely as politically charged as Rogers's; whereas Rogers had sought to invigorate the national discourse with the foolishness from Washington, Carson's late-night antics were designed to provide a sedative. Filmmaker Billy Wilder called *The Tonight Show* the Valium and Nembutal of the nation. Neither did Carson equal Rogers's ubiquitous visibility in print and film or on stage and radio, but the overwhelming power of television to trump all competitors more than compensated.[6]

Carson's success gave him ample leverage to dictate terms to NBC, which was desperate to maintain the revenue stream that the comedian was pouring into the network. In late 1974, feeling overworked and overexposed despite a recently renegotiated contract that called for Mondays off, he demanded that NBC stop airing reruns of the show on Saturday nights—relabeled *The Best of Carson*—in order to save the rebroadcasts for weeknights when he was absent. Reluctant to give the time slot and its revenue back to local affiliates, NBC hustled to fill the ninety minutes with a new variety-comedy show. It considered several options and numerous hosts, from popular singer Linda Ronstadt to game-show host Bert Convy.[7]

Herbert Schlosser, NBC's new president, rejected these possibilities and tapped thirty-year-old writer Lorne Michaels to be executive producer of a show tentatively called *NBC's Saturday Night*. Michaels had earned a name for himself by producing comedy specials and films in his native Canada and was already well known to NBC as one of the funniest of the offbeat writers for *Rowan and Martin's Laugh-In*. During the next several months Michaels assembled a collection of writers and performers from his days on *Laugh-In* and his relationships with the creators of the acidly satiric magazine *The National Lampoon*, as well as from his connections with the Second City and the Committee, to create *Saturday Night Live*. The show debuted on October 11, 1975, and quickly became a sensation for its ability to deliver what millions of Americans were now openly prepared to buy. In addition to daring one-liners and physical slapstick, this included political humor and particularly presidential satire.

Saturday Night Live finally pulled together all the formative elements that had helped shape the performance of presidential comedy as it evolved during the mid-twentieth century. Political references in the show's sketches and the standup routines of celebrity hosts such as George Carlin, Lily Tomlin, Dick Cavett, and Richard Pryor during the first season recalled the humor of Will Rogers in the *Follies*, Mort Sahl at the hungry i, and the Smothers Brothers on CBS. The topicality that was first brought to comedy performance by Rogers's declaration, "All I know is just what I read in the papers," then was refashioned by Sahl's working from a rolled-up daily newspaper during the 1950s, and constituted the heart of *TW3*'s brief but provocative run in the mid-1960s found its latest place with "Weekend Update," a satiric news broadcast that lampooned newsmakers from Washington to Hollywood. The segment went on to become an inspiration for future hits such as *The Daily Show* and *The Colbert Report*.

While he recognized real talent among the creators and cast of *Saturday Night Live* and acknowledged its many very clever moments, Johnny Carson was not a big fan of the show. Once he vacated the time slot, however, and consented to the network's creation of this playful new expression of comedic performance that had been incubating for decades, his ongoing approval became less relevant, especially as *Saturday Night Live*'s ratings began to rise. Carson himself had subverted convention when he presciently assessed the national mood and started to ridicule Richard Nixon, but ultimately the comedic response to contemporary events—many of them inside the White House—got ahead of him. His unilateral decision to stop joking at Nixon's expense was noted but not widely emulated. Carson maintained his sky-high ratings, but he was no longer alone at the top. In comparison to the funny goings-on live from New York every Saturday night, the vision of late-night comedy created by Steve Allen and refined by Carson was the ritualized stuff of the establishment. The "boomer humor" born of the ironic response to the cold war notion that security could be achieved only through the prospect of nuclear extinction, and infused with even greater cynicism by the collapse of faith in institutional leadership during the 1960s and early 1970s, permanently found its place center stage. As they aged, those on the leading edge of the baby boom, represented by Lorne Michaels and his *Saturday Night Live* performers, gained executive influence in producing humor for the masses that was forged by insurgents from Mort Sahl and Lenny Bruce to the Smothers Brothers and others in the crucible of anticommunism, the civil rights movement, and the Vietnam War. The power of Michaels and his contemporaries increased as their cohort continued to extend its dominance of the consumer marketplace, and especially as the baby boom's trailing edge—now of college age but no longer threatened by the prospect of being drafted to fight a lost war—found that protest no longer required marching.

They discovered a more comfortable means of rebellion couched in the satire that was now readily available in the party setting of 11:30 on Saturday nights in between commercials for beer and movies. Dissent could be effectively articulated through a laughing response to the show and its comedians who joked defiantly and hilariously at the expense of established authority. The moniker "the Not Ready for Prime Time Players"—the name of the show's resident troupe of performers that included Chevy Chase, Gilda Radner, Dan Aykroyd, John Belushi, and other veterans of what had been considered "sick" humor—belied the reality that their work was quickly coming to dominate mainstream comedy culture. As Americans gathered in groups around television sets to enjoy *Saturday Night Live*—much as they had gathered around record players to hear *The First Family* in 1962—jokers of all types came together as a reimagined and reinvigorated company of comedians. As for the president, he could decide to join in or remain aloof, but both choices were fraught with political peril.[8]

Gerald Ford soon began to appreciate his predicament. The wide gulf between the American people and the presidency broadened further as his occasional gaffes gave his reputation as an "accidental president" unintended and unfortunate new meaning. *Saturday Night Live* was the most popular contributor to this impression as Chevy Chase regularly impersonated Ford merely through slapstick clumsiness—by falling down, say, or attempting to answer the telephone and stapling his ear instead. The show capitalized on the awareness that Americans—frustrated by the circumstances that had propelled Ford into office without their votes—sought to exercise their suffrage with laughing ridicule. Ford's verbal and physical missteps became metaphors for not only what detractors considered his personal inadequacies for the job but also the low expectations for the presidency in general following the Johnson and Nixon years. As a clown, the humiliated chief executive was expected to perform pratfalls. The entertainment and news media alike fixated on Ford's mistakes in order to accommodate these audience expectations and to capitalize on the realization that a good laugh at the president could sell both airtime and product. Ford initially hoped that the skits as well as reporters' questions about his balance and intelligence would soon run their course and disappear. But as he admitted in his autobiography, "I was wrong." From the moment he first slipped in Salzburg, "every time I stumbled or bumped my head or fell in the snow, reporters zeroed in on that to the exclusion of almost everything else."[9]

As 1975 came to a close and Ford started to plan his run for a full term the following year, his staff debated how to combat the persistent image of ineptitude. His plight was similar to that of Herbert Hoover. When Hoover was confronted by a crisis of confidence during the Great Depression, his standing as an honorable, hardworking public servant was undermined by a sullenness that rendered him unable to refute Will Rogers's description of him during their joint broadcast in 1931 as "a very human man" at a time when extraordinary leadership was needed. Schooled by history and aware of the ascendance of political humor during the intervening decades, Ford was determined not to duplicate Hoover's stolidity or the humorlessness of Lyndon Johnson and Richard Nixon. He was endowed with a quiet warmth that exuded good cheer—despite an outward demeanor that could strike people as stiff and dull—and he appreciated the importance of laughter. Keenly aware of the need to rehabilitate the image of the office, Ford took steps to project a more open and affable presidential style. He began the tradition of holding news conferences in the aesthetically pleasing White House Rose Garden during the spring and summer and was the first incumbent president to appear on a weekly news program, NBC's *Meet the Press*. He became only the third president—after Eisenhower and Nixon—to use a professional television adviser when he hired veteran news producer Robert Mead. Mead, who had assisted in the Nixon White House, eagerly went to work for Ford in order to, as he said, "apply some energy towards the right objectives [instead] of all the wrong [ones]." Within days of taking office, Ford also engaged comedy writer Robert Orben, who had written for Dick Gregory and *The Red Skelton Show*. Orben eventually became director of Ford's speechwriting department and manufactured a steady supply of anecdotes and one-liners for the president's many addresses.[10]

With these initiatives Ford illustrated his understanding that the country was at a cultural as well as a political crossroads, even if he was unsure which direction the nation would choose. In hiring Orben as well as actor and comedy writer Don Penny to help craft his speeches, he perceived the need to institutionalize the presidency's performance of humor in response to new realties. Jokes at the expense of the president no longer were simply the product of a few bold comedy entrepreneurs who were easily ignored and unlikely to find a consistently large mainstream audience. Rather, satire and other forms of ridicule were becoming commercially subsidized and mass-produced commodities. The failures and pratfalls of presidents, the comics' ability to mine them quickly for laughs, and the electronic media's expanding capability and eagerness to broadcast them for profit meant that political humor was no longer differentiated from humor in general in the minds of the American audience. Despite chafing in private at some jokes that he later admitted had tested his forbearance and, he claimed, put deep teeth marks in his favorite pipes, Ford was determined both to project good cheer and get laughs of his own.[11]

• • •

Nothing confirmed the mass commercialization of political satire more clearly than the meteoric popularity of Saturday Night Live, which quickly earned a viewership rivaling the size of Johnny Carson's, in large part owing to the frequent ridicule of the president purveyed by its brightest star, Chevy Chase. In the spring of 1976 Ford shared the rostrum with Chase at the Radio-Television Correspondents Association Dinner in Washington in what turned out to be a showcase for two comedians joined in an uneasy tango that each was intent on leading. After Ford was seated, the band reprised "Hail to the Chief," this time to announce Chase's entrance. Flanked by Saturday Night Live co-stars John Belushi and Dan Aykroyd playing Secret Service agents, he stumbled and tripped his way across the banquet hall, hit his head on the lectern, and informed the crowd, "I have asked the Secret Service to remove the salad fork embedded in my left hand." Chase's caricature capitalized on the hard-won precedents set by Will Rogers and Vaughn Meader, but as with David Frye's mimicry of Richard Nixon, there was hardly a hint of deference.[12]

Determined not to be upstaged, Ford was well prepared for what he knew were both of his roles. On prominent display as the object of the joke, he sat a few feet away from Chase, smoking his pipe and laughing appreciatively, projecting good-natured tolerance. When it came time for his performance as comedian, he purposely got caught in the tablecloth as he rose to speak and haplessly watched his "speech"—actually a sheaf of blank paper— cascade to the floor. After this precisely choreographed bit of slapstick, he launched into a routine crafted by Bob Orben and Don Penny that began with a playful tribute to his comic assailant: "I really enjoyed his fine performance. Mr. Chevy Chase, you're a very, very funny suburb." He went on to poke fun at show people with a comic reversal that acknowledged the intertwining of entertainment and politics: "I *like* the people in show business. In fact, all my life I have had nothing but respect and admiration for show business personalities. It's just that I wouldn't want my daughter voting for one." Both comics scored laughs, and the president could take delight in knowing that the professional did not steal this particular show (figs. 8 and 9).[13]

Three weeks later, emboldened by the appreciative laughs and favorable press, the Ford White House took the battle to Chase's turf. Ron Nessen, Ford's press secretary, decided to accept an invitation to host Saturday Night Live that had been offered partly in jest by Al Franken, one of the show's writers, when the two happened to meet at a campaign event in New Hampshire. Nessen reflected in his memoir that he had hoped "the sting could be taken out of the ridicule of Ford's alleged bumbling by co-opting it." He

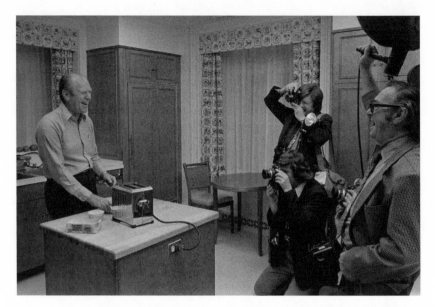

FIGURE 8. *Gerald Ford jokes with the press while demonstrating his English muffin toasting technique in the White House residence kitchen in 1974. Courtesy Gerald R. Ford Library, Ann Arbor, Michigan.*

maintained that he did not discuss his plan with Ford before agreeing to take part, although Nessen's appearance had certainly been approved by the time of the Radio-Television Correspondents dinner, where Ford made mention of it in his remarks. Ford also agreed to appear, if only fleetingly and on videotape. Lorne Michaels took a small television crew to the White House to film the president delivering the show's trademark open, "Live from New York, it's Saturday night!" as well as the quip, "I'm Gerald Ford and you're not," a takeoff on another of Chase's signature lines, "I'm Chevy Chase and you're not," which Chase used to introduce the "Weekend Update" segment. Confident that he could salvage his boss's image, show Ford to be a good sport, and possibly make inroads with younger voters in an election year, Nessen traveled to New York to host *Saturday Night Live* on April 17, 1976.[14]

Although Nessen had been a television correspondent for NBC News for twelve years prior to joining the Ford administration, he appeared out of his element once immersed in the show's industrial-strength ridicule. Ford's taped introduction from the White House earned rousing applause and recalled the novelty of Richard Nixon's brief cameo on *Laugh-In* eight years earlier, but the president's fortunes seemed to fall from there. Nessen participated in some innocuous skits, including a series peppered throughout

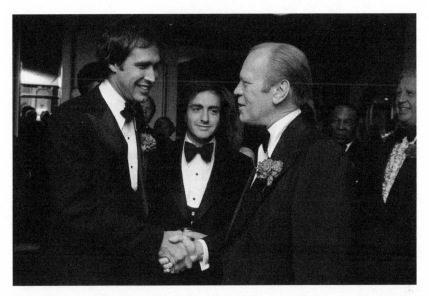

FIGURE 9. *Chevy Chase and Gerald Ford exchange pleasantries at the Radio-Television Correspondents Association Dinner in Washington, D.C., in 1976. Lorne Michaels, the executive producer of* Saturday Night Live, *stands between them. Courtesy Gerald R. Ford Library, Ann Arbor, Michigan.*

the show that featured him in costume playing "Press Secretaries through History," but other sketches were more biting. Most memorably, he played opposite Chevy Chase in another of Chase's scathing caricatures of Ford as a blank-eyed buffoon, but instead of tempering the parody with his presence, Nessen's participation lent the image of Chase's Ford accidentally stabbing himself with a letter opener the aura of authenticity. Some thought the exchange between the comedian president and the actual press secretary just zany enough to be taken for early reality television:

> CHASE AS FORD: Brief me on my schedule tomorrow, Ron.
> NESSEN: All right, sir. You'll be awakened at 5:30 a.m. in the usual manner.
> CHASE AS FORD: Ron, Betty and I are getting sick and tired of the twenty-one-gun salute. . . . Couldn't someone just speak in my ear or set the alarm clock?
> NESSEN: We tried the alarm clock at the beginning, if you'll remember, sir. When it rang, you answered the telephone and broke your ankle.[15]

Even the portions of the broadcast that did not feature Nessen had unfortunate consequences. Given Ford's introducing the show and Nessen's hosting it, mock ads for a jam called "Dog Vomit" and for a carbonated vaginal douche named "Autumn Fizz," and punk rocker Patti Smith's singing the lyric "Jesus died for somebody's sins, but not mine" the night before Easter Sunday, seemed to carry presidential approval. Few could avoid at least a passing thought of the president when cast member Gilda Radner—playing partially deaf and daft senior citizen Emily Litella—wondered why there was so much fuss about the upcoming "presidential erections." Paradoxically, even as Ford was associated with the show in this way, the stiff formality of his appearance in the videotaped clips and Nessen's decision to wear a powder blue polyester suit among a cast and crew mostly wearing jeans and sneakers exposed the profound disconnect between the presidency—and the political establishment in general—and the hip audience Nessen hoped to attract.[16]

Public response to Nessen's appearance was mixed. Negative correspondence received by the White House outpaced positive feedback by a three-to-two margin, with viewers alternately using adjectives such as "vulgar" and "disgusting" or "courageous" and "refreshing" to describe the performance. The news media, however, were nearly unanimous in interpreting it as a failure and further proof of Ford's ineptitude. At his regular press briefing the following Monday, Nessen was besieged by collegial heckling as well as hard questions about his network debut as a comedian. Did the president watch it? With Mrs. Ford? Did the president have any reservations about his participation? Did he scold Nessen about it? Did Ford approve of the Federal Communications Commission's permitting mixed audiences to see the show? Nessen squirmed as he attempted to minimize the performance and tried to move on to other topics, but to no avail. Many journalists criticized the president and Nessen in their newspaper columns. Even Ford's television adviser, Robert Mead, argued that it might be "acceptable for Gerald Ford" to participate, "but not for the Office of the President," although by 1976 fewer Americans recognized the distinction. The White House and self-appointed gatekeepers of popular culture continued to wrangle over the propriety of presidential ridicule as they had following the release of *The First Family*, but times had changed. *Saturday Night Live*'s ratings continued to soar, and by the end of that season it was NBC's second most profitable program, behind only *The Tonight Show*.[17]

Ford was narrowly defeated by Democrat Jimmy Carter in that November's election. His popular image remained that of a stumblebum, and Nessen later acknowledged that his hosting *Saturday Night Live* failed to lessen that impression. Even Ford admitted in retrospect that "it was probably" a tactical mistake to take part in the show, but his and Nessen's participation was ultimately neither a gain nor a great loss. His laughable public image was probably unavoidable, given the circumstances under which he became president, the popular distrust—even hostility—toward the office, and a growing willingness to use satire openly to express it. Despite Ford's efforts, most Americans laughed in agreement the following year when comic Woody Allen observed in his film *Annie Hall* that politicians ranked one notch below child molesters. Still, Ford's broader strategy was ultimately effective. In his attempt to rid the presidency of its imperial pretensions, he decided to make it as accessible as possible, and while this came at the expense of his political future, it paid dividends to his successors. Ford regenerated the presidency's use of humor and institutionalized it in unprecedented ways by taking comedic risks and employing writers to produce jokes. Just as significantly, he put it in the service of Republicans for the first time since the wryly subtle wit of Calvin Coolidge. He set the stage for Ronald Reagan, George H. W. Bush, and their successors by reinventing a dual role for the office that portrayed the president as both able to receive humor with good cheer and capable of performing it. Neither Ford nor his staff understood the cultural shift at work. Bob Orben later complained that humor toward the president should not cross the line by becoming mockery. "So many public figures are being brought down by ridicule," he observed. "Where are our heroes coming from . . . ? It's important to have leaders we respect." In fact the office had forfeited its moral authority and heroic cachet during the previous two administrations, leaving ridicule, for many, the last best hope for expressing their dissatisfaction. Nevertheless, Ford strove to recapture that respect. Don Penny remarked years later that after the disastrous Nixon experience, "courage and comedy in the White House started with Gerald Ford."[18]

Meanwhile, the popularity and influence of *Saturday Night Live* continued to solidify. In September 1976 the show inaugurated what would come to be recognized as its hallmark contribution to political pop culture—the mock presidential debate. With Ford and Democratic nominee Jimmy Carter locked in what would prove a tight race and about to debate each other the following week, the comedians—led by host Lily Tomlin— mischievously preempted reality. Chevy Chase took to the podium as Ford and Dan Aykroyd as Carter for what would be a landmark performance. The sketch played off Ford's love of football and not so subtly planted the thought that the president had played too often without a helmet:

LILY TOMLIN AS MODERATOR RUTH CLUSEN: Now, at the request of President Ford, Mr. Tommie Bell, the senior linesman of the National Football League, will toss the coin to determine who will be asked the first question.

CHEVY CHASE AS GERALD FORD: I'll take the side with the head on it.

UNIDENTIFIED ACTOR AS TOMMIE BELL: Heads it is. The president will receive. . . .

JANE CURTIN AS JOURNALIST LIZ MONTGOMERY: Mr. President, Governor Carter has accused you of hiding in the White House instead of meeting the people. How do you answer that charge?

CHASE AS FORD: I was not hiding. I was simply lost for a little while. The Secret Service found me and now everything is just fine. . . .

JOHN BELUSHI AS JOURNALIST TOM BURKE: Governor Carter, . . . your son Chip has admitted to smoking marijuana. . . . What is your attitude on the decriminalization of marijuana?

DAN AYKROYD AS JIMMY CARTER: Mr. Burke, as much as I love my son Chip, if I were to come upon him smoking marijuana, I would have him arrested. . . .

TOMLIN AS CLUSEN: Mr. President, rebuttal?

CHASE AS FORD: No, thank you. I've just had dinner.

The live audience—both in NBC's Studio 8H and in front of television sets at home and at parties nationwide—howled as the president of the United States was laid low and his opponent, portrayed as aloof and morally self-righteous, came off only slightly more favorably. Letters of protest were overwhelmed by ratings that further confirmed *Saturday Night Live* as among the nation's favorite programs. As viewers flocked to it, so did advertisers.[19]

With the triumph of *Saturday Night Live* and the tribulations of Gerald Ford, this exuberant dance of comedians—shaping the relationship between the people and their presidents—moved toward its postmodern denouement. The performance of political standup, particularly that aimed at the presidency, took on a mass-produced form and widespread popularity similar to that which had institutionalized vaudeville a century earlier and which persists today. As its commercial viability bloomed, crowds of new performers and other producers were drawn to a widening array of outlets for this hot commodity. NBC revived *Laugh-In* in 1977, which had left the air four years earlier, this time with a format more similar to that of *Saturday Night Live*, featuring political satire as well as physical comedy performed by guest hosts and a troupe of young unknown comedians, including Robin Williams. In 1980 ABC debuted *Fridays*, a thinly veiled copy of *Saturday Night Live* that included future *Seinfeld* co-star Michael Richards. Richard Pryor briefly starred in his own comedy-variety show on NBC in 1977, although the daring comic's material proved ill suited to the 8 pm slot on Tuesday nights. Several of his sketches provoked battles with NBC censors, and his portrayal of the first African American president—in a skit that included an endorsement of Black Panther co-founder Huey Newton to head the FBI and ended with the president attacking a reporter for making insinuating comments about his mother—seemed to many to take presidential humor at least one joke too far by putting a black man in the White House. Pryor quit the show after one month rather than fight the continual battles.[20]

As for televised comedy talk shows, the legacy first popularized by Steve Allen and Jack Paar and then made legendary by Johnny Carson proliferated even further, informed by the success of *Saturday Night Live*. In 1980 Carson—still enjoying superstar influence and still looking for more time off—negotiated a new contract with NBC that paid him $5 million a year and shortened *The Tonight Show* to sixty minutes. Faced with a challenge similar to that which produced *Saturday Night Live*, the network decided to showcase frequent Carson stand-in David Letterman with his own show following *The Tonight Show*. *Late Night with David Letterman* premiered in 1982 and gave viewers staple segments including "Stupid Pet Tricks" and "Small Town News" as well as another monologue and another venue for laughing at the president. When Letterman moved to CBS in 1993 after Jay Leno was chosen over him to replace Carson on his retirement from *The Tonight Show*, NBC named former *Saturday Night Live* writer Conan O'Brien to replace Letterman. In the course of a few years, a new host of comedians took their standup routines and sat down behind multiplying desks and microphones. There they began to dominate more and more airtime and purveyed jokes, parody, and satire that took on the president even as their material adopted a predictable, crowd-pleasing familiarity. Entrepreneurial comics joined corporate America to produce, in Mort Sahl's words, "rebellion by the pound."[21]

●　●　●

With the country still sobered by the backwash of Watergate, along with severe economic "stagflation" and a lost war in Vietnam, few Americans were specifically looking to put a comedian in the White House in 1976. But Gerald Ford was right when he sensed their desire for a chief executive who was not only honest and capable but also accessible and able to relate comfortably to a national community held together predominantly by the images and rhetoric of entertainment. Given both the successes and failures of presidents from Franklin Roosevelt to Richard Nixon and the commodification of humor lobbed at the White House by comedians turned celebrities, there was growing pressure on the president to project himself more openly as celebrity in chief.[22]

Jimmy Carter proved unable to fill the bill. Forthright and intelligent, Carter was a born-again Christian, former Georgia governor, and peanut farmer whose down-home informality and modest national credentials—unsullied by Washington politics—appealed to Americans looking to return to the nation's founding simplicity in its bicentennial year. His toothy, engaging smile, however, belied a seriousness that rarely gave way to humor and struck many as arrogance and a presumption of moral superiority. Carter very reluctantly followed Ford's lead and brought a humorist—Jerry Dolittle—onto his speechwriting staff, but he rejected much of what Dolittle wrote for him and proved inept at performing the rest. To Ford aide Don Penny, who also worked for Carter, it seemed that the president lacked the soul of a humorist: "I observed his lack of humor. I looked in Carter's eyes and I saw buttons. The second time I looked into his eyes I saw his feet." Carter, for his part, was unrepentant: "If the American people wanted Bob Hope for their president, they should have elected him." His humorlessness was emblematic of an administration that failed to extricate the nation from its profound economic malaise and international crises including the seizure of the American embassy and its staff in Tehran, Iran, in 1979. Even worse, he failed to project the star power required to convince Americans that they had the capacity to conquer these challenges. By 1980 Americans were looking for a new headliner, and in the parlance of the show business world that produced him, Ronald Reagan "nailed" the part.[23]

More than any other president, Reagan was a born comedian, a natural. His personal journey to distinction and fame followed a path that harked back to those blazed by Will Rogers, Samuel Clemens, and Charles Browne and exemplified the transformational odyssey of self-invention that had become a hallmark of the national mythology. Raised in the early twentieth century, a period of dynamic tensions between conservatism and progressivism, the rural tradition and the promise of the burgeoning modern cities, Reagan moved with his family to six different cities in six years before finally settling in small-town Dixon, Illinois, west of Chicago, where his Irish American father was a struggling shoe salesman but a more dedicated alcoholic. Graduating from tiny Eureka College in the depths of the Great Depression, the young Reagan gravitated toward the opportunities of the cosmopolitan West in increments of self-discovery, first to Davenport and Des Moines, Iowa, where as a radio sportscaster he cast himself as "Dutch Reagan," then to Hollywood in 1937, where, with no film training or experience, he landed a contract with Warner Brothers mostly on the basis of his handsome looks and cheerful manner. As with Browne's transformation into Artemus Ward and Clemens's into Mark Twain, Ronald Reagan redefined himself through performance and good humor as he negotiated the modern American frontiers between old truths and new opportunities and between authenticity and illusion.[24]

Reagan knew how to tell a story, deliver a punch line, and make people laugh, but he ultimately applied these skills to politics rather than to a career as a standup comic, although the two vocations already coincided in peculiar ways in the glazed reality of Hollywood and sunny southern California. With his film career waning by the early 1950s, he began to give talks to local civic groups. Then he accepted an offer by General Electric to host its half-hour television show, *G.E. Theater*, and serve as something of a corporate cheerleader by speaking at G.E. plants across the country. In the process, he perfected his skills before a live crowd, and by giving voice to his fervent anticommunism and his dislike for what he maintained was a bloated and intrusive central government, he completed his transformation from liberal Democrat to conservative Republican. In 1964 he drew national attention by delivering an impassioned speech in support of presidential candidate Barry Goldwater. While he could not prevent Goldwater's staggering defeat by Lyndon Johnson, Reagan caught the attention of party leaders, who sensed his magical quality before an audience. More particularly, in contrast with the fear-mongering doomsday seriousness characteristic of many conservatives, Reagan projected a beaming smile and ready humor. In this he consciously and deliberately emulated Franklin Roosevelt, whose indomitable optimism — if not his politics — Reagan continued to idolize throughout his life. Here was a cheerful conservative.[25]

Reagan's effervescent nature, topped off as it was by his sparkling love of a good joke, did much to win him the White House in 1980. Americans were weary of a national mood that roamed between grief, melancholia, fear, and outrage over the events of the previous two decades since John F. Kennedy's assassination, and they eagerly responded to Reagan, who evoked the same buoyant spirit of bold, energetic nationalism espoused by Kennedy and Franklin Roosevelt, even as he rejected their ideology in favor of a conservatism that believed government was too big and the military too small. Reagan believed that America needed to be reminded of its grand exceptionalism. The presidency, he insisted, functioned in large part to project this greatness. If Gerald Ford was modestly successful in rehabilitating the office, Reagan was intent on exalting it with cinematic magnificence.[26]

He did so with relish, and his humor was central to his success. Like Roosevelt and Kennedy, he effectively utilized one-liners and anecdotes to promote specific programs and policies in speeches that charmed the media and often frustrated congressional leaders, who found themselves merrily circumvented. He employed jokes to blunt the edge of his ideological attacks on social programs and his positions on controversial issues. "I've been getting some flak about ordering the production of the B-1 [bomber]," he admitted on one occasion. "How did I know it was an airplane? I thought it was a vitamin for the troops." More significantly, he used humor instinctively to reimagine for Americans a nostalgic sense of ideal possibility. His unshakably upbeat manner, often expressed through the "Morning in America" metaphor that he called on frequently and that became the theme of his 1984 reelection campaign, dovetailed luminously with Ford's pronouncement years earlier that the "long national nightmare" of Watergate was over. Reagan lent the dark-to-bright imagery a utopian brilliance. His jaunty rhetoric implied not only that a new era of opportunity and promise was dawning but also that the previous twenty years could and should be forgotten. Many Americans came to interpret his smiling confidence as celebratory reassurance that the incongruities between the nation's ideals and its realities—the "Great American Joke" that had seemed so laughably intractable for two centuries—were well on their way to being reconciled. America stood, as Reagan often said, as a shining "City upon a Hill," recalling the idealized Puritan image first expressed by Governor John Winthrop in 1630 and reinforced by Reagan's Illinois upbringing in the Disciples of Christ Church. The president saw this City in very tangible terms, and without realizing it, he recalled for his fellow citizens the long-standing national reverence for humor—from the days of jest-books, Benjamin Franklin, and Seba Smith—as one of its foundational components.[27]

Americans in general responded enthusiastically to these images because Reagan simultaneously embodied the showman president and the comic-heroic everyman. As Reagan biographer Lou Cannon observed, the president steadfastly believed that "he was not really a politician at all, but simply an actor on loan from Hollywood." The intertwining of Reagan's Hollywood and political careers characterized his presidency throughout his two terms. In 1988 his leading lady, Nancy Reagan, demonstrated that eight years in the White House had not changed this outlook when she observed that the time had come "for the Bushes to step into the political leading roles and for the Reagans to step into the wings." The majority of Americans not only were unconcerned by such references; they were enthralled by the illusion. Reagan played into the rhetoric of celebrity and show that had been incubating in American culture since the days of Artemus Ward's fascination with "the show bizniss." This fascination accelerated along with mass media and dallied increasingly with presidential politics over the next century until—as Lenny Bruce maintained—the distinction between performance and reality was virtually nonexistent by the time television mania took hold in the 1950s and early 1960s, although it would be another twenty years before sheer showmanship manifested itself openly in the White House.[28]

The public knew in 1980 and 1984 that they were voting for the consummate showman president; they came to expect illusion from Reagan and were not unduly alarmed when it was revealed as such. As they had during the postwar 1920s and 1950s following other periods of national trauma, Americans chose to engage in entertaining diversion and—as historian Richard Hofstadter wrote—"sentimental appreciation rather than . . . critical analysis" where governance was concerned. It mattered little that Reagan spoke tenderly about religious faith yet rarely attended church, or championed the family unit but was the first divorced president and was estranged from his children. He often quipped, "Government does not solve problems; it subsidizes them," yet he left a much larger government billions of dollars deeper in debt than the one he inherited. But by performing the presidency sincerely, which included the talent to *take* as well as *make* jokes, Reagan did what Americans had done since the birth of the republic: he used humor to ingratiate himself into community with fellow citizens while distinguishing himself at the same time. Paradoxically, while Reagan reestablished the imperial presidency to its greatest height in a generation, he successfully portrayed himself as a Washington outsider standing in solidarity with common citizens in mocking opposition to the very bureaucracy over which he held executive power. The public applauded when he compared feeding tax dollars to the government with feeding a stray dog: "It just follows you home and sits on your doorstep asking for more." To many, including young people, who gave him large majorities against Jimmy Carter in 1980 and Democratic nominee Walter Mondale in 1984, he was a wisecracking hero patriotically standing up to the abuses of big government. This heroic legend crystallized early in his presidency when, after an assassination attempt nearly took his life, he managed to cut up with the physicians who tended to his wounds. At a news conference following the shooting, Reagan press aide Lyn Nofziger recounted to reporters the president's quip as he was being wheeled by his doctors into surgery: "I hope all you fellows are Republicans." Such one-liners may have been apocryphal, but it did not matter. Reagan performed as billed, supplying good humor and—with his full recovery—a happy and courageous Hollywood ending. In the process, he hard-wired humor to heroism more profoundly than any other president since Franklin Roosevelt.[29]

As a result, an enthusiastically positive "zeitgeist" developed around Reagan that not only blunted most of the sharp humor aimed at him but also insulated him personally from serious charges of wrongdoing, particularly with regard to the constitutional abuses of the Iran-contra scandal during his second term. Congresswoman Pat Schroeder called him the "Teflon president" because nothing negative ever seemed to stick to him. Reagan maintained a stealth offensive of charm that frustrated critics even as it completely disarmed them, and his flair for storytelling and self-deprecating humor added to what Bob Orben called a "balance of goodwill" that always remained high. A quick, deflecting one-liner was frequently enough to do the trick. "Just for the record, I'm speaking in jest here," he said to a group of photojournalists in 1988. "Of course, some of you think I've been doing that for eight years now."[30]

For the same reasons, Reagan also managed to upstage the professional comedians despite the rapid commercialization of presidential ridicule. In contrast to his more immediate predecessors and, later, Bill Clinton and George W. Bush, the popular president largely eclipsed the iconoclasts who sought to take him to task, whether for attempting to cut social programs or for his large expenditures on the military. There was much humor directed at Reagan, of course, but it was more than neutralized in the public mind by the performance of the real star, the president himself. In this way, making fun of Reagan was reminiscent of the adulatory spoofs of John Kennedy such as *The First Family*. Mainstream comics most frequently poked fun at Reagan's age and intellect or issues ancillary to these, such as his leisurely work schedule and his disengagement from day-to-day governing; but their material was generally soft parody or gentle ribbing that did little to disturb the consensus of approval. Often it barely masked open admiration. Mort Sahl observed during the 1984 campaign that when "Reagan goes to a home for the elderly and meets an 80-year-old man, he thinks, 'When I was your age I was working.'" Some barbs were sharper, but they were darting punch lines that flew by and rarely stabbed. Mark Russell, the comedian and pianist whose jovial routines first made him a local favorite in Washington, D.C.'s, Shoreham Hotel during the 1960s and later on PBS, once asked: "What do you get when you combine James Dean and Ronald Reagan? Rebel without a Clue." Peggy Noonan, one of Reagan's speechwriters, later registered one of the most trenchant gibes when she needled her former boss with a nod to the rhetoric of Winston Churchill—"The battle for the mind of Ronald Reagan was like the trench warfare of World War I: never have so many fought so hard for such barren terrain."[31]

Ironically, it was not *Saturday Night Live* or its budding crop of imitators but *The Tonight Show*—Johnny Carson's old reliable late-night serving of comedic comfort food—that more consistently lampooned the Reagan White House. By 1980 all of the original stars of *Saturday Night Live*, including Lorne Michaels, had departed the show for more lucrative projects, leaving it short on consistent talent and vision until Michaels was enticed back in 1985. There was a relative dearth of political satire on the show, and some among the writers and cast voiced frustration that part of its founding mission had been forfeited at a time when it was most needed. The show's tradition of presidential impersonation established by Chevy Chase continued during the Reagan years—performed by Harry Shearer, Randy Quaid, and Phil Hartman, among others—but these efforts lacked consistency. Carson, meanwhile, earned laughs with his regular impressions of the president. Sporting rouge on his cheeks to approximate Reagan's ruddy complexion, a black wig, and a blank expression, Carson often spoofed the president's age while reveling in the conflation of politics and show business that Reagan so blatantly personified:

> REPORTER: Mr. President . . .
> CARSON AS REAGAN: Yes, that's what it says on my checks. My Social Security card also says number one, but I think that's for when it was issued. . . .
> REPORTER: Mr. President, you've called the Soviet Union the Evil Empire—
> CARSON AS REAGAN: That used to be MGM, but I think Louis B. Mayer may have died. I may have, too. [It's] so hard to keep track.
> REPORTER: Well, let me ask you a different question. . . .
> CARSON AS REAGAN: Yes, I've already forgotten that one.
> REPORTER: What do you plan to do about Red China?
> CARSON AS REAGAN: Replace some of it with blue china. . . . Say, how do you like the movies now that they're talkies?[32]

Carson's jokes could be more acidic, such as his ridicule of Reagan's choice of advisers and staff members, 138 of whom were prosecuted on criminal or ethics charges and left the administration under a variety of circumstances: "There is a power struggle going on between President Reagan's advisors. Moe and Curly are out. Larry is still in." The popularity of such jests—emanating from the master impresario, Carson, in the world capital of illusion, Hollywood—befitted both Reagan's show business pedigree and the mood of a nation either comfortable with or resigned to its Hollywood presidency. Predictably, Reagan always managed to recapture center stage and defuse the comedians by becoming one. Regarding the competence of his conservative right-wing administration, he freely joked, "Sometimes our right hand doesn't know what our far-right hand is doing." As for the age issue: "[House Speaker Thomas P. "Tip"] O'Neill once asked me how I keep myself looking so young for the cameras. I told him I have a good makeup team. It's the same people who've been repairing the Statue of Liberty." Most famously, when his age became more of a concern in 1984 as the seventy-three-year-old president faced a challenge from fifty-six-year-old

Walter Mondale, Reagan was ready. Asked during their second televised debate whether he had any doubt about his ability to meet the demands of the office, he saw his cue: "Not at all, . . . and I want you to know that . . . I will not make age an issue of this campaign. I am not going to exploit for political purposes my opponent's youth and inexperience." The hall erupted, and even Mondale made no attempt to disguise his appreciation. The issue was smothered by laughter, and Mondale's election hopes were similarly smothered by Reagan's landslide victory two weeks later.[33]

Ronald Reagan was a king of comedy. With his mastery of humor as performance art, he took the presidency beyond performative parity to temporary supremacy over both the professional standups who were beginning to dominate popular culture and a sophisticated national audience that was not merely receptive to humor directed at the president but proving insatiable in its appetite for it. He accomplished this largely by nature but also by nurture. Reagan applied his instinctive talent to skills honed by the hard experience and easy laughter of predecessors from Abraham Lincoln to Jack Kennedy, from Mark Twain to Will Rogers to Johnny Carson, and from two presidents named Roosevelt. He took full command of the stage set by Gerald Ford by building on Ford's amiability and following his precedent of importing comedy writers onto his speechwriting staff. Much of Reagan's material was his own, but he understood the new economy of political humor at least as well as Ford. To keep up with the comedy writers filling the private sector, the president's survival demanded that they work in the public sector as well. Reagan synthesized these many influences and capitalized on them. Landon Parvin, chief comedy writer during Reagan's first term, understood even before Reagan left office how his administration had redefined the landscape of presidential humor: "I don't think people realize how he has changed what is going to be expected of a politician." In fact this realization had been dawning for most of the previous century. Those who followed Reagan could only hope to equal his performance with their own. Parvin went on to craft jokes for both George H. W. and George W. Bush and wrote the routine performed by Laura Bush at the White House Correspondents' Association dinner in 2005.[34]

• • •

Reagan's legacy reverberated in other directions as well. In its ideological zeal for deregulating government, his administration sought to remove what it considered the roadblocks to free enterprise, and none of these initiatives had more impact on popular culture than the changes to American broadcasting. Cable television began to threaten the three commercial networks—ABC, CBS, and NBC—with booming subscription numbers during the 1970s, and popular channels including HBO, which debuted in 1972, ESPN in 1979, and CNN in 1980, grew even faster during the Reagan years. The Cable Act of 1984 allowed cable channels to charge viewers as much as the market would bear, and dozens of new networks continued to appear, including the Fox Network in 1986 and Comedy Central, which debuted on April Fool's Day, 1991.[35]

Other profound effects on broadcasting came from actions taken by the Federal Communications Commission and, in the words of Reagan's FCC chairman Mark Fowler, its "policy of 'unregulation.'" Believing television to be "just another appliance . . . [a] toaster with pictures," Fowler and the FCC granted licenses to hundreds of new stations, lifted restrictions on the number of commercials aired during a program, and increased the number of stations a company was allowed to own in a single market. In 1987 it dissolved what had been known as the "Fairness Doctrine," the requirement in place since 1934 that obligated broadcasters—as "public trustees"—to confront controversial issues in a balanced way, giving "equal opportunities" to opposing views. No longer encumbered by such mandates, and facing increased competition from all sides, producers began to generate programming that was more daring and likely to attract viewers because of provocative content, be it violence, sex, or a particular political perspective. The network restrictions that once censored the Smothers Brothers and TW3 as well as Lenny Bruce, Mort Sahl, and other "sick comedians" further evaporated in the friction between cultural propriety and economic profit.[36]

These developments radically affected the quantity and diversity of what Americans saw and heard on mass media. They also accelerated the intertwining of popular and political culture and gave renewed power to the commercial producers of humor at the expense of the presidency. Television shows proliferated that dashed old formulas and assumptions and openly showcased digs at the president. *The Simpsons*, which premiered in 1989, was similar to other shows that subverted the family sitcom, such as *Married . . . with Children* and *Roseanne*, but it became the longest-running situation comedy in the history of the medium—and a metaphor, even a worldview for many—thanks largely to its satiric commentary on all manner of authority. This has included, at some point, virtually every president in American history, each one cheerily reduced to an animated cartoon. The cascade of late-night shows influenced by Johnny Carson was accompanied by an even larger wave of sketch and comedy-talk offerings in the wake of deregulation and the boom in cable television, including *Not Necessarily the News* on HBO and *MadTV* and *In Living Color* on the Fox Network, all of which included liberal servings of political parody and satire. Just as significantly, the end of the Fairness Doctrine combined with the intense competition for ratings permanently blurred the boundaries between news reports, editorial commentary, political campaigning, and entertainment. This not only initiated intense new debates among journalists, salespeople, politicians, comedians, and other show business figures over who carries more legitimacy in the public exchange of information and ideas, but also set the stage for the success of self-described "fake news" programs such as *The Daily Show*, which premiered on Comedy Central in 1996, and its popular spin-off, *The Colbert Report*, in 2005.[37]

Ronald Reagan's adoration of show business, in combination with his administration's promotion of it through deregulation, empowered the comedians of mass media tremendously. In the process, his influence also inadvertently presented subsequent presidents with new challenges that threatened to typecast them once again as the fool—the butt of the joke—and even more definitively than Gerald Ford had been. The marketplace for political humor is now an ever louder, more crowded bazaar, much more congested than during Ford's administration. The points of sale for broad parody, cutting impersonation, elaborate satire, and cheap one-liners speckle the airwaves and the Internet. The influence once wielded by Johnny Carson is even more extensive and diffuse, no longer concentrated in one personality, to be sure, but refracted through a large and growing cast of comedian luminaries—Jay Leno, David Letterman, Conan O'Brien, Jon Stewart, and Stephen Colbert shining brightly among them—who have become household names. The standup showmen dominate the scene.

As for showman presidents, they play on, understanding that the distance from the public once afforded by traditional deference vanished with Herbert Hoover and that—as Will Rogers and Franklin Roosevelt first taught—the president can ill afford not to harness the power of humor for political gain and popular support. But Ronald Reagan has been a hard act to follow for two reasons. In personal terms, the glow of his charismatic good cheer proved largely impossible for his successors to eclipse, just as Harry Truman and Lyndon Johnson discovered in the wake of Franklin Roosevelt and John Kennedy. The second reason is more vexing. Reagan's buoyant humor masked a serious dislike for government that resonated strongly with many of the Americans who elected and reelected him. When he stepped—as Nancy Reagan said—"into the wings" of southern California at the end of his eight-year run, this dislike not only remained but deepened into zealous vituperation among conservatives, especially when, after four more years under Reagan's vice president, George H. W. Bush, executive control over the despised federal government passed in 1992 to Democrat Bill Clinton, whom many of them considered the antithesis of their hero in every respect. The jocular disdain for government that Reagan emanated was replaced by much more caustic ridicule of Clinton's policies, his private life, and even—with the exposure in 1998 of his sexual relationship with White House intern Monica Lewinsky—his private parts. Comedians of all political persuasions, both onstage and in the workplace, gorged on the farcical excesses of Clinton's personal follies and peculiarities, whether the "feel your pain" rasp of his voice, his cravings for fast food, or the Lewinsky affair and subsequent impeachment. Any hesitation to mock the presidency had long since vanished, owing to the rise of earlier comedians and the fall of earlier presidents, but Clinton faced a new brand of comic. Presented with the first two-term Democratic president since Roosevelt and therefore a threat to Reagan's legacy, conservatives took full advantage of the media landscape left behind by Reagan's deregulation, bursting as it was with new opportunities to be heard but devoid of any restraints under the Fairness Doctrine. Talk radio became their stage. The popularity of the format ballooned under Reagan's FCC; the number of talk radio stations—barely two hundred at the beginning of Reagan's first term—quadrupled by Clinton's election in 1992. New voices, captured by microphones from behind desks essentially identical to Jay Leno's and David Letterman's, railed mercilessly against Clinton's presidency and at what they considered even more unpardonable: Clinton's complicity in what conservatives viewed as the acts of cultural warfare during the 1960s and 1970s, including Lyndon Johnson's Great Society, the civil rights movement, the Vietnam War, and the women's movement. Their audiences, listening from behind the wheel or at work and calling in with a jab of their own, delighted in assaulting with laughter the man they considered the kingpin of the liberal left.[38]

This new strain of comedian was and continues to be epitomized by talk radio giant Rush Limbaugh. An itinerant disc jockey during the 1970s, he was hired and fired by numerous stations across the country, finally landing a job in Sacramento, California, where he began to build an audience. A syndication deal took him to New York City, where he premiered his national broadcast in August 1988. The timing was perfect; Limbaugh's appearance dovetailed seamlessly with the departure of the Republicans' heroic but soft-hearted president. Taking over as the second half of their right-wing tag team, Limbaugh soon replaced Reagan as the laughing—or in Limbaugh's case, sneering—oracle of American conservatism. The day Clinton was inaugurated, he unveiled an "America Held Hostage" graphic on his short-lived television show, thus beginning an eight-year running attack on the Clinton White House filled with derision and including large doses of dark humor at the president's expense, including one-liners and stinging but immensely popular vocal impersonations of Clinton by comedian Paul Shanklin. Equipped with a biting sense of both humor and timing, Limbaugh is a talented satirist whose take-no-prisoners intensity has been vociferously condemned by his critics but embraced by the estimated 14 million weekly members of his laughing chorus, most of whom refer to themselves as "dittoheads." Although his radio influence and large—if intensely partisan—populism is vaguely reminiscent of Will Rogers's, his is relentlessly more strident. Any hints of reconciliation, accommodation, or equanimity have been exorcized as signs of capitulation in the high-stakes culture wars between red and blue states that resemble the zero-sum comedy wars waged by Abbie Hoffman and others decades ago. Yet now as then, such humor resonates. What is more, it sells.[39]

Much remains the same, but much more has changed over the past two hundred years. Artemus Ward and Mr. Dooley could never have imagined—although Will Rogers and Mark Twain could—that in the early twenty-first century the political comedians would be invested with the sort of comprehensive sovereignty that presidents and candidates can only dream of: political influence, economic power, and cultural celebrity. Comics have acquired the influence to sway political discourse and grab headlines; they appear on the news more frequently than presidents with their jokes and gibes, and even shape the identities of those who are or would be president. Al Gore discovered this when he ran against George W. Bush in 2000. Four days after the first televised debate, the encounter was spoofed on *Saturday Night Live*, with comedian Will Ferrell playing a dim-bulb George Bush spouting malapropisms and his co-star Darrell Hammond a stiffly clownish Gore. Rather than accept the exaggerated caricature with good cheer, and fearful that the show's 7 million viewers would accept Hammond's impersonation as the truth, Gore's staff worked to correct their candidate's perceived deficiencies. This resulted in Gore's struggling to depict himself differently in the second and third debates, which contributed, according to journalist Howard Fineman, "to the lasting impression that Gore is a political changeling incapable of presenting himself honestly." Such perceptions might have been less consequential at other times, but in 2000—when the presidency hung by a chad—every punch line, if not every vote, counted. Gore's experience further demonstrated the stealthy power of laughter: the comedian's lessons still must be mastered. Subsequent White House hopefuls could only continue to smile and joke, laugh and learn.[40]

EPILOGUE

߀ack to the Future

*O*N APRIL 17, 2008, Stephen Colbert broadcast his half-hour satiric send-up of political infotainment, *The Colbert Report*, from the birthplace of American democratic government: Philadelphia. In the wake of the latest debate between the Democratic candidates for the presidential nomination, and just prior to that month's Pennsylvania primary, all the leading players gathered in the University of Pennsylvania's Zellerbach Theater, where the show had been in residence all week, to play their parts and share a few laughs. The apparently immortal Ben Franklin—inventor, founding father, and pioneering political funnyman—sitting off to the side as Colbert's special sidekick for the week, proudly announced he had just invented the toaster. Colbert informed the three-hundred-year-old comedian turned foil that he was a century too late. Then, one by one, Democratic presidential hopefuls Hillary Clinton, John Edwards, and Barack Obama made their entrance to share some fleeting one-on-one time with the star. Clinton demonstrated her ability to solve a sudden crisis by fixing Colbert's mammoth but malfunctioning rear projection screen, and Edwards, who by this time was out of contention for the nomination, came on to discuss the importance of universal health care but wound up admitting, to the audience's delight, that what he really wanted was a jet ski, maybe two. Finally, as the pièce de résistance, Obama materialized via video link from a campaign rally—his own audience behind him, Colbert's in front—to complain jovially about what he called Republicans' and the media's fixation with "manufactured political distractions," such as whether his decision to wear an American flag lapel pin or not was a question of patriotism. Colbert, of course, held court throughout as the merriment swirled around the eye of his comic approval. He dispensed one-liners and satiric commentary while earnestly playing the character—that of a bombastic right-wing demagogue—that earned him the attention of millions of fans four nights a week on Comedy Central, as well as second place on *Time* magazine's readers' list of the most influential people of 2008.[1]

The Colbert broadcast exemplified the postmodern dance of the comedians. All those involved performed the various roles that have become commercialized rituals in the national culture. In the process of vying to be the next president of the United States, candidates auditioned to become celebrity in chief by displaying a stage persona that now requires first and foremost a sense of humor and a knack for spontaneously making jokes as well as taking them. Clinton and Obama understood—as did Republican nominee John McCain, who appeared frequently on the *Late Show with David Letterman* and more than a dozen times on *The Daily Show with Jon Stewart* during the election cycle—that the perils of being upstaged by the public's happy memories of Ronald Reagan, John Kennedy, or Franklin Roosevelt could be politically fatal. In paying tribute to Colbert and his audience, candidates could lay claim to these former presidents' genial pedigree. As for Colbert, he commanded center stage—just as Stewart, Letterman, Bill Maher, and Jay Leno did in their own venues—as a powerful critic whose joking commentaries shaped cultural impressions and helped determine political futures, much as Will Rogers dominated stage, radio, and print during the 1920s and 1930s. Rogers's syndicated newspaper column—his "daily telegrams"—had become Stewart's *Daily Show* and Colbert's nightly *Report*. But whereas Rogers's influence was unrivaled and uniquely tied to his talents, as well as to the willing cooperation of a laughing president in step with the comedian and a public eager to take its cue from both men, the intervening decades and the passing parade of other presidents and comics begat legions of political comedians. Their punch lines now are packaged in bulk and digitally mass-produced, subject not to presidential approval or questions of propriety but to insatiable consumer demand.[2]

Some continue to object to the proliferation of presidential ridicule out of traditional respect for the office. Many argue that such performances—to the extent that they demean presidents and force candidates to suspend "serious" campaigning to crack jokes—are themselves examples of the manufactured political distractions referred to by Obama on *The Colbert Report*. But such reticence has long since been laughed down by overriding commercial imperatives that have institutionalized jabs at the president and made them virtually inseparable not just from nonpolitical humor but even from other forms of political discourse. The visual, electronic, and print media are saturated with posters, books, and broadcasts that poke fun at every aspect of presidential life. World Wide Web sites such as JibJab.com, TheOnion.com, About.com's bulging clearinghouse of political humor, and—with the arrival of the Obama administration—TeleprompterPresident.com offer no end of jokes, satire, sound bites, and images trampling the office and those in it.

On television, where *TW3* and *The Smothers Brothers Comedy Hour* were banished from the marketplace during the 1960s, *The Tonight Show*'s once virtual monopoly on presidential humor has been utterly busted by the ripple effects of Johnny Carson's influence, which launched not only *Saturday Night Live* in 1975 but also subsequently the careers of Jay Leno and David Letterman with their highly rated shows, and by extension the television celebrity of Jon Stewart, Stephen Colbert, Will Ferrell, Bill Maher, Conan O'Brien, Jimmy Kimmel, and others. The monologue, the top ten list, the "word," and other nightly staples have become daily requirements for feeding workplace conversation and the twenty-four-hour news cycle, as cable news organizations reprise the funniest gags numerous times daily. For three weeks in October 2008, NBC super-sized *Saturday Night Live* by also producing *Saturday Night Live Weekend Update Thursday* during prime time to capitalize on the sensational spike in popularity of the show generated by the remarkable impersonation of the Republican vice presidential nominee, Alaska governor Sarah Palin, by one of the show's most popular stars, Tina Fey. More than four decades after it preempted *TW3* in advance of the 1964 election, and thirty-two years after the Not Ready for Prime Time Players first spoofed a presidential debate on *Saturday Night Live*, NBC embraced presidential satire and injected it into its schedule wherever it could. In the fall of 2009 Jay Leno also moved to prime time on NBC, carrying with him his monologue and many of the other political ingredients of *The Tonight Show*, ceded to Conan O'Brien, whose *Late Night* was in turn inherited by *Saturday Night Live* alumnus Jimmy Fallon.

Political comedians are everywhere. Though professional humorists' faces are represented on U.S. currency only by Benjamin Franklin on the hundred-dollar bill, their performances have become legal tender for exchanging laughs and selling all manner of products worth millions. On the same day George W. Bush left office in January 2009, Will Ferrell made his Broadway debut in a one-man show, *You're Welcome America: A Final Night with George W Bush*, which reunited the comedian with the impersonation that launched his national celebrity during the 2000 campaign. Leno's and Colbert's faces have graced packages of snack chips, and Colbert even appeared in an issue of Marvel Comics' *The Amazing Spider-Man* in 2008, beating out Barack Obama, who starred alongside the same superhero in a January 2009 issue commemorating the president's inauguration.[3]

The ebb and flow of events and national traumas continue to affect the tidal wave of humor leveled at the chief executive, but they have done little to alter the cultural or economic basis for it. Both supply and demand clearly surge during election years, and likewise when a president's approval ratings dip. National tragedy still carries a chilling effect, but the cold soon melts in the heat of resurgent laughter—sparked by catharsis, cynicism, or hope, and fueled by the drive for profits. As in the aftermath of the Kennedy assassination in 1963, most Americans had little tolerance for presidential satire or other comedic commentary immediately following the terrorist attacks of September 11, 2001. Comedian Bill Maher was fired and his ABC program, *Politically Incorrect*, was canceled not long after when Maher seemed to compare favorably the courage of the al Qaeda terrorists—who personally flew airliners into buildings—with that of American leaders who, he said, "have been the cowards, lobbing cruise missiles from 2,000 miles away." Nevertheless, Maher soon bounced back with a standup comedy tour and a new show on HBO. As for *Saturday Night Live*, it opened its twenty-seventh season on schedule less than three weeks after the attacks, but the show was largely a tribute to those who had been lost and to American resilience, and its ridicule was kept far away from George W. Bush. "Can we be funny?" producer Lorne Michaels asked New York mayor Rudolph Giuliani in the opening of the show. "Why start now?" replied the mayor, happy to provide a cathartic punch line, and the laughter slowly resumed. After four somber months, David Letterman was among the first to break the tacit moratorium against presidential ridicule by alluding—to his audience's delight—to Bush's briefly choking on a pretzel while watching a football game on TV in the White House. The humor aimed at Bush was benign—a mild reference to a president of the United States unable to successfully eat a snack food— but within a few seconds, as if to make up for lost time and his necessarily soft treatment of the commander in chief, Letterman managed to get in a few more caustic jibes at Vice President Dick Cheney and former president Bill Clinton for good measure:

> Just about now, a military tribunal is convicting a pretzel. . . . [The president] was out cold for four seconds. Fortunately, it was the same four seconds that Dick Cheney was conscious. . . . This, of course, is not the first choking episode in the White House. The last time, the president actually got caught in someone else's mouth.

Neither Cheney's nor Clinton's reaction earned coverage, but Bush was quick to acknowledge the moment and join in the fun, wisecracking the next day: "My mother always said when you're eating pretzels, chew before you swallow. Listen to your mother."[4]

Occasionally the supply of jokes is depressed despite soaring demand, underscoring the economic and cultural significance of humor many considered treasonous not long before. In November 2007 the Writers Guild of America voted to strike in the wake of stalled negotiations with producers over compensation for Internet and DVD content. The work stoppage idled twelve thousand film and television writers, including those for *The Daily Show*, *The Colbert Report*, *The Tonight Show*, and other programs, and halted the industrialized manufacture of one-liners and other humorous commodities for three months. The period coincided with some of the lowest approval ratings for George W. Bush to date, yet the mainstream comedians were largely silent, and their networks lost millions of dollars. In contrast with the 1950s and 1960s, when sponsors shuddered at the prospect of alienating viewers with presidential satire, in 2007 they quaked at the thought of television without it. Anxious to stem the losses and satisfy audience demand, several comics returned to the air in early January, fully one month before the strike was settled, although in most cases without the contributions of their writers. David Letterman's production company, Worldwide Pants, Inc., entered into an interim agreement with the Writers Guild and returned at full strength. Jay Leno maintained that he had a right to compose and perform his own material on *The Tonight Show* despite his membership in the union, attracting the ire of Writers Guild officials. Leno's actions drew attention both to the high-stakes debate over the commercial distinction between creativity and performance and to the value in the twenty-first-century economy of Leno's—or any comedian's—labor and the resulting laughter. The economics and the politics of humor had converged. Most important for everyone, by early 2008 the strike was over and the laughs were turned back on, just in time to revitalize the balance sheets for the new year and take aim at the presidential primary season.[5]

These comedic performances are highly valued, not only because they possess formidable commercial value as entertainment, but also because they are endowed with political legitimacy and authority in a popular culture in which the meaning of performance and its relationship to reality is highly contested. As the findings of the Pew Research Center for the People and the Press discussed at the beginning of this book show, many Americans, especially young people, rely on programs such as *The Daily Show*, *Saturday Night Live*, and *The Colbert Report* not merely for entertainment but for political news as well, and the audiences for these shows—which tend to be young overall—are among the most knowledgeable about news in general. This overlapping of playful diversion with serious discussion of news is not surprising, given the widespread deregulation in the communications industry during the 1980s and the intense competition network television faced from cable outlets and video recording devices that led to the thinning, then virtual disappearance, of any consistent line separating entertainment from journalism. In the grab for high ratings, news organizations have contributed to the confusion with their penchant for sensationalism, blatant promotions of entertainment programming thinly veiled as hard news stories, and the exaltation of bombastic talk-show hosts and infotainment pundits in the guise of traditional journalists. Indeed audiences have long since abandoned the conventional understanding of television journalism as it became ritualized during the 1960s and 1970s. In response, Stewart and Colbert, for their part, perform as commentators and broadcasters of what Stewart calls "fake news" on sets bedecked with video monitors displaying reporters "on location" and all the other slick trappings of conventional news operations. They openly mock the time-honored ritual of "real" news with their meticulous satire of it and by virtue of their comedy credentials. By frankly acknowledging the absurdity of the performance and reveling in it, but with an honest and rigorous inquisitiveness, The Daily Show and The Colbert Report ironically open up the possibility of legitimate political discourse. The result is political satire that nearly 2 million viewers daily find refreshing, informative, and credible. Bill Moyers, a longtime journalist and former aide to Lyndon Johnson, observed that "you simply can't understand American politics in the new millennium without The Daily Show."[6]

In so effectively satirizing what he and millions of other Americans consider the forfeited authority of television journalism, Stephen Colbert and his fellow comedians have cunningly further complicated the distinction between fact and fancy. During the premiere episode of The Colbert Report in October 2005, he inaugurated his regular "Word" segment with a term of his own invention. "Truthiness," he explained, is truth that "comes from ... the gut," that one feels intuitively rather than pursuing intellectually and critically. In choosing "truthiness" as its Word of the Year in 2006, the American Dialect Society defined it as "the quality of preferring concepts or facts one wishes to be true, rather than concepts or facts known to be true." Colbert credits the rise to prominence of "truthiness" to George W. Bush's presidency. "It doesn't seem to matter what facts are," he observed in a 2006 interview. "Perception is everything. It's certainty." Many people admired Bush, he went on, because he was "certain of his choices as a leader, even if the facts that back him up don't seem to exist. It's the fact that he's certain that is very appealing." Similarly, The Colbert Report capitalizes on this relativism, as well as America's insatiable attraction to show business and celebrity and television journalists' abdication of their own authority, in order to interrogate the function of political satire. The concept of truthiness has been expanded to include playful questions as to what extent comedy news shows such as Colbert's program and The Daily Show—ostensibly mere entertainment—now perform a serious function in the national culture.[7]

This fuzzy threshold between spectacle and reality, between comedy and seriousness, also has permeated the relationship between the people and the presidency. The fusing of politics and entertainment means that politicians—presidents most visibly and significantly—must play to both arenas, often simultaneously. When Barack Obama performed on *The Colbert Report* in 2008, he was standing on his own stage at a "town hall" campaign event and appeared by means of a live video feed that connected him to the theater where Colbert's show was under way. Obama's audience, to whom he had been speaking about the severity of the economic crisis and the wars in Iraq and Afghanistan, could be seen in the background. The comedian's sat before him. Colbert's huge video projection screen served as a common proscenium arch linking the two performances in a mirror image. The spectacle on two stages was part stump speech, part comedy routine, and the boundary between them was transparent, to the extent it existed at all. Presidents and would-be presidents must negotiate the delicate balance between projecting seriousness equal to the sober responsibilities of the office prescribed by the Constitution and identifying with a populace that has been brought into intimate proximity to the presidency and increasingly equates leadership with a sense of humor. By their ability to command the stage and elicit laughter from large groups of people, comedians exude authority and strengthen the bonds of community among those present. Presidents, in seeking to accomplish the same things, frequently find value in performing as comedians, although the circumstances of such performances are not always sharply delineated.[8]

For this reason, mock candidacies of comedians and other celebrities—though still consumer staples during each election cycle—have lost much of their novelty and cultural potency. The humor of campaigns such as those by Will Rogers and Gracie Allen was founded on the silly incongruity of a comedian playing the president. Now, thanks to the cumulative actions of comics, presidents, and American citizens during the past century, the comedian and the president have merged to the point where the thought of a standup comic running for office is no longer laughably provocative. (Indeed, by 2008 political satirist and former *Saturday Night Live* star Al Franken could not only run a legitimate campaign for the U.S. Senate, but also win over incumbent Norm Coleman, if by the slimmest of margins.) Pat Paulsen's mock presidential campaign in 1968 was the last to tickle the public imagination in a significant way by effectively critiquing the presidency through a comedian's candidacy.

Similarly, as Al Gore discovered in 2000, presidential impersonation has been endowed with a humor that is no longer based solely on incongruity but founded on the laughably porous—often indistinguishable—division

between performer and politician. As a result of the prevalence of impersonation, especially on television, many Americans see and hear the mimic
at least as often as the president, a familiarity that creates uncertainty as
to which image is more truthful. Will Rogers and his radio audience were
the first to experience this phenomenon—briefly and on a much smaller
scale—with his imitation of Calvin Coolidge in 1928, but the commercial
proliferation of both comic impersonation and the electronic media has replaced the prospect of *mistaken* identity with that of *conflated* identity. This
transition was heralded by Vaughn Meader's adulatory but audaciously ac-
curate impersonation of John F. Kennedy on the *Talent Scouts* program,
then with *The First Family* in 1962. The signature catchphrases from Dana
Carvey's imitation of George H. W. Bush during the late 1980s and early
1990s, especially his rhetorical parodies ("Not gonna do it," "Wouldn't be
prudent"), were routinely attributed to Bush himself, even though the president rarely if ever uttered those phrases. Toward the end of his term, Bush
had to limit his use of one of his favorite expressions—"a thousand points of
light"—after he realized that audiences could no longer take it seriously in
the wake of Carvey's imitation.[9]

This "truthy" melding of comedic and presidential identity found its
ultimate expression in the election of 2008, when Tina Fey's uncanny
impersonation of Sarah Palin, and Palin's own subsequent appearance on
the show, made *Saturday Night Live* a site of both merry confusion and
substantive debate over the effects of political satire, much as it was when
Ron Nessen hosted the program three decades before. When Fey poked fun
at the lack of foreign policy experience of the vice presidential nominee,
who would be, if elected, one tragedy away from the presidency, or when
she prompted peals of laughter simply by repeating largely verbatim Palin's
convoluted response to a question by CBS news anchor Katie Couric, Fey
indelibly defined Palin for many. When the two identically dressed women
passed each other onstage during Palin's appearance on the show two weeks
before the election, the moment transcended illusion as a joke and became
what executive producer Lorne Michaels called "a heightened reality" that
was replayed on news programs, the Internet, and in the minds of numerous
Americans when they entered the voting booth. For her part, Palin eschewed
appearances on Sunday morning news roundtables but agreed to appear
on *Saturday Night Live*, leaving many observers angry and frustrated at the
McCain campaign for its refusal to make her available for "hard" interviews. Others, however, embraced her decision as an act of valiant defiance
against what they considered the left-leaning bias of the media. More significantly, her *Saturday Night Live* appearance was largely accepted within
the popular culture as interchangeable with conventional news broadcasts.

Realizing that she could potentially score more political points by appearing as a comedic performer than more formally as a candidate, Palin and her advisers demonstrated their understanding of the political economy of humor in the twenty-first century. Palin used humor in a calculated attempt to compensate for her lack of weightier presidential credentials. Although the McCain ticket was defeated at the polls, many Americans viewed her television performances in zero-sum terms: her failure to answer hard questions was compensated for by her willingness to be lampooned and her ability to crack jokes in return. The clear winners, meanwhile, were *Saturday Night Live*, whose ratings skyrocketed to their highest levels in fourteen years the week of the Palin appearance, and NBC. The network realized enormous revenues from the Obama-Biden campaign, which placed numerous ads on the show to reinforce its own candidates' strengths and what it considered Palin's lack of qualifications, and to counteract any public relations boon her performance might inspire.[10]

The slippery, multifaceted reception of political humor and its myriad effects on political and popular culture have generated intense debate as to its significance or insignificance. Columnists, scholars, and other social commentators—even comedians—have argued for its radicalism on the one hand or its essential conservatism on the other. Depending on the perceived state of the union, their political allegiance, and the party in power, they either decry humor's ability to demean and subvert authority or celebrate this same iconoclasm as an articulation of democracy holding national leaders to account—or else deny its significance entirely. In April 2006, when Stephen Colbert mercilessly satirized George W. Bush at that year's White House Correspondents' Association dinner by, among other things, reprising his thoughts on "truthiness" while standing a few feet away from the president who he believed personified the concept, most of the news establishment responded first by ignoring or dismissing his comments completely, then by condemning them. Columnist Richard Cohen of the *Washington Post* argued that Colbert, in disrespecting the tradition of the presidency and taking unfair advantage of Bush's sense of decorum, "was not just a failure as a comedian but rude." This was in contrast to *New York Times* columnist Frank Rich's charge the year before—following Laura Bush's crowd-pleasing performance—that it was the Bush administration that had shamelessly used humor to manipulate both the event and the journalists attending it in order to mute criticism and boost the president's popularity. After the 1976 election Chevy Chase remarked with conviction and satisfaction that his impersonations had contributed directly to the defeat of Gerald Ford. By contrast, scholar Mark Crispin Miller maintains that television has completely neutralized the potential of humor as a comic weapon to subvert the powerful.

Instead, he says, it uses the mere mirage of jocular individualism "not to question the exalted" but to promote cynically the television culture of consumption and the status quo. Mort Sahl concurred, saying in a 2003 interview that true satire has been replaced in the performances of many comedians by an elitist fascination with their own celebrity and a self-serving ridicule devoid of serious political content; "bitchery," he said, "has replaced satire." As long ago as 1985, in his popular lament over the effects of the media culture, *Amusing Ourselves to Death*, educator and social critic Neil Postman charged that in their passive embrace of the "politics of image," Americans were trapping themselves in "a perpetual round of entertainments" in which "serious discourse dissolves into giggles." The debate still rages over whether the mass production of laughter and its distribution through the dulling conformity of television has utterly sapped humor directed at the presidency of its political potency, sacrificing the laughing *citizen* to the giddy and trivial pleasures of the laughing *consumer*.[11]

* * *

The cast members of this history—citizens, presidents, and other show people—demonstrate how Americans have calculatedly and creatively made use of humor in diverse ways for their own benefit and their own times. They have done so as consumers, by buying or rejecting the wares available to them, be they Benjamin Franklin's almanacs, Will Rogers's daily telegrams, Franklin Roosevelt's grinning bon mots, or Lenny Bruce's jazzed obscenities. In the early twenty-first century, digital entertainment manifested as television and streaming video dominates the culture, flooding the marketplace with jokes, sketches, and impersonations that often and easily submerge the potency of humor in the mere salesmanship of celebrity and spectacle, and producing only kidding ritual without meaning. Mass media, however, retain their potential for disseminating the voices of witty if often unwitting insurgents against convention. Artemus Ward used the stage to audition for his fellow Americans new means of intertwining performance, humor, and politics. Subsequent comedians—Will Rogers, Franklin Roosevelt, Vaughn Meader, John Kennedy, Dick Gregory, and Ronald Reagan among them—have used subsequent media, from mass-produced print and radio to film and television, to shape and reshape the dialogue between the American people and their president. Today this potential is realized not so much by the prescribed nightly capsules of jolly but tranquillizing jokes dispensed on *Late Night* and *The Tonight Show*. Rather it bears fruit in the audacious humor of Jon Stewart, Stephen Colbert, *Saturday Night Live*, Rush Limbaugh, and others who continue to play with the innate volatility of laughter in daring and often uncomfortable ways. At their best, these jesters produce satiric performances that are fundamentally democratic, for effective satire is essentially inquisitive. It is not content to poke fun and cash in on a quick punch line. It uses laughter more deliberately, to urge a purposeful, egalitarian response from the audience—be it uproarious hilarity, the shock of absurdity, or dark outrage—followed by public dialogue and then, possibly, protest, reform, or some other corrective. During the 1960s the Smothers Brothers, the producers of TW3, and Mort Sahl were vilified for allegedly trivializing the institutions of national authority and weakening American society through satire. More than a century ago the English poet and critic Matthew Arnold excoriated America for its "addiction to the 'funny man'" Mark Twain, whom he considered both "a national misfortune" and proof of the inferiority of American civilization. In satirically holding the president of the United States to account and by encouraging debate over the definition of broadcast journalism and truth itself, Colbert and Stewart have provoked similar criticism, yet these Americans, like their predecessors, have had a definite impact. Rather than draining culture, as Neil Postman feared, laughter continues to irrigate it to produce new and useful societal understandings.[12]

In addition to acting as consuming members of the audience, Americans simultaneously play the complementary roles of comic entrepreneur and performer using all available means. This, too, is nothing new. Charles Browne traveled through the public sphere of his day as a typesetter and journalist, eventually reinventing himself as the comic showman Artemus Ward in order to enrich himself with fame and fortune. Samuel Clemens exulted in the typographical "Machine Culture" of his time to make not just a point but a profit. Each of those who followed—from Finley Peter Dunne to Stephen Colbert—has been similarly motivated by celebrity and commercial gain. Such ambitions did not necessarily constrict Ward's or other comedians' ability to affect political culture; in many ways they drove it.[13]

Presidents have come to understand much the same thing. "Politics," said nineteenth-century writer Ambrose Bierce, is "the conduct of public affairs for private advantage." While cynical perhaps, Bierce's observation echoes the incongruity of "the Great American Joke": American ideals are forever confounded by the human imperfections and self-interests of those pursuing them. For over a century presidents have learned to exploit laughter to advance both their policies and their celebrity. Barack Obama, Jay Leno, and their audience collectively demonstrated this on March 19, 2009, when Obama made an extended appearance on *The Tonight Show* and became the first sitting president to do so. Obama used the comedian's medium to explain his administration's responses to the financial challenges facing the country and the comedian's craft to buoy Americans' spirits; the event was a postmodern fireside chat. Simultaneously, he magnified his own star power. Leno, meanwhile, was happy to perform the public service of helping the president combat serious times with warm laughter while also competing for punch lines and being fully aware that Obama's historic appearance would enrich his personal and professional fortunes. Viewers, for their part, responded in diverse ways—with laughter, by contributing supportive or disparaging assessments of the president's policies, or by cracking their own jokes and commanding a tiny part of the limelight for themselves. To the extent that humor remains an expression of the American tug-of-war between self-interest and communal well-being, everyone is a comedian.[14]

This tradition continues to represent the best hope for political comedy. The satiric voices of professional comics are not the only ones being heard, despite the loudness of their presence in popular culture and the hand-wringing of those who fear that effective humor has been lost to laughing apathy and consumerism. Were he truly still among us—as *The Colbert Report* fancied he was in 2008—Benjamin Franklin might observe to his fellow citizens that they have no less a sense of humor than their ancestors, and no less need to exercise its political power, yet they possess extraordinary access to a public sphere now bulging with new tools for expressing it. He might equate the computer keyboard and mouse to his boxes of type and his printing press. He would no doubt marvel at Webcams and audio software, and at today's interpersonal media—e-mail, blogs, texting, Twitter, YouTube, and Facebook, which includes the option to identify oneself publicly as a comedian—which have the potential to reach a national, even global, audience within moments. Indeed, while television remains dominant, it is increasingly the inspiration for the wider public performance of jokes and comical videos on the Internet which continue to satirize and otherwise poke fun at authority and frequently gain enormous currency. In late 2008, research by the Nielsen Company showed that television viewing and use of the Internet are complementary activities that go on simultaneously, suggesting that watching television is not a wholly passive activity but rather one that regularly generates response of some kind—the response of American citizens declaring their sovereign control over political power. They frequently take jabs at the president, and they are also frequently very funny.[15]

In 1933 Franklin Roosevelt said, "I sometimes think that the saving grace of America lies in the fact that the overwhelming majority of Americans are possessed of two great qualities—a sense of humor and a sense of proportion." Americans continue to profit from humor even as they carry on the debate over its value to democracy. Nevertheless, presidents, professional jokers, and the American people—comedians all, performing across the boundaries of popular entertainment, radical dissent, and political opportunism—have conspired to bring the performance of political comedy permanently to center stage. There it remains, part mischievous insurgency, part political sideshow, part show business spectacle. The American company of comedians endures, performing a dance that has become a ritual of national culture, though the question who leads at any given time remains very much in play.[16]

NOTES

Prologue

1. Daniel Kurtzman, "Laura Bush Video: White House Correspondents' Dinner," About.com, April 30, 2005, politicalhumor.about.com/od/multimedia/v/laurabush-video.htm (accessed April 25, 2008).
2. Ibid.
3. Victor Turner, *The Anthropology of Performance* (New York: PAJ Publications, 1988), 25; Richard Schechner, *The Future of Ritual: Writings on Culture and Performance* (London: Routledge, 1995), 1.
4. Victor Turner, *From Ritual to Theatre: The Human Seriousness of Play*, Performance Studies Series (New York: PAJ Publications, 1982), 30–44.
5. Ibid.
6. Brian Sutton-Smith, "Games of Order and Disorder," paper presented to the symposium "Forms of Symbolic Inversion," sponsored by the American Anthropological Association, Toronto, December 1, 1972, quoted ibid., 28.
7. See Joseph Boskin, *Rebellious Laughter: People's Humor in American Culture* (Syracuse: Syracuse University Press, 1997); Arthur Power Dudden, ed., *American Humor* (New York: Oxford University Press, 1987); and Jesse Bier, *The Rise and Fall of American Humor* (New York: Octagon, 1981).
8. Pew Research Center for the People and the Press, news release, "What Americans Know: 1989–2007: Public Knowledge of Current Affairs Little Changed by News and Information Revolutions" (Washington, DC, April 15, 2007), 13; Pew Research Center, *Trends 2005* (Washington, DC: Pew Research Center, 2005), 46–47; Heritage, posting to Common Ground Common Sense forum, May 1, 2005, www.commongroundcommonsense.org/forums/lofiversion/index.php/t27905.html (accessed April 28, 2008); Frank Rich, "Laura Bush's Mission Accomplished," *New York Times*, May 8, 2005.
9. Rogers branded himself a "ropin' fool" in the film of that title, which he wrote and produced in 1921.
10. For the rise of commercial television and consumer culture, see Lizabeth Cohen, *A Consumers' Republic: The Politics of Mass Consumption in Postwar America* (New York: Alfred A. Knopf, 2003); and Lynn Spigel, *Welcome to the Dreamhouse: Popular Media and Postwar Suburbs* (Durham: Duke University Press, 2001). For a discussion of the heroic quality of the standup comedian in postwar America, see David Marc, *Comic Visions: Television Comedy and American Culture*, 2nd ed. (Malden, MA: Blackwell, 1997), 10–15.
11. Arthur Power Dudden, *Pardon Us, Mr. President! American Humor on Politics* (South Brunswick, NJ: A. S. Barnes, 1975), 83.

12. Artemus Ward, *Artemus Ward, His Book* (New York: Carleton, 1862), 176, 79.
13. Hal Erickson, *"From Beautiful Downtown Burbank": A Critical History of Rowan and Martin's Laugh-In, 1968–1973* (Jefferson, NC: McFarland, 2000), 167–68.
14. Sheldon Cherney, "An Analysis of the Use of Humor in Presidential Campaign Speeches, 1940–1952" (Ph.D. diss., University of Southern California, 1956), 1–2.
15. Bedřich Smetana and Karel Sabina, *The Bartered Bride: A Lyric Opera in Three Acts* (London: Boosey and Hawkes, 1945); Joseph Boskin, *Rebellious Laughter: People's Humor in American Culture* (Syracuse: Syracuse University Press, 1997).
16. Louis D. Rubin Jr., "The Great American Joke," *South Atlantic Quarterly* 72, no. 1 (1973): 83.
17. E. B. White and Katharine S. White, eds., *A Subtreasury of American Humor* (New York: Coward-McCann, 1941), xvii.

1. An American Company of Comedians

1. Ward, *Artemus Ward, His Book*, 179–85.
2. Ibid., 186; John J. Pullen, *Comic Relief: The Life and Laughter of Artemus Ward, 1834–1867* (Hamden, CT: Archon Books, 1983), 3.
3. Daniel Wickberg, *The Senses of Humor: Self and Laughter in Modern America* (Ithaca: Cornell University Press, 1998), 41–45.
4. Paul Starr, *The Creation of the Media: Political Origins of Modern Communication* (New York: Basic Books, 2004), 130; Walter Blair and Hamlin Hill, *America's Humor: From Poor Richard to Doonesbury* (Oxford: Oxford University Press, 1978), 30–31; Benedict Anderson, *Imagined Communities: Reflections on the Origin and Spread of Nationalism*, rev. and extended ed. (London: Verso, 1991); Jürgen Habermas, *The Structural Transformation of the Public Sphere: An Inquiry into a Category of Bourgeois Society*, trans. Thomas Burger, Studies in Contemporary German Social Thought (Cambridge: MIT Press, 1989).
5. Wickberg, *The Senses of Humor*, 74–84.
6. See Alexis de Tocqueville, *Democracy in America*, trans. George Lawrence, 1st ed. (New York: Harper & Row, 1966); Mary P. Ryan, *Civic Wars: Democracy and Public Life in the American City during the Nineteenth Century* (Berkeley: University of California Press, 1997); Claude Lefort, *Democracy and Political Theory*, trans. David Macey (Minneapolis: University of Minnesota Press, 1988); LeRoy Ashby, *With Amusement for All: A History of American Popular Culture since 1830* (Lexington: University Press of Kentucky, 2006), 21; Robert C. Toll, *Blacking Up: The Minstrel Show in Nineteenth-Century America* (New York: Oxford University Press, 1974), 13, 55–56.
7. Benjamin Franklin, *The Prefaces, Proverbs, and Poems from Poor Richard's Almanacks for 1733–1758* (Franklin Center, PA: Franklin Library, 1984), 49; Blair and Hill, *America's Humor*, 32; Well-Fed Domine Double-Chin Esq. [pseud.], *Feast of Merriment. A New American Jester. Being a Most Curious Collection of Witty Jests — Merry Stories — Smart Repartees — Droll Adventures — Funny Jokes . . .* (Philadelphia, 1795), 64, v.
8. *Beers's Almanac and Ephemeris . . . for . . . 1793*, quoted in Robert K. Dodge, *Early American Almanac Humor* (Bowling Green, OH: Bowling Green State University Popular Press, 1987), 9.

9. *The Autobiography of Benjamin Franklin* (New York: Walter J. Black, 1941), 132.

10. *Beers's Almanac and Ephemeris . . . for . . . 1793*, quoted in Dodge, *Early American Almanac Humor*, 11; Paul M. Zall, ed., *Ben Franklin Laughing: Anecdotes from Original Sources by and about Benjamin Franklin* (Berkeley: University of California Press, 1980), 130.

11. Gordon S. Wood, *The Americanization of Benjamin Franklin* (New York: Penguin, 2004), 147–51; David McCullough, *John Adams* (New York: Simon & Schuster, 2001), 405–6; Starr, *The Creation of the Media*, 56; George Washington, *Rules of Civility & Decent Behaviour in Company and Conversation: A Book of Etiquette* (Williamsburg, VA: Beaver Press, 1971), 10; Sedition Act, Public Law 74, 5th Cong., 2nd sess. (July 14, 1798).

12. Stephen Hess and Sandy Northrop, *Drawn & Quartered: The History of American Political Cartoons* (Montgomery, AL: Elliott & Clark, 1996), 36–38.

13. Tocqueville, *Democracy in America*, 49; Washington Irving, "Rip Van Winkle: A Posthumous Writing of Diedrich Knickerbocker," in *The Comic Tradition in America: An Anthology of American Humor*, ed. Kenneth S. Lynn (New York: Norton, 1968), 45.

14. Seba Smith, *My Thirty Years Out of the Senate* (New York: Oaksmith, 1859), 33–34.

15. Ibid., 36, 207.

16. Artemus Ward, *The Complete Works of Artemus Ward (Charles Farrar Browne)* (New York: G. W. Dillingham, 1898), 4.

17. Starr, *The Creation of the Media*, 88–90; Ward, *Artemus Ward, His Book*, 17–18.

18. Pullen, *Comic Relief*, 27; Ward, *Artemus Ward, His Book*, 18.

19. Charles Browne, "Our Speech," *Cleveland Plain Dealer*, January 18, 1859, quoted in Pullen, *Comic Relief*, 29.

20. Pullen, *Comic Relief*, 16.

21. Blair and Hill, *America's Humor*, 173; Bruce C. Daniels, *Puritans at Play: Leisure and Recreation in Colonial New England* (New York: Palgrave Macmillan, 1995), 17; Worthington C. Ford et al., eds., vol. 12, *Journals of the Continental Congress, 1774–1789* (Washington, DC: Government Printing Office, 1904–37), 1018. For the popularity of nineteenth-century stage performance and its use in the culture wars of the time, see Lawrence W. Levine, *Highbrow/Lowbrow: The Emergence of Cultural Hierarchy in America* (Cambridge: Harvard University Press, 1988).

22. Charles Chester Cole, *The Social Ideas of the Northern Evangelists, 1826–1860* (New York: Columbia University Press, 1954), 113.

23. Ward, *Complete Works*, 59; Pullen, *Comic Relief*, 46–48.

24. "Artemus Ward—Mr. Charles F. Browne's Lecture," *Boston Daily Advertiser*, December 7, 1861, quoted in Pullen, *Comic Relief*, 44; Artemus Ward, T. W. Robertson, and Edward P. Hingston, *Artemus Ward's Lecture* (London: J. C. Hotten, 1869), 105–6; Ward, *Complete Works*, 21; Pullen, *Comic Relief*, 106.

25. Artemus Ward, "High-Handed Outrage at Utica," in *Complete Works*, 36–37.

26. Pullen, *Comic Relief*, 1–3.

27. Charles E. Schutz, *Political Humor: From Aristophanes to Sam Ervin* (Rutherford, NJ: Fairleigh Dickinson University Press, 1977), 191, 45.

28. Edwin M. Stanton quoted in Benjamin P. Thomas, *"Lincoln's Humor" and Other Essays* (Urbana: University of Illinois Press, 2002), 12; Forrest McDonald,

The American Presidency: An Intellectual History (Lawrence: University Press of Kansas, 1994), 298, 398.

29. Ward, *Complete Works*, 430–31.
30. Ibid., 104.
31. Rubin, "The Great American Joke."
32. Henri Bergson, *Laughter: An Essay on the Meaning of the Comic*, trans. Cloudesley Brereton and Fred Rothwell (New York: Macmillan, 1924), 4; Turner, *The Anthropology of Performance*, 41.

2. Dance Partners

1. William Dean Howells quoted in Pullen, *Comic Relief*, 26; Ward, *Complete Works*, 25.
2. Richard Hofstadter, *The Age of Reform* (New York: Vintage Books, 1955), 136; Howells quoted in Fred Kaplan, *The Singular Mark Twain: A Biography* (New York: Doubleday, 2003), 3.
3. Mark Twain quoted in Geoffrey C. Ward, Dayton Duncan, and Ken Burns, *Mark Twain* (New York: Alfred A. Knopf, 2001), 235.
4. *Mark Twain*, directed by Ken Burns (Walpole, NH: Florentine Films, 2001); Marc, *Comic Visions*, 3–4; Stephen Ponder, *Managing the Press: Origins of the Media Presidency, 1897–1933* (New York: Palgrave, 2000), 3; Starr, *The Creation of the Media*, 252–58; Ben Procter, *William Randolph Hearst: The Early Years, 1863–1910* (New York: Oxford University Press, 1998), 101; Hess and Northrup, *Drawn & Quartered*, 52–67.
5. Ashby, *With Amusement for All*, 73, 105, 107; Richard Butsch, *The Making of American Audiences: From Stage to Television, 1750–1990* (Cambridge: Cambridge University Press, 2000), 103–4; Arthur Frank Wertheim, *Vaudeville Wars: How the Keith-Albee and Orpheum Circuits Controlled the Big-Time and Its Performers* (New York: Palgrave Macmillan, 2006), 10, 35–62.
6. Robert W. Snyder, *The Voice of the City: Vaudeville and Popular Culture in New York* (Chicago: Ivan R. Dee, 2000), 28; Butsch, *The Making of American Audiences*, 102–18.
7. Michael A. Genovese, *The Power of the American Presidency, 1789–2000* (New York: Oxford University Press, 2001), 97.
8. Pullen, *Comic Relief*, 82; Fred W. Lorch, *The Trouble Begins at Eight: Mark Twain's Lecture Tours* (Ames: Iowa State University Press, 1968), 15–17; Twain quoted in Mark Twain and Paul Fatout, *Mark Twain Speaks for Himself* (West Lafayette, IN: Purdue University Press, 1978), 124.
9. Lorch, *The Trouble Begins at Eight*, 20.
10. Ward, Duncan, and Burns, *Mark Twain*, 54, 55 (Bret Harte quote); Lorch, *The Trouble Begins at Eight*, 33–34; Kaplan, *The Singular Mark Twain*, 289.
11. Twain quoted in Ward, Duncan, and Burns, *Mark Twain*, 48; Kaplan, *The Singular Mark Twain*, 257, 335.
12. Ron Powers, *Mark Twain: A Life* (New York: Free Press, 2005), 277; Kaplan, *The Singular Mark Twain*, 247.
13. Mark Twain, *The Mysterious Stranger*, quoted in *The Assault of Laughter: A Treasury of American Political Humor*, ed. Arthur P. Dudden (New York: Thomas

Yoseloff, 1962), 523; Mark Twain, "The United States of Lyncherdom," in *Mark Twain: Collected Tales, Sketches, Speeches, and Essays, 1891–1910*, ed. Louis J. Budd (New York: Literary Classics of the United States, 1992), 479–86; Powers, *Mark Twain*, 609, 607, 593 (Twain quotes); Roy Blount Jr., "America's Original Superstar," *Time*, July 14, 2008, 51–52; William McKinley quoted in Genovese, *The Power of the American Presidency*, 108; Ward, Duncan, and Burns, *Mark Twain*, 203, 201 (Twain quote); Twain quoted in Kaplan, *The Singular Mark Twain*, 583.

14. Powers, *Mark Twain*, 492; Mark Twain, "Mark Twain as a Presidential Candidate," *New York Evening Post*, June 9, 1879, quoted in Twain and Fatout, *Mark Twain Speaks for Himself*, 116–17.

15. Twain quoted in William M. Gibson, *Theodore Roosevelt among the Humorists: W. D. Howells, Mark Twain, and Mr. Dooley* (Knoxville: University of Tennessee Press, 1980), 35, 25, 34, 29; Theodore Roosevelt quoted ibid., 22.

16. Twain quoted in Grace Eckley, *Finley Peter Dunne* (Boston: Twayne, 1981), 26.

17. Finley Peter Dunne quoted ibid., 34.

18. James DeMuth, *Small Town Chicago: The Comic Perspectives of Finley Peter Dunne, George Ade, Ring Lardner* (Port Washington, NY: Kennikat Press, 1980), 6–9.

19. Ibid.; Stanley Trachtenberg, ed., *American Humorists, 1800–1950*, vol. 1 (Detroit: Gale Research, 1982), 125.

20. Dunne quoted in DeMuth, *Small Town Chicago*, 30–31.

21. Finley Peter Dunne, *Mr. Dooley in Peace and in War* (Boston: Small, Maynard, 1899), 81–82.

22. Finley Peter Dunne, Elmer Ellis, and Franklin P. Adams, *Mr. Dooley at His Best* (New York: Charles Scribner's Sons, 1938), 99–103.

23. Ibid.; Dunne quoted in Gibson, *Theodore Roosevelt among the Humorists*, 43.

24. Charles Fanning, *Finley Peter Dunne & Mr. Dooley: The Chicago Years* (Lexington: University Press of Kentucky, 1978), 243; Eckley, *Finley Peter Dunne*, 29; Roosevelt quoted in Dudden, *The Assault of Laughter*, 285; Gibson, *Theodore Roosevelt among the Humorists*, 47; Dunne quoted in Philip Dunne, ed., *Mr. Dooley Remembers: The Informal Memoirs of Finley Peter Dunne* (Boston: Little, Brown, 1963), 209.

25. Lewis L. Gould, *The Modern American Presidency* (Lawrence: University Press of Kansas, 2003), 10–11; Louis Brownlow quoted in Ponder, *Managing the Press*, 23–24.

26. Arthur Wallace Dunn, *Gridiron Nights: Humorous and Satirical Views of Politics and Statesmen as Presented by the Famous Dining Club* (New York: Frederick A. Stokes, 1915), 4, 32; Sheryl Gay Stolberg, "Obama to Skip Gridiron Club Dinner," *New York Times*, March 13, 2009; Jim Free quoted in "Humor and the Presidency," session 1, September 18, 1986, videotape AV88-11-011, Ford Library Administrative Files, Gerald R. Ford Library (hereafter cited as GRFL), Ann Arbor, MI.

27. Genovese, *The Power of the American Presidency*, 105; Dunn, *Gridiron Nights*, 19, 7.

3. A Presidential Crinoline

1. Unspecified quotation by DeMille on display at the Will Rogers Memorial Museum (hereafter cited as WRMM), Claremore, OK.

2. Ben Yagoda, *Will Rogers: A Biography* (Norman: University of Oklahoma Press, 2000), 10–14, 32–35; Betty Rogers, *Will Rogers: His Wife's Story* (Norman: University of Oklahoma Press, 1979), 27–29.

3. Jim Hopkins quoted in Yagoda, *Will Rogers*, 38; Rogers, *Will Rogers*, 47–56.

4. *Will Rogers' Weekly Articles*, vol. 5, *The Hoover Years: 1931–1933*, ed. Steven K. Gragert (Stillwater: Oklahoma State University Press, 1982), 76.

5. Stephen Langley, *Theatre Management in America: Principle and Practice; Producing for the Commercial, Stock, Resident, College, and Community Theatre*, rev. ed. (New York: Drama Book Publishers, 1980), 90; David Nasaw, *Going Out: The Rise and Fall of Public Amusements* (New York: BasicBooks, 1993), 3.

6. Nasaw, *Going Out*, 35, 27; Wertheim, *Vaudeville Wars*, xvii, 121–23; Kathy Peiss, *Cheap Amusements: Working Women and Leisure in Turn-of-the-Century New York* (Philadelphia: Temple University Press, 1986); Marvin A. Carlson, *Performance: A Critical Introduction*, 2nd ed. (New York: Routledge, 2004), 19; Turner, *From Ritual to Theatre*, 33, 37; Albert F. McLean Jr., *American Vaudeville as Ritual* (Lexington: University of Kentucky Press, 1965).

7. Will Rogers and Donald Day, *The Autobiography of Will Rogers* (Boston: Houghton Mifflin, 1949), 19; Yagoda, *Will Rogers*, 58.

8. Yagoda, *Will Rogers*, 59; Rogers, *Will Rogers*, 91–92.

9. Rogers, *Will Rogers*, 86, 90–91; unidentified newspaper clipping quoted in *The Papers of Will Rogers*, vol. 3, *From Vaudeville to Broadway, September 1908–August 1915*, ed. Arthur Frank Wertheim and Barbara Bair (Norman: University of Oklahoma Press, 2001), 91, 116.

10. *Washington Times* quoted in Yagoda, *Will Rogers*, 82.

11. Ashby, *With Amusement for All*, 115–19.

12. Rogers and Day, *The Autobiography of Will Rogers*, 38; George Martin, "The Wit of Will Rogers," *American Magazine*, November 1919, 34.

13. *Will Rogers' Weekly Articles*, vol. 1, *The Harding–Coolidge Years: 1922–1925*, ed. James M. Smallwood and Steven K. Gragert (Stillwater: Oklahoma State University Press, 1980), 194.

14. Yagoda, *Will Rogers*, 13; Gulf radio broadcast, November 26, 1933, "Will Rogers Radio Broadcasts, 1933–1935," WRMM, 67.

15. Unidentified clipping quoted in Wertheim and Bair, *The Papers of Will Rogers*, 3:257–58.

16. Rogers and Day, *The Autobiography of Will Rogers*, 12; Yagoda, *Will Rogers*, 30; Wertheim and Bair, *The Papers of Will Rogers*, 3:59; Theodore Roosevelt to Will Rogers, August 4, 1918, Will Rogers Papers, doc. 1975.21.0150, Will Rogers Memorial Museum, Claremore, OK. (hereafter cited as WRP-WRMM); Smallwood and Gragert, *Will Rogers' Weekly Articles*, 1:150.

17. Wertheim and Bair, *The Papers of Will Rogers*, 3:355.

18. Smallwood and Gragert, *Will Rogers' Weekly Articles*, 1:193–95.

19. Ibid., 1:196; George M. Cohan quoted in Yagoda, *Will Rogers*, 146; Smallwood and Gragert, *Will Rogers' Weekly Articles*, 1:193; Rogers, *Will Rogers*, 164; Joseph Tumulty to Rogers, March 14, 1924, no. 18RF, WRP-WRMM.

20. For examples, see *Will Rogers at the Ziegfeld Follies*, ed. Arthur Frank Wertheim (Norman: University of Oklahoma Press, 1992), 145–46; *Will Rogers' Daily Telegrams*, ed. James M. Smallwood and Steven K. Gragert, 4 vols. (Stillwater: Okla-

homa State University Press, 1978), 1:xiii; John Barry, "Claremore Cowboy: Will Rogers, Journalist," *Boston Globe*, August 22, 1935; "The Most Publicized Man in America," box 14, miscellaneous file, WRMM; Lary May, *The Big Tomorrow: Hollywood and the Politics of the American Way* (Chicago: University of Chicago Press, 2002), 17.

21. Gould, *The Modern American Presidency*, 43–47.

22. Ibid., 33.

23. William McAdoo quoted in David Greenberg, *Calvin Coolidge* (New York: Times Books, 2006), 7; Wertheim, *Will Rogers at the Ziegfeld Follies*, 146; Yagoda, *Will Rogers*, 189–90; unidentified clipping quoted in *The Papers of Will Rogers*, vol. 4, *From the Broadway Stage to the National Stage, September 1915–July 1928*, ed. Steven K. Gragert and M. Jane Johansson (Norman: University of Oklahoma Press, 2005), 231; Rogers, *Will Rogers*, 167–68.

24. Greenberg, *Calvin Coolidge*, 9 (Dorothy Parker quote), 10; Will Rogers, "How to Escape a Lecture," *Good Housekeeping*, March 1935, 25, 214; Charles Curtis to Will Rogers, April 28, 1930, WRP-WRMM, 1975.31.0501; Rogers to Herbert Hoover, ca. July 5, 1932, no. 45aAW, WRP-WRMM.

25. Arthur Frank Wertheim, *Radio Comedy* (New York: Oxford University Press, 1979), 3; Butsch, *The Making of American Audiences*, 174–76, 186–87; Greenberg, *Calvin Coolidge*, 102.

26. Alfred Balk, *The Rise of Radio, from Marconi through the Golden Age* (Jefferson, NC: McFarland, 2006), 40–43; Steven K. Gragert, ed., *Radio Broadcasts of Will Rogers* (Stillwater: Oklahoma State University Press, 1983), 2.

27. Rogers, *Will Rogers*, 169–70; "Talk by Mr. Will Rogers, Montclair High School, Montclair, New Jersey, April 16th, 1928," 1975.23.0019, WRP-WRMM, 24–25.

28. V. V. McNitt to Rogers, telegram, January 6, 1928, 1975.31.0501, WRP-WRMM; Smallwood and Gragert, *Will Rogers' Daily Telegrams*, 1:170.

29. Will Rogers, *Letters of a Self-Made Diplomat to His President* (Claremore, OK: Will Rogers Heritage Press, 1988).

30. Rogers to Calvin Coolidge, January 1928, file 1595, President's Personal File (PPF), Calvin Coolidge Memorial Room, Forbes Library, Northampton, MA. For the sake of clarity I have corrected Rogers's eccentric spelling and often confusing use of capitalization and punctuation. No word usage has been altered.

31. Greenberg, *Calvin Coolidge*, 76, 101–5.

32. Calvin Coolidge to Rogers, January 11, 1928, 1975.21.0147, WRP-WRMM; Smallwood and Gragert, *Will Rogers' Daily Telegrams*, 1:170.

33. For Hoover's role in the commercialization of radio, see Susan Smulyan, *Selling Radio: The Commercialization of American Broadcasting, 1920–1934* (Washington, DC: Smithsonian Institution Press, 1994); Yagoda, *Will Rogers*, 306.

34. Gragert, *Radio Broadcasts of Will Rogers*, 14.

35. David M. Kennedy, *The American People in the Great Depression: Freedom from Fear*, pt. 1 (Oxford: Oxford University Press, 1999), 38, 162–63, 91; Smallwood and Gragert, *Will Rogers' Daily Telegrams*, 3:36.

36. Will Rogers, "Bacon and Beans and Limousines," in Gragert, *Radio Broadcasts of Will Rogers*, 66–67.

37. Stuart M. Crocker to Rogers, telegram, October 24, 1931, no. 135CL, WRP-WRMM.

38. Roosevelt quoted in William R. Brown, *Imagemaker: Will Rogers and the American Dream* (Columbia: University of Missouri Press, 1970), 16; Stephanie Koziski, "The Stand-Up Comedian as Anthropologist: Intentional Culture Critic," *Journal of Popular Culture* 18, no. 2 (1984): 57–76.

39. Will Rogers, *How We Elect Our Presidents*, ed. Donald Day (Boston: Little, Brown, 1952), 3; Steven K. Gragert, ed., *"He Chews to Run": Will Rogers' Life Magazine Articles, 1928* (Stillwater: Oklahoma State University Press, 1982), 4, 109; Eddie Cantor and David Freedman, *Your Next President!* (New York: Ray Long and Richard R. Smith, 1932).

40. Heywood Broun, "Here's Candidate Par Excellence!" *Washington Star*, July 6, 1924; Joseph H. Carter, *Never Met a Man I Didn't Like: The Life and Writings of Will Rogers* (New York: Avon Books, 1991), 168; Rogers, *Will Rogers*, 278; Smallwood and Gragert, *Will Rogers' Weekly Articles*, 1:301.

41. Typed notes by Rogers for introducing James Rolph, October 1, 1930, 1975.14.0181, WRP-WRMM; Gragert, *Radio Broadcasts of Will Rogers*, 92.

42. Rogers, *How We Elect Our Presidents*, 123.

43. Frances Perkins, "First Impressions," in *The Roosevelt Treasury*, ed. James N. Rosenau (Garden City, NY: Doubleday, 1951), 39.

44. Yagoda, *Will Rogers*, 178; Joseph A. Stout Jr. and Peter C. Rollins, eds., *Convention Articles of Will Rogers* (Stillwater: Oklahoma State University Press, 1976), 8.

45. Stout and Rollins, *Convention Articles of Will Rogers*, 56.

46. Smallwood and Gragert, *Will Rogers' Daily Telegrams*, 1:260, 2:233.

47. Smallwood and Gragert, *Will Rogers' Weekly Articles*, 5:192; Rogers's undated type-written notes titled "Roosevelt," 1975.25.0009, WRP-WRMM.

48. Rogers to Franklin Roosevelt, telegram, November 25, 1932, President's Personal File (PPF) 599, "Rogers, Will" file, Franklin D. Roosevelt Library (hereafter cited as FDRL), Hyde Park, NY. Sentence punctuation, sentence case, and paragraphing have been added. Original spelling and punctuation within sentences have been retained.

49. M. S. Venkataramani, ed., *The Sunny Side of FDR* (Athens: Ohio University Press, 1973), 241; Coolidge quoted in Kennedy, *The American People*, 34; Greenberg, *Calvin Coolidge*, 7; John Gunther, *Roosevelt in Retrospect: A Profile in History* (New York: Harper & Brothers, 1950), 121–22, 34 (Edwin M. Watson quote); *Complete Presidential Press Conferences of Franklin D. Roosevelt*, 24 vols., vols. 1–2, 1933 (New York: Da Capo Press, 1972), x, xii.

50. John Tebbel and Sarah Miles Watts, *The Press and the Presidency: From George Washington to Ronald Reagan* (New York: Oxford University Press, 1985), 441; *Complete Presidential Press Conferences of Franklin D. Roosevelt*, 1:1–3. The Ananias Club refers to a biblical figure struck dead for lying.

51. *Complete Presidential Press Conferences of Franklin D. Roosevelt*, 1:85.

52. Ibid., 5:302, 3:137.

53. Ibid., 2:161–62.

54. Unidentified person quoted in Arthur A. Sloane, *Humor in the White House: The Wit of Five American Presidents* (Jefferson, NC: McFarland, 2001), 78; Gunther, *Roosevelt in Retrospect*, 56; *Complete Presidential Press Conferences of Franklin D. Roosevelt*, 4:96.

55. *Complete Presidential Press Conferences of Franklin D. Roosevelt,* 1:xv.

56. William E. Leuchtenburg, *Franklin D. Roosevelt and the New Deal, 1932–1940* (New York: Harper & Row, 1963), 44; Franklin Roosevelt quoted in Waldo W. Braden and Earnest Brandenburg, "Roosevelt's Fireside Chats," *Speech Monographs* 22, no. 5 (1955): 293; Roosevelt quoted in Lawrence W. Levine and Cornelia R. Levine, *The People and the President: America's Conversation with FDR* (Boston: Beacon Press, 2002), 31, xi.

57. Levine and Levine, *The People and the President,* x.

58. Gragert, *Radio Broadcasts of Will Rogers,* 72–77.

59. Gulf radio broadcast, May 7, 1933, "Will Rogers Radio Broadcasts, 1933–1935," WRMM, 8–9.

60. Ibid., 12–13; Franklin Roosevelt, "Address of the President Delivered by Radio from the White House: May 7, 1933," Mid-Hudson Regional Information Center, Franklin D. Roosevelt Presidential Library, Hyde Park, NY, www.mhric.org/fdr/chat2.html (accessed June 27, 2008); Yagoda, *Will Rogers,* 303.

61. Henry L. Mencken, "Last Words: A Short Essay on Democracy," in *School of Cooperative Individualism,* ed. Edward J. Dodson, www.cooperativeindividualism.org/mencken_democracy.html (accessed July 2, 2008); Roosevelt to Rogers, June 1, 1932, FDR Governorship Papers, ser. 1, container 68, "Will Rogers file," FDRL.

62. Louis McHenry Howe to Rogers, July 17, 1934, PPF 599, "Rogers, Will" file, FDRL.

63. *FDR: Day by Day—The Pare Lorentz Chronology* (electronic database), FDRL; Frank M. Russell to Stephen Early, May 20, 1933, Official File (OF) 228, box 1, "National Broadcasting Company, 1933–1945" file, FDRL; Early to Russell, May 20, 1933, OF 228, FDRL.

64. Rogers quoted in T. Harry Williams, *Huey Long* (New York: Alfred A. Knopf, 1969), 836.

65. Gulf radio broadcast, November 19, 1933, "Will Rogers Radio Broadcasts, 1933–1935," WRMM, 62–63.

66. Rogers to Stephen Early, telegram, November 21, 1933, PPF 599, "Rogers, Will" file, FDRL. Sentence punctuation and sentence case added.

67. Early to Rogers, telegram, November 21, 1933, PPF 599, "Rogers, Will" file, FDRL. Sentence punctuation and sentence case added.

68. Sloane, *Humor in the White House,* 76; Franklin Roosevelt, *FDR's Fireside Chats and Speeches,* audiocassette (Plymouth, MN: Metacom, 1995).

69. Visit by the author to the Roosevelt home in Hyde Park, NY. National Park Service personnel confirmed that the conspicuous placement of the framed cartoons next to the front door was personally supervised by Franklin Roosevelt and that he refused to remove them, even when King George VI visited in 1939.

70. Gulf radio broadcast, November 26, 1933, "Will Rogers Radio Broadcasts, 1933–1935," WRMM, 67–68; Turner, *From Ritual to Theatre,* 32.

71. *Complete Presidential Press Conferences of Franklin D. Roosevelt,* 6:99–101.

72. May, *The Big Tomorrow,* 11.

73. Rae Shirley to Roosevelt, telegram, August 24, 1935, PPF 200B, "Public Reaction, August 24, 1935" file, FDRL.

74. Marvin H. McIntyre "M.H.M." to Roosevelt, June 9, 1937, PPF 599, FDRL; Roosevelt to McIntyre, June 10, 1937, PPF 599, FDRL; M. LeHand to James G.

Blaine, November 20, 1935, PPF 599, FDRL; "Radio Address of the President from Hyde Park, New York[,] . . . November 4, 1938," PPF 599, FDRL.

75. Yagoda, *Will Rogers*, 237.

4. New Frontiers

1. U.S. Department of State, *Peace and War: United States Foreign Policy, 1931–1941* (Washington, DC: U.S. Government Printing Office, 1942), 598–607; Tony Hendra, *Going Too Far* (New York: Doubleday, 1987), 25; Lizabeth Cohen, *A Consumer's Republic: The Politics of Mass Consumption in Postwar America* (New York: Alfred A. Knopf, 2003).

2. Gary W. Coville, "Gracie Allen's 1940 Presidential Campaign," *American History Illustrated* 25, no. 5 (1990): 63–65.

3. Gould, *The Modern American Presidency*, 109. For a discussion of "domestic containment" in the United States during the first two decades of the cold war, see Elaine Tyler May, *Homeward Bound: American Families in the Cold War Era* (New York: Basic Books, 1988).

4. Stephen E. Kercher, *Revel with a Cause: Liberal Satire in Postwar America* (Chicago: University of Chicago Press, 2006), 44–46, 61–71, 79–83; Hendra, *Going Too Far*, 78–81.

5. Alan Havig, *Fred Allen's Radio Comedy* (Philadelphia: Temple University Press, 1990), 130–52, 205; Kercher, *Revel with a Cause*, 79–83, 348 (Groucho Marx quote).

6. David Marc, *Comic Visions: Television Comedy and American Culture*, 2nd ed. (Malden, MA: Blackwell, 1997), 10–11; Wickberg, *The Senses of Humor*, 204.

7. Marc, *Comic Visions*, 35, 61; Stephen Wagg, *Because I Tell a Joke or Two: Comedy, Politics, and Social Difference* (London: Routledge, 1998), 246–47, 250; Stefan Kanfer, *Ball of Fire: The Tumultuous Life and Comic Art of Lucille Ball* (New York: Alfred A. Knopf, 2003), 153.

8. Wickberg, *The Senses of Humor*, 203–4; Bob Hope quoted in Bob Hope, *Bob Hope's Dear Prez, I Wanna Tell Ya!* (Los Angeles: General Publishing Group, 1996), 24; William Robert Faith, *Bob Hope: A Life in Comedy* (Cambridge, MA: Da Capo Press, 2003), 167; Todd S. Purdum, "Bob Hope, Before He Became the Comedy Establishment," *New York Times*, April 20, 2003; Wagg, *Because I Tell a Joke or Two*, 251, 253; Gerald R. Ford, *Humor and the Presidency* (New York: Arbor House, 1987), 50.

9. Gould, *The Modern American Presidency*, 103–4; Ashby, *With Amusement for All*, 296; Richard W. Waterman, Robert Wright, and Gilbert St. Clair, *The Image-Is-Everything Presidency* (Boulder, CO: Westview Press, 1999), 108.

10. David McCullough, *Truman* (New York: Simon & Schuster, 1992), 362; Harry Truman quoted in *The Truman Wit*, ed. Alex J. Goldman (New York: Citadel Press, 1966), 47; Truman quoted in *Give 'Em Hell, Harry*, ed. Mark Goodman (New York: Award Books, 1975), 111.

11. William E. Leuchtenburg, *In the Shadow of FDR: From Harry Truman to Bill Clinton*, 2nd ed. (Ithaca: Cornell University Press, 1983), 18, 20 (David Lilienthal quote); Wickberg, *The Senses of Humor*, 202; McCullough, *Truman*, 493.

12. Boskin, *Rebellious Laughter*, 89; Kercher, *Revel with a Cause*, 2–3; Malcolm Muggeridge quoted in Dudden, *Pardon Us, Mr. President!* 41; C. Wright Mills, *White Collar: The American Middle Classes*, 50th anniversary ed. (New York: Oxford University Press, 2002), 108.

13. Cohen, *A Consumers' Republic*, 257–74.

14. David Halberstam, *The Fifties* (New York: Fawcett Columbine, 1993), 224–32; Cohen, *A Consumers' Republic*, 150, 332–33.

15. John Kenneth Galbraith quoted in Genovese, *The Power of the American Presidency*, 147.

16. Jason Ankeny, "Tom Lehrer Biography," All Music (Santa Clara, CA: Macrovision, 2008), http:www.allmusic.com/cg/amg.dll (accessed August 14, 2008); Allan M. Winkler, *Life under a Cloud: American Anxiety about the Atom* (Urbana: University of Illinois Press, 1999), 99–100; Tom Lehrer, *Songs by Tom Lehrer*, LP, Reprise, RS-6216.

17. Stan Freberg, *The Stan Freberg Show: Direct from the Famous CBS Radio Broadcasts* (Schiller Park, IL: Radio Spirits, 1997), liner notes and disc 1; Kercher, *Revel with a Cause*, 328.

18. Steve Allen et al., "State of the Nation's Humor," *New York Times Magazine*, December 7, 1958, 26, 27, 114.

19. Robert Rice, "The Fury," *New Yorker*, July 30, 1960, 34; Mort Sahl quoted in Boskin, *Rebellious Laughter*, 79; Sahl quoted in Ashby, *With Amusement for All*, 315.

20. Rice, "The Fury"; Gerald Nachman, *Seriously Funny: The Rebel Comedians of the 1950s and 1960s* (New York: Pantheon, 2003), 56; Mort Sahl, *Heartland* (New York: Harcourt Brace Jovanovich, 1976), 19; Kercher, *Revel with a Cause*, 209; "The Tiger & the Lady," review of *The Next President*, *Time*, April 21, 1958, 76; Rogers quoted in Ray Robinson, *American Original: A Life of Will Rogers* (New York: Oxford University Press, 1996), 146; "Comedians: Will Rogers with Fangs," *Time*, July 25, 1960, 42; Mort Sahl, *The Next President*, LP, Verve, MGV-15021.

21. Mort Sahl, interview with Terry Gross, *Fresh Air*, WHYY, December 23, 2003; Kercher, *Revel with a Cause*, 203.

22. Hendra, *Going Too Far*, 40, 51; Kercher, *Revel with a Cause*, 121–34.

23. Hendra, *Going Too Far*, 6–10; Boskin, *Rebellious Laughter*, 57–59.

24. Boskin, *Rebellious Laughter*, 62–70.

25. Alfred Bester, "Mort Sahl: The Hip Young Man," *Holiday*, September 1958, 91; Susan Sontag quoted in Boskin, *Rebellious Laughter*, 73; Dudden, *Pardon Us, Mr. President!* 41.

26. *Will Rogers' Weekly Articles*, vol. 3, *The Coolidge Years, 1927–1929*, ed. James M. Smallwood and Steven K. Gragert (Stillwater: Oklahoma State University Press, 1981), 1.

27. Mort Sahl, *The Future Lies Ahead: Mort Sahl, Iconoclast*, LP, Verve, MGV-15002.

28. Mort Sahl, *Mort Sahl at the hungry i*, LP, Verve, MGV-15012.

29. Nat Hentoff, "The Iconoclast of the Night Club," *Reporter Magazine*, January 9, 1958, 35, 36.

30. Bergson, *Laughter*, 20–21.

31. Roland Gelatt, *The Fabulous Phonograph: From Edison to Stereo* (New York: Appleton-Century, 1965), 290–93; David Morton, *Off the Record: The Technology*

and Culture of Sound Recording in America (New Brunswick, NJ: Rutgers University Press), 38–39.

32. Thomas Hine, *The Rise and Fall of the American Teenager* (New York: Harper-Collins, 1999), 238; Gelatt, *The Fabulous Phonograph*, 293, 308–9.

33. Kercher, *Revel with a Cause*, 209.

34. Jack Ragotzy, *Co-Star: The Record Acting Game*, LP, Roulette, CS-115; R. S. Taylor, "Records from the Comedians," *Atlantic Monthly*, November 1961, 166.

35. Ronald L. Smith, *Goldmine Comedy Record Price Guide* (Iola, WI: Krause Publications, 1996), 393; Rosalyn Krokover, "Sight & Sound," *McCalls*, February 1961, 6; Carlton Brown, "Long-Playing Laughter," *Good Housekeeping*, December 1960, 30.

36. Gilbert Millstein, "New Sick and/or Well Comic," *New York Times Magazine*, August 7, 1960, 36; Kercher, *Revel with a Cause*, 136; Bob Newhart, *Deluxe Edition: The Button-Down Mind of Bob Newhart*, LP, Warner Brothers, 2N/2NS1399, liner notes.

37. "Bob Newhart: Unbuttoned," *American Masters*, PBS, July 20, 2005; Newhart, *Deluxe Edition: The Button-Down Mind of Bob Newhart*.

38. Newhart, *Deluxe Edition: The Button-Down Mind of Bob Newhart*.

39. "The Third Campaign," *Time*, August 15, 1960, 42; *New York Times* quoted in Cherney, "Analysis of Humor in Campaign Speeches," 1–2.

40. Wickberg, *The Senses of Humor*, 199–202 (Eisenhower quote 199); Newhart, *Deluxe Edition: The Button-Down Mind of Bob Newhart*; Sahl quoted in "The Third Campaign," 42.

41. Sahl, *Heartland*, 87–88, 80–81; Sahl quoted in Pierre Berton, ed., *Voices from the Sixties* (New York: Doubleday, 1967), 105.

42. John F. Kennedy quoted by Sahl, *Fresh Air* interview, December 23, 2003; Theodore H. White, *The Making of the President, 1960* (New York: Atheneum, 1961), 324; Kennedy quoted in Bill Adler, *The Complete Kennedy Wit* (New York: Citadel Press, 1967), 67; Kennedy quoted in Gerald C. Gardner, ed., *The Quotable Mr. Kennedy* (New York: Abelard Schuman, 1962), 63.

43. John F. Kennedy and Theodore C. Sorensen, *"Let the Word Go Forth": The Speeches, Statements, and Writings of John F. Kennedy* (New York: Delacorte Press, 1988), 105; Kennedy quoted in Sloane, *Humor in the White House*, 102.

44. Gerald Gardner, *All the Presidents' Wits* (New York: Beech Tree Books, 1986), 220; Richard Reeves, *President Kennedy: Profile of Power* (New York: Simon & Schuster, 1993), 326; *The Wit of John F. Kennedy*, LP, Challenge, PCHG-CH618S.

45. *The Wit of John F. Kennedy*.

46. Kennedy and Sorensen, *"Let the Word Go Forth,"* 12; Reeves, *President Kennedy*, 326; Norman Mailer, "Superman Comes to the Supermart," *Esquire*, November 1960, 119–27; Joseph P. Kennedy quoted in Geoffrey C. Ward et al., "The Kennedys: 1900–1980," in *The American Experience*, videotape (Boston: Shanachie Entertainment Corporation, 1992).

47. John F. Kennedy to Bob Newhart, June 18, 1963, White House Central Name File (hereafter cited as WHCNF), "Newhall" file, John Fitzgerald Kennedy Library, Boston (hereafter cited as JFKL); Kercher, *Revel with a Cause*, 222; Judith Campbell Exner quoted in Ward et al., "The Kennedys: 1900–1980."

48. Vaughn Meader quoted in David Isay, "Lives: 'Nov. 22, 1963, the Day I Died,'" *New York Times Magazine*, November 21, 1999, 124.

49. Videotape, "Talent Scouts," July 3, 1962, VA2437, University of California–Los Angeles Film and Television Archive (hereafter cited as UCLA-FTA), Los Angeles.

50. Kercher, *Revel with a Cause*, 232.

51. James Hagerty quoted in Nicholas J. Cull, "No Laughing Matter: Vaughn Meader, the Kennedy Administration, and Presidential Impersonations on the Radio," *Historical Journal of Film, Radio, and Television* 17, no. 3 (1997): 384–85.

52. Meader quoted in Ronald L. Smith, *The Stars of Stand-Up Comedy: A Biographical Encyclopedia* (New York: Garland, 1986), 147–48.

53. Peter Bunzel, "A Kennedy Spoof Full of 'Vigah,'" *Life*, December 14, 1962, 83; Taylor Branch, *Parting the Waters: America in the King Years, 1954–63* (New York: Simon and Schuster, 1988), 674–75.

54. "The First Family," *Time*, November 30, 1962, 20; Bob Booker and Earle Doud, *The First Family*, LP, Cadence, CLP-3060.

55. Booker and Doud, *The First Family*.

56. "Follow-the-Meader," *Newsweek*, January 14, 1963; Bunzel, "A Kennedy Spoof Full of 'Vigah,'" 84–85; Earle Doud and Bob Booker, *The First Family Photo Album* (Greenwich, CT: Fawcett Publications, 1963).

57. Presidential news conference, December 12, 1962, excerpted on *The Wit of John F. Kennedy*.

58. Pierre Salinger, *With Kennedy* (New York: Doubleday, 1966), 316; "'Good-Night, Jackie . . . Good-Night, Bobby . . . ,'" *Newsweek*, December 3, 1962, 29; Pierre Salinger to Daniel Hart, February 8, 1963, White House Central Subject Files (hereafter cited as WHCSF), box 832, "PR 15-6 Impersonations" file, JFKL; Malcolm Kilduff to Pierre Salinger, memorandum, November 29, 1962, WHCSF, box 832, "PR 15-6 Impersonations" file, JFKL; Pierre Salinger to John F. McCullough, April 12, 1963, WHCSF, box 832, "PR 15-6 Impersonations" file, JFKL.

59. Tony Zimmerlie to Kennedy, January 16, 1963, WHCSF, box 832, "PR 15-6 Impersonations" file, JFKL; Salinger to Tom Crabtree, March 9, 1963, WHCSF, box 832, "PR 15-6 Impersonations" file, JFKL; George I. Silberberg to Kennedy, May 9, 1963, WHCSF, box 832, "PR 15-6 Impersonations" file, JFKL; Lee C. White to Silberberg, June 10, 1963, WHCSF, box 832, "PR 15-6 Impersonations" file, JFKL; Silberberg to White, June 15, 1963, WHCSF, box 832, "PR 15-6 Impersonations" file, JFKL.

60. Robert Gregory to Kennedy, n.d., WHCSF, box 832, "PR 15-6 Impersonations" file, JFKL; Charles B. Craver to Kennedy, December 3, 1962, WHCSF, box 832, "PR 15-6 Impersonations" file, JFKL; Kenneth O'Donnell to Craver, December 6, 1962, WHCSF, box 832, "PR 15-6 Impersonations" file, JFKL.

61. Vaughn Meader to Kennedy, telegram, June 26, 1962, WHCNF, "Vaughn Meader" file, JFKL. Sentence punctuation and sentence case added.

62. Liner notes on album cover of Booker and Doud, *The First Family*.

63. Michael Ross, Ron Friedman, and Larry Siegel, *Have Some Nuts!!*, LP, Verve, V/V6-15042; Smith, *The Stars of Stand-Up Comedy*, 148.

64. Isay, "Lives: 'Nov. 22, 1963, the Day I Died.'"

5. All Lies and Jest

1. *Inside the Making of Dr. Strangelove*, directed by David Naylor, DVD (Culver City, CA: Columbia Pictures, 2000); "TV's $40,000,000 JFK Coverage," *Variety*, November 27, 1963.

2. Hendra, *Going Too Far*, 165; Lenny Bruce quoted in Cull, "No Laughing Matter," 394.

3. "Fate of the Myna Bird," *Time*, January 10, 1964, 78; Isay, "Lives: 'Nov. 22, 1963, the Day I Died.'"

4. Mort Sahl, *The New Frontier*, LP, Reprise, R-5002.

5. "The Third Campaign," 42; Kercher, *Revel with a Cause*, 242, 243 (Kennedy quote); Sahl, *The New Frontier*; Nat Lehrman, "Playboy Interview: Mort Sahl," *Playboy*, February 1969, 60.

6. "Mars Broadcasting, Inc.," n.d., box 832, "PR 15-6 Impersonations" file, JFKL; Salinger to Mars Broadcasting, Inc., telegram, February 13, 1963, WHCSF, box 832, "PR 15-6 Impersonations" file, JFKL; Robert V. Whitney to K. B. Willson, February 15, 1963, WHCSF, box 832, "PR 15-6 Impersonations" file, JFKL.

7. Hendra, *Going Too Far*, 166.

8. Tocqueville, *Democracy in America*, 67.

9. Hine, *The Rise and Fall of the American Teenager*, 257; David Farber, *The Age of Great Dreams: America in the 1960s* (New York: Hill and Wang, 1994), 4; Young Americans for Freedom, "Sharon Statement," www.yaf.com/statement/ (accessed March 27, 2008); Tom Hayden, *The Port Huron Statement: The Visionary Call of the 1960s Revolution* (Berkeley: Thunder's Mouth Press, 2005), 5.

10. Winkler, *Life under a Cloud*, 172; Todd Gitlin, *The Sixties: Years of Hope, Days of Rage* (New York: Bantam Books, 1993), 35; Joseph Boskin, *Humor and Social Change in Twentieth-Century America* (Boston: Trustees of the Public Library of the City of Boston, 1979), 96.

11. Kercher, *Revel with a Cause*, 358–71, 388–89.

12. "As Broadcast" script, folder 8, box 129, Leland Hayward Papers (hereafter cited as LHP), Billy Rose Theatre Division, New York Public Library for the Performing Arts (hereafter cited as BRTD-NYPLPA), New York; "As Broadcast" script, folder 10, box 128, LHP, BRTD-NYPLPA. Punctuation has been added for clarity.

13. "As Broadcast" script, folder 8, box 129, LHP, BRTD-NYPLPA; "As Broadcast" script, folder 16, box 128, LHP, BRTD-NYPLPA.

14. Kercher, *Revel with a Cause*, 379–88; Harry Castleman and Walter J. Podrazik, *Watching TV: Six Decades of American Television*, 2nd ed. (Syracuse: Syracuse University Press, 2003), 164, 172, 174; R. Manesse to *That Was the Week That Was*, postcard, October 2, 1964, folder 2, box 118, LHP, BRTD-NYPLPA; Peter M. Nakahara to National Broadcasting Company, November 23, 1965, folder 8, box 120, LHP, BRTD-NYPLPA.

15. Nachman, *Seriously Funny*, 397–99, 403; Lenny Bruce, *How to Talk Dirty and Influence People* (New York: Fireside, 1992), 22–24.

16. Hendra, *Going Too Far*, 116; Ben Alba, *Inventing Late Night: Steve Allen and the Original Tonight Show* (Amherst, NY: Prometheus Books, 2005), 173; Lenny Bruce, "How to Relax Your Colored Friends at Parties," on *Howls, Raps & Roars:*

Recordings from the San Francisco Poetry Renaissance, compact disc, Fantasy, 4FCD-4410-2.

17. Lenny Bruce quoted in Nachman, *Seriously Funny*, 404.

18. Bruce, *How to Talk Dirty and Influence People*, 185; Lenny Bruce, "Ike, Sherm, and Nick," on *The Lenny Bruce Originals*, vol. 1, compact disc, Fantasy, FCD-60-023.

19. Nachman, *Seriously Funny*, 394; John Leonard, "TV: From Variety Show to Talk Show, the Sullivan and the Carson of It All," *New York Times*, October 29, 1975; Alba, *Inventing Late Night*, 157.

20. Marc, *Comic Visions*, 57–61; Kercher, *Revel with a Cause*, 354.

21. Hope quoted in William Robert Faith, *Bob Hope: A Life in Comedy* (Cambridge, MA: Da Capo Press, 2003), 389; Hendra, *Going Too Far*, 129–30.

22. Nachman, *Seriously Funny*, 413, 417, 391, 429; Kercher, *Revel with a Cause*, 416, 421, 418; Shawn Price, "New Release Is a Showcase for a Comedy Giant, Lenny Bruce," *Orange County Register*, October 17, 2004; George Carlin, *George Carlin: Class Clown*, LP, Little David, LD1004LP.

23. Lenny Bruce, "Johnson," on *Lenny Bruce: The Berkeley Concert*, LP, Bizarre, 2XS-6329.

24. Dick Gregory quoted in Nachman, *Seriously Funny*, 407.

25. Dick Gregory and Robert Lipsyte, *Nigger* (New York: E. P. Dutton, 1964), 158–60; Dick Gregory and Sheila P. Moses, *Callus on My Soul: A Memoir* (Atlanta: Longstreet Press, 2000), 47. Paragraph breaks have been added.

26. Gregory and Lipsyte, *Nigger*, 161; Gregory quoted in Kercher, *Revel with a Cause*, 288.

27. Gregory quoted in Mel Watkins, *On the Real Side: A History of African American Comedy from Slavery to Chris Rock* (Chicago: Lawrence Hill Books, 1999), 495, 496.

28. Watkins, *On the Real Side*, 490; Dick Gregory, *East and West*, LP, Colpix, CP420; Gregory quoted in Smith, *The Stars of Stand-up Comedy*, 96.

29. Gregory, *East and West*.

30. Arthur M. Schlesinger Jr., *The Imperial Presidency* (1973; reprint, Boston: Mariner Books, 2004), xxvii.

31. Robert Dallek, *Flawed Giant: Lyndon Johnson and His Times, 1961–1973* (New York: Oxford University Press, 1998), 122–24; Barry Goldwater quoted in Robert Schnakenberg, *Distory: A Treasury of Historical Insults* (New York: St. Martin's Press, 2004), 50; Doris Kearns Goodwin, *Lyndon Johnson and the American Dream* (New York: St. Martin's Griffin, 1991), 341; Alvin Shuster quoted in Dudden, *Pardon Us, Mr. President!*, 28.

32. Goodwin, *Lyndon Johnson and the American Dream*, 79, 248; Robert Dallek, *Lyndon B. Johnson: Portrait of a President* (New York: Oxford University Press, 2004), 52–53, 75–77; Barbara Garson, *MacBird* (New York: Grove Press, 1967).

33. "American Humor: Hardly a Laughing Matter," *Time*, March 4, 1966, 47; Boskin, *Rebellious Laughter*, 93; Abbie Hoffman, *Revolution for the Hell of It* (New York: Thunder's Mouth Press, 2005), 45.

34. *LBJ Menagerie*, LP, Jubilee, JGM-2068; Christopher Weeks, *LBJ in the Catskills*, LP, Warner Brothers, W1662; Kenny Solms and Gail Parent, *Here Comes the Bird*, LP, Atlantic, SD-8159; Marty Allen and Steve Rossi, *Meet the Great Society*, LP,

Mercury, SR-61015; George Abbott quoted in "American Humor: Hardly a Laughing Matter," 47.

35. Lew Irwin and the Credibility Gap, An *Album of Political Pornography*, LP, Blue Thumb, BTS-2.

36. Hendra, *Going Too Far*, 188, 186, 199–201.

37. Dallek, *Lyndon B. Johnson: Portrait of a President*, 298; Lawrence E. Mintz, "Standup Comedy as Social and Cultural Mediation," in *American Humor*, ed. Arthur Power Dudden, 85–96 (New York: Oxford University Press, 1987), 91.

38. Muhammad Ali, undated comments before a live audience, www.float-like-a-butterfly.de/bioe.htm (accessed August 18, 2008).

39. Allen J. Matusow, *The Unraveling of America: A History of Liberalism in the 1960s* (New York: Harper Torchbooks, 1984), 412; Todd Gitlin, *The Sixties: Years of Hope, Days of Rage* (New York: Bantam Books, 1993), 233; "The Banners of Dissent," *Time*, October 27, 1967; Hoffman, *Revolution for the Hell of It*, 47.

40. Gitlin, *The Sixties*, 235; Matusow, *The Unraveling of America*, 413; Abbie Hoffman, *The Autobiography of Abbie Hoffman* (New York: Four Walls Eight Windows, 2000), 144.

41. Gitlin, *The Sixties*, 236–37; Abbie Hoffman quoted ibid., 236.

42. Gitlin, *The Sixties*, 6; Ashby, *With Amusement for All*, 348–52.

43. Alba, *Inventing Late Night*, 268; *Smothered: The Censorship Struggles of the Smothers Brothers Comedy Hour*, directed by Maureen Muldaur, DVD (Santa Monica, CA: Muldaur Media, 2002).

44. Nachman, *Seriously Funny*, 447; Muldaur, *Smothered*.

45. Muldaur, *Smothered*; Pete Seeger, *Waist Deep in the Big Muddy and Other Love Songs*, LP, Columbia, CS9505; Allan M. Winkler, *"To Everything There Is a Season": Pete Seeger and the Power of Song* (New York: Oxford University Press, 2009), 128–32; Smith, *The Stars of Stand-Up Comedy*, 201.

46. Muldaur, *Smothered*.

47. Ibid.; unidentified CBS executive quoted in Nachman, *Seriously Funny*, 452.

48. *Pat Paulsen for President*, October 20, 1968, videotape, VA22834, UCLA-FTA; Hendra, *Going Too Far*, 217–18.

49. Pat Paulsen quoted in "Pat Paulsen," Norwegian American Homepage, ed. Roger M. Grace, www.lawzone.com/half-nor/paulsen.htm (accessed October 30, 2007); Kennedy quoted in Ramin Setoodeh, "Revenge of the Rodent," *Newsweek*, November 24, 2008.

50. *Pat Paulsen for President*.

51. Ibid.

52. Ibid.

53. Ibid.

54. Hendra, *Going Too Far*, 217.

55. *Pat Paulsen for President*.

56. Lincoln quoted in Pullen, *Comic Relief*, 2–3.

57. *Smothers Brothers Comedy Hour*, November 10, 1968, videotape, VA7751, UCLA-FTA.

58. Richard Nixon quoted in Herbert S. Parmet, *Richard M. Nixon: An American Enigma* (New York: Pearson Longman, 2008), 68; Roger Ailes quoted in Joe

McGinniss, *The Selling of the President, 1968* (New York: Trident Press, 1969), 103; Bergson, *Laughter*, 37.

59. "Nixon: Part II, Triumph," in *The American Experience*, directed by Elizabeth Deane, DVD (Boston: WGBH Educational Foundation, 1990); Rick Perlstein, *Nixonland: The Rise of a President and the Fracturing of America* (New York: Scribner, 2008), 84, 86; Nixon quoted in Farber, *The Age of Great Dreams*, 225; Norman Mailer quoted in Stanley I. Kutler, *The Wars of Watergate: The Last Crisis of Richard Nixon* (New York: Norton, 1992), 67.

60. Nixon quoted in Deane, "Nixon: Part II, Triumph"; Perlstein, *Nixonland*, 330.

61. Erickson, *"From Beautiful Downtown Burbank,"* 117 (Jack Gould quote), 167–68.

62. "Nixon's New-Found Humor," *Time*, February 7, 1969; Bill Adler, *The Wit and Humor of Richard Nixon* (New York: Popular Library, 1969); Bill Adler, ed., *The Kennedy Wit* (New York: Citadel Press, 1964).

63. John Morton Blum, *Years of Discord: American Politics and Society, 1961–1974* (New York: Norton, 1991), 351, 320, 334, 333.

64. Russell Baker, "Sunday Observer: Vintage Farce," *New York Times*, December 30, 1973; Dudden, *Pardon Us, Mr. President!*, 24; Boskin, *Rebellious Laughter*, 92, 93; Nixon quoted in "Watergate Tapes Online," washingtonpost.com (accessed May 19, 2008).

65. David Frye, *Richard Nixon: A Fantasy*, LP, Buddah, 1600.

66. David Frye, *I Am the President*, LP, Elektra, EKS-75006; John Kenneth Galbraith quoted in Dudden, *Pardon Us, Mr. President!*, 24.

67. Frye, *Richard Nixon: A Fantasy*; Faith, *Bob Hope: A Life in Comedy*, 374–77.

68. Richard Severo and Bill Carter, "Johnny Carson, Low-Key King of Late-Night TV, Dies at 79," *New York Times*, January 24, 2005; Stephen Cox, *Here's Johnny! Thirty Years of America's Favorite Late-Night Entertainer*, rev. ed. (Nashville: Cumberland House, 2002), 185, 186, 56; Museum of Television and Radio, *Stand-Up Comedians on Television* (New York: Harry N. Abrams, 1996), 94.

6. Rebellion by the Pound

1. Johnny Carson quoted in Ed McMahon, *Here's Johnny! My Memories of Johnny Carson, the Tonight Show, and Forty-six Years of Friendship* (Waterville, ME: Thorndike Press, 2005), 180–81; Kenneth Tynan, *Show People: Profiles in Entertainment* (New York: Simon and Schuster, 1979), 152.

2. Douglas Brinkley, *Gerald R. Ford* (New York: Times Books, 2007), 76; Gerald R. Ford in televised remarks after his swearing-in as vice president of the United States by Chief Justice Warren E. Burger before a joint session of Congress in the United States Capitol, Washington, DC, December 6, 1973.

3. Ford, televised remarks, December 6, 1973.

4. Brinkley, *Gerald R. Ford*, 67; Thomas M. DeFrank, *Write It When I'm Gone: Remarkable Off-the-Record Conversations with Gerald R. Ford* (New York: G. P. Putnam's Sons, 2007), 105; Gerald R. Ford, televised inaugural address in the White House, August 9, 1974; "The Failure of Mr. Ford," *New York Times*, September 9, 1974.

5. Richard Reeves, "Ladies and Gentlemen, the President of the United States,"

New York, November 25, 1974; Ron Nessen, *It Sure Looks Different from the Inside* (Chicago: Playboy Press, 1978), 165; Johnson quoted in Schnakenberg, *Distory*, 53; Brinkley, *Gerald R. Ford*, 6.

6. John Leonard, "Reviews: 'Tube of Plenty' and 'Television,'" *New York Times*, November 30, 1975; Leonard, "TV: From Variety Show to Talk Show, the Sullivan and the Carson of It All"; Laurence Leamer, *King of the Night: The Life of Johnny Carson* (New York: William Morrow, 1989), 269; Billy Wilder quoted in Tynan, *Show People*, 128.

7. Leamer, *King of the Night*, 269; Tim Brooks and Earle Marsh, *The Complete Directory to Prime Time Network and Cable TV Shows, 1946–Present*, 7th rev. ed. (New York: Ballantine Books, 1999), 1038; Tom Shales and James A. Miller, *Live from New York: An Uncensored History of Saturday Night Live* (Boston: Little, Brown, 2002), 3–4.

8. Leamer, *King of the Night*, 261.

9. *NBC Saturday Night Live with Ron Nessen*, videotape, April 17, 1976, F765, GRFL; Gerald R. Ford, *A Time to Heal: The Autobiography of Gerald R. Ford* (New York: Harper & Row, 1979), 289.

10. Philip Shabecoff, "Aides Say Ford Ignores Skepticism about Ability," *New York Times*, December 29, 1975; Judith H. Dobrzynski, "Robert Mead, 61, News Producer for Networks and Advisor to Ford," *New York Times*, May 19, 1996; Terry O'Donnell to Gerald Ford, memo, November 18, 1975, WHCSF, box 150, "PR 16-1 11/1/75-1/9/76" file, GRFL; Robert Mead quoted in Alexis St. John, "Is Show Biz Coming to the Oval Office?" *Forecast!* n.d., WHCNF, "Mead, Robert" file, GRFL, 33; Robert Orben, "Speeches, Humor, and the Public," in *The Ford Presidency: Twenty-two Intimate Perspectives of Gerald R. Ford*, ed. Kenneth W. Thompson (Lanham, MD: University Press of America, 1988), 235.

11. Gerald R. Ford, *Humor and the Presidency* (New York: Arbor House, 1987), 49.

12. Nessen, *It Sure Looks Different from the Inside*, 173 (Chevy Chase quote); Russell L. Peterson, *Strange Bedfellows: How Late-Night Comedy Turns Democracy into a Joke* (New Brunswick, NJ: Rutgers University Press, 2008), 178.

13. "President's Remarks at Radio-Television Correspondents Dinner, Thursday, March 25, 1976," speech draft, March 25, 1976, Paul Theis and Robert Orben Files, box 47, "4/3/76—Gridiron Dinner" file, GRFL.

14. Nessen, *It Sure Looks Different from the Inside*, 173; "President's Remarks at Radio-Television Correspondents Dinner"; Shales and Miller, *Live from New York*, 75–76.

15. *NBC Saturday Night Live with Ron Nessen*; Nessen, *It Sure Looks Different from the Inside*, 174.

16. *NBC Saturday Night Live with Ron Nessen*.

17. Correspondence, WHCSF, box 48, "FG 6-11/Nessen, Ron; 4/27/76" file, GRFL; "News Conference no. 480," transcript, April 19, 1976, Ronald H. Nessen Files, box 18, "April 19, 1976 (no. 480)" file, GRFL; "'Surrogate' Television Appearances Campaign," memo, n.d., Helen M. Collins Files, box 3, "Television Office—General" file, GRFL; Shales and Miller, *Live from New York*, 173.

18. Nessen, *It Sure Looks Different from the Inside*, 177; Ford, *Humor and the Presidency*, 47–48; *Annie Hall*, directed by Woody Allen (Los Angeles: United Artists Corporation, 1977); Robert Orben quoted in "Political Satire Can Shape the Country's Perceptions," *U.S. News & World Report*, clipping, Robert T. Hartmann

Papers, box 145, "Orben, Bob," file, GRFL; Don Penny quoted in "Humor and the Presidency," session 1, September 18, 1986, videotape AV88-11-013, Ford Library Administrative Files, GRFL.

19. Michael Cader, *Saturday Night Live: The First Twenty Years* (Boston: Cader Books, 1994), 199.

20. Castleman and Podrazik, *Watching TV*, 270, 268, 287; "Obama Was Obviously Not the First Black President," video recording, www.doubleviking.com (accessed December 29, 2008).

21. Leamer, *King of the Night*, 285; Alba, *Inventing Late Night*, 302–4; Sahl, *Fresh Air* interview, December 23, 2003.

22. For a complete discussion of the modern intersection of the presidency and show business beyond the performance of humor, see Alan Schroeder, *Celebrity-in-Chief: How Show Business Took Over the White House* (Boulder, CO: Westview Press, 2004).

23. Gardner, *All the Presidents' Wits*, 63–64, 69 (Penny quote), 63 (Carter quote).

24. Jules Tygiel, *Ronald Reagan and the Triumph of American Conservatism*, 2nd ed. (New York: Pearson Longman, 2006), 2; Lou Cannon, *President Reagan: The Role of a Lifetime* (New York: Public Affairs, 2000), 186, 16–17; Garry Wills, *Reagan's America* (New York: Penguin, 2000), 110–11.

25. Tygiel, *Ronald Reagan*, 86–88; Sean Wilentz, *The Age of Reagan: A History, 1974–2008* (New York: HarperCollins, 2008), 132–33; Wills, *Reagan's America*, ix.

26. Wilentz, *The Age of Reagan*, 7.

27. Cannon, *President Reagan*, 23; Ronald Reagan quoted in Gardner, *All the Presidents' Wits*, 37; John Winthrop, "A Model of Christian Charity," in *Winthrop Papers*, vol. 2 ([Boston]: Massachusetts Historical Society, 1931), 295.

28. Cannon, *President Reagan*, 713, 4 (Nancy Reagan quote); Cannon, *President Reagan*, 187.

29. Wilentz, *The Age of Reagan*, 136; Richard Hofstadter, *The American Political Tradition and the Men Who Made It* (New York: Vintage Books, 1989), xxxiii; Genovese, *The Power of the American Presidency*, 176; Cannon, *President Reagan*, 713, 7; Reagan quoted in Gardner, *All the Presidents' Wits*, 48; "Humor and the Presidency," session 4, September 19, 1986, videotape AV88-11-005, Ford Library Administrative Files, GRFL.

30. Alleen Pace Nilsen and Don L. F. Nilsen, "Political Cartoons: Zeitgeists and the Creation and Recycling of Satirical Symbols," in *Laughing Matters: Humor and American Politics in the Media Age*, ed. Jody C. Baumgartner and Jonathan S. Morris (New York: Routledge, 2008), 67–79; Wills, *Reagan's America*, xxv; Orben quoted in Cannon, *President Reagan*, 95; Ronald Reagan, *Ronald Reagan: The Wisdom and Humor of the Great Communicator*, ed. Frederick J. Ryan Jr. (San Francisco: Collins Publishers, 1995), 97.

31. Sahl quoted in Gerald Gardner, *Campaign Comedy: Political Humor from Clinton to Kennedy* (Detroit: Wayne State University Press, 1994), 104, 103 (Mark Russell quote); Peggy Noonan quoted in Wilfrid Sheed, "His Sentiments Exactly," *New York Times*, February 4, 1990.

32. Castleman and Podrazik, *Watching TV*, 263; McMahon, *Here's Johnny!* 226–27.

33. Wilentz, *The Age of Reagan*, 202; McMahon, *Here's Johnny!*, 226; Reagan quoted in Cannon, *President Reagan*, 130; Ryan, *Ronald Reagan*, 102; "Second

Reagan-Mondale Debate," The American Presidency Project (Santa Barbara, CA: Gerhard Peters, 1999–2008), www.presidency.ucsb.edu/showdebate.php?debateid=12 (accessed October 14, 2008).

34. Landon Parvin quoted in Gardner, *All the Presidents' Wits*, 26.

35. Ashby, *With Amusement for All*, 455–57, 461.

36. Ibid., 457, 456 (Fowler quote); Wilentz, *The Age of Reagan*, 195–96; Val E. Limburg, "Fairness Doctrine: U.S. Broadcasting Policy" (Chicago: Museum of Broadcast Communications, 2008), www.museum.tv/archives/etv/F/htmlF/fairnessdoct/fairnessdoct.htm (accessed December 8, 2008); Ashby, *With Amusement for All*, 458.

37. Ashby, *With Amusement for All*, 462; Castleman and Podrazik, *Watching TV*, 349; Chris Turner, *Planet Simpson: How a Cartoon Masterpiece Defined a Generation* (Cambridge, MA: Da Capo Press, 2004), 8; Wilentz, *The Age of Reagan*, 196.

38. Wills, *Reagan's America*, xxii; Ashby, *With Amusement for All*, 446.

39. Howard Kurtz, *Hot Air: All Talk, All the Time* (New York: Times Books, 1996), 236–37; Jon Meacham, "What Will Rogers Could Teach the Age of Limbaugh," *Washington Monthly*, January–February 1994, 17; Zev Chafets, "Late-Period Limbaugh," *New York Times Magazine*, July 6, 2008.

40. Chris Smith and Ben Voth, "The Role of Humor in Political Argument: How 'Strategery' and 'Lockboxes' Changed a Political Campaign," *Argumentation and Advocacy* 39 (Fall 2002): 114, 117, 123 (Howard Fineman quote).

Epilogue

1. *The Colbert Report*, Comedy Central, April 17, 2008; "The Time 100," *Time*, May 12, 2008.

2. Schroeder, *Celebrity-in-Chief*, 3.

3. *The Amazing Spider-Man*, issue no. 573 (New York: Marvel Entertainment, 2008); *The Amazing Spider-Man*, issue no. 583 (New York: Marvel Entertainment, 2009).

4. Bill Maher quoted in Jake Tapper, "The Salon Interview: Bill Maher," Salon.com, December 11, 2002, dir.salon.com/story/people/interview/2002/12/11/maher/index.html (accessed November 20, 2008); *Saturday Night Live* with Reese Witherspoon, Rudolph Giuliani, and Paul Simon, NBC, September 29, 2001; *Late Show with David Letterman*, CBS, January 14, 2002; Bush quoted in Kenneth R. Bazinet, "Bush Bounces Back," *New York Daily News*, January 15, 2002.

5. Michael Cieply, "Writers Begin Strike as Talks Break Off," *New York Times*, November 5, 2007; Joseph Carroll, "Congress' Approval Rating at 20%; Bush's Approval at 32%," Gallup (Washington, DC: Gallup, Inc., November 20, 2007), www.gallup.com/poll/102829/Congress-Approval-Rating-20-Bushs-Approval-32.aspx (accessed October 25, 2008); Bill Carter, "Leno Faces Writers Guild Action over Monologues," *New York Times*, January 5, 2008.

6. Pew Research Center, *Trends 2005*, 47; Pew Research Center, "What Americans Know: 1989–2007," 13; Geoffrey Baym, "*The Daily Show*: Discursive Integration and the Reinvention of Political Journalism," *Political Communication* 22 (2005): 260–63, 260 (Bill Moyers quote).

7. Stephen Colbert, "October 17, 2005: The Word—Truthiness," Colbert Nation, October 17, 2005, www.colbertnation.com/the-colbert-report-videos/24039/

october-17-2005/the-word—truthiness (accessed October 7, 2008); "Merriam-Webster's Words of the Year 2006," Merriam-Webster Online, www.merriam-webster.com/info/o6words.htm (accessed January 6, 2009); Stephen Colbert quoted in Nathan Rabin, "Stephen Colbert," A.V. Club, January 25, 2006, www.avclub.com/articles/stephen-colbert,13970/ (accessed January 20, 2009); Baym, "The Daily Show," 273–74.

8. The Colbert Report, April 17, 2008.

9. Peterson, Strange Bedfellows, 180; Michael Ventre, "Comedians Leave Voters with Great Impression," MSNBC.com, October 9, 2008, www.msnbc.msn.com/id/27072074 (accessed October 28, 2008).

10. Saturday Night Live with Anna Faris, Tina Fey, and Amy Poehler, NBC, September 27, 2008; Saturday Night Live with Sarah Palin, Tina Fey, and Josh Brolin, NBC, October 18, 2008; Rick Kissell, "Sarah Palin Boosts 'SNL' Ratings," Variety.com, October 19, 2008, www.variety.com/article/VR1117994302.html?categoryid=1064&cs=1 (accessed November 22, 2008).

11. "Colbert Roasts President Bush: 2006 White House Correspondents Dinner," video recording, video.google.com/videoplay?docid=-869183917758574879 (accessed December 12, 2008); Richard Cohen, "So Not Funny," Washington Post, May 4, 2006; Rich, "Laura Bush's Mission Accomplished"; Schroeder, Celebrity-in-Chief, 284; Mark Crispin Miller, "Prime Time: Deride and Conquer," in Watching Television: A Pantheon Guide to Popular Culture, ed. Todd Gitlin (New York: Pantheon, 1986), 223; Sahl, Fresh Air, December 23, 2003; Neil Postman, Amusing Ourselves to Death: Public Discourse in the Age of Show Business (New York: Penguin, 2006), 155, 156.

12. Baym, "The Daily Show," 267, 270–73; Matthew Arnold, Civilization in the United States: First and Last Impressions of America (Boston: Cupples and Hurd, 1888), 177; Postman, Amusing Ourselves to Death, 156.

13. Powers, Mark Twain, 521.

14. Ambrose Bierce, The Devil's Dictionary (Sioux Falls, SD: NuVision Publications, 2007), 135; The Tonight Show, NBC, March 19, 2009.

15. Gary Holmes, "TV Viewing and Internet Use Are Complementary, Nielsen Reports," Nielsen.com, October 31, 2008, www.nielsen.com/media/2008/pr_081031.html (accessed November 3, 2008).

16. Roosevelt quoted in Wickberg, The Senses of Humor, 202–3.

INDEX

Adams, John, 23; and Sedition Act of 1798, 23
Agnew, Spiro, 185, 190–91
Alda, Alan, 132, 146
Ali, Muhammad, 168–69
Allen, Fred, 102–3; censorship of, 103, 104, 142; influence of, 103, 112–13
Allen, Gracie, 101, 104, 105, 175, 221; mock presidential candidacy (1940), 101
Allen, Steve, 113, 151, 153, 178, 188, 194, 203; as comedy visionary, 153–55
Alvin and the Chipmunks, 175
Arnold, Matthew, on Twain, 225
Artemus Ward, His Book, 16, 32, 33, 45
Aykroyd, Dan, 116, 195, 197; imitation of Carter, 12, 201–2

Ball, Lucille, 104, 105; appearance before House Committee on Un-American Activities (HUAC), 105
Benny, Jack, 101, 104, 105, 172
Berle, Milton, 104
Bierce, Ambrose, 225
blackface minstrelsy, 19, 30, 110, 160
Block, Herbert. *See* Herblock
Browne, Charles Farrar, 11, 16–18, 32, 45, 101; attitudes toward performance, 28–30; death of, 16, 50; Howells on, 37; as journalist, 17, 23, 26–28, 225; and Maine, 16–17, 26, 130, 132; as personification of American spirit, 17, 19–20; as standup comedian, 11, 16, 20, 30, 35–36, 109, 225; and Twain's career, 44. *See also* Ward, Artemus
Bruce, Lenny, 114, 160, 165, 170, 174, 187, 194; compared with Ward, 155; influence on political humor, 150–53,

156–58, 185; on LBJ, 157; on Meader's career, 139–40; obscenity charges against, 156–57; on performance versus reality, 150–52, 206; posthumous pardon of, 156
Burns, George, 101, 172
Bush, George H. W., 13, 201, 210, 212; Carvey imitation of, 222
Bush, George W., 208, 210, 219; and 2000 election, 214; Ferrell imitation of, 214, 217; and "truthiness," 220; and 2005 White House Correspondents' Association dinner, 1–3, 6–8; and 2006 White House Correspondents' Association dinner, 223
Bush, Laura, 1–4, 6–8, 210, 223

Carlin, George, 156, 194
Carson, Johnny: compared with Rogers, 193; cultural power of, 12, 154, 188–93; influence on late-night comedy, 203, 211–12, 217; on Nixon, 188, 190, 192, 194; on Reagan, 208–9; and *Saturday Night Live*, 12, 193–94. *See also* *Tonight Show, The*
Carter, Jimmy: defeat of Ford, 200; lack of humor, 203–4; Reagan's victory over, 207; and *Saturday Night Live*, 12, 201–2
Carvey, Dana, 13, 222
Cedric the Entertainer (Cedric Antonio Kyles), 2
Chase, Chevy, 199, 209; imitation of Ford, 12, 195, 197–99, 201–2; impact on 1976 election, 223
Cheney, Dick, 2, 218
Cheney, Lynne, 1, 2
"child" jokes, 116–17, 145